D0953590

Acclaim for *The Corporate Athlete*

"Today's challenging business climate requires every top executive to be perfectly fit both mentally and physically. *The Corporate Athlete* is must reading for everyone who wants to manage his or her business, career, or profession effectively while living a balanced life. Buy it—it's a great investment."

> —Leonard Lauder, Chairman and Chief Executive Officer of the Estee Lauder Companies, Inc.

"As Jack Groppel so aptly explains, the rigor of corporate athletics is often even more demanding than that of professional athletes. In my world, one does not have the luxury of an off-season. By following Groppel's advice and changing one bad habit per day, even those who are barely surviving in the corporate world can become ultimate corporate athletes. This book is for all those striving for the gold."

> —Arthur M. Blank, CEO and President, The Home Depot

"The tools in this book will enhance performance and enable executives to achieve their potential both inside and outside of the workplace. This book will change your life!"

> —Beatrice Cassou, Managing Director, Morgan Stanley Dean Witter

"As a coach, I must guide players on how to maximize their talent and skill under extreme pressure. This coaching is physical, emotional, mental, and even spiritual. *The Corporate Athlete* will do the same for you in business and in life—it will be your coach."

> —Lou Holtz, author of *Winning Every Day: The Game Plan for Success*

"Brilliant . . . *The Corporate Athlete* takes the lessons learned from elite athletes and applies them to people like us who are duking it out, day in and day out in the corporate world. Now I have more energy than ever, I look better, I feel better, I'm in the zone when I need to be, and I am more at peace with myself and my life than ever before."

> —Sherri Sklar, Vice President, Business Development, ABT Corporation

"Dr. Groppel applies many of the same principles and techniques that I used to help me win my gold medal to the corporate world. He will have you performing like an Olympian at the office."

> —Dan Jansen, Olympic Gold Medal Speed Skater

"*The Corporate Athlete* is the answer to increase performance in the corporate world. It's clear, comprehensive, and makes sense. Jack Groppel's approach offers practical suggestions that lead to better health, increased productivity, and a better corporate environment."

> —Zig Ziglar, author of *See You at the Top,* motivational teacher

"If you feel like all you ever do is work, work, work and that burnout is just around the corner, you really must read and digest *The Corporate Athlete.* This is *the* book to teach you how to perform your job at the highest level possible while maintaining maximal health and happiness."

> —Jim Courier, French Open Champion and former World No. 1 Tennis Player

"Outstanding . . . *The Corporate Athlete* is a truly comprehensive program to help you achieve both your personal and your professional goals. It will help you take control of your life and effect positive physical, mental and spiritual change."

> —Darlene Hamrock, Regional Vice President, Clinique

"You cannot be intimidated by the geographical challenges of global business. In the first four months of 1999 I traveled around the world twice; all the flights were at night as my days were filled with nonstop meetings. I felt great at the beginning and at the end of all my travel. The recipe for beating the jet lag monster is contained in *The Corporate Athlete.*"

> —Peter J. Cathey, President and CEO, World Duty Free Inflight, Inc.

"Wow! This is an incredible book. Every person in business should read it from cover to cover, and apply it every day."

> —Brian Tracy, author of *Maximum Achievement*

"*The Corporate Athlete* works! Dr. Groppel gives the reader insight into how lifestyle affects our moods, energy levels, and overall health."

> —Mike Richter, Goalie, New York Rangers

"I highly recommend it!"

—Tom Hopkins, Master Sales Trainer, Author of *Sales Closing for Dummies*

"The strategies found in *The Corporate Athlete* will serve as a model of how to live your life. With the demanding schedules and especially with the travel requirements in business today, *The Corporate Athlete* will keep you centered. And it will stay with you for life."

— Claudine M. McIntee, Vice President, Morgan Stanley Dean Witter

"Dr. Jack Groppel is the world's leading authority in the translation of scientific sport science research and information into popular language. He has helped thousands of athletes, coaches and executives become the very best they can be."

—E. Paul Roetert, Ph.D., FACSM, Director, American Sport Education Program

"Dr. Jack Groppel is one of the most knowledgeable, caring, and professional individuals I have worked with in my career. Whatever Jack has to say about improving performance—no matter where the workplace—is worth reading about."

—Pam Shriver, top tennis player

"As the leader goes, so goes the organization. Leaders must be able to project a positive 'bring it on' approach to challenging conditions. The wisdom shared by Dr. Jack Groppel in *The Corporate Athlete* should be a big part of any leader's development."

— Rodger Price, Director of Leadership Development, Johnson Controls Automotive Systems Group

"Failure is not an option. I always must be on when I'm performing my job. Whether I'm driving a race car in excess of 230 miles per hour or managing my own business, I rely heavily on the training program found in *The Corporate Athlete*. This book is for anyone who strives to excel."

— Eddie Cheever, 1998 Indianapolis 500 champion

"Whether it is your personal life or your business life or if your goal is to win the U.S. Open, the fitter you are physically, mentally, nutritionally, and spiritually, the better equipped you will be to meet the challenges that lie ahead. You will find all the answers in *The Corporate Athlete*."

—David Leadbetter, author of *David Leadbetter's Faults and Fixes*

"In today's global, competitive world where you are either a Corporate Athlete or sitting on the bench, you need to take care of yourself mentally and physically. This book tells you how."

—Albert J. Dunlap, author of *Mean Business*

"Until *The Corporate Athlete*, I was always in a constant, unrelenting state of go, go, go! Dr. Jack Groppel's material has trained me how to pace myself both personally and professionally."

—Jodie Abendroth, Director of Operations, Peter Lowe International, Inc.

"Jack delivers the 'how' in how to be mentally tough!"

—Augie Nieto, President and CEO, Life Fitness, Inc.

"The airline business is demanding, both professionally and physically. Jack Groppel's program offers a no-nonsense approach to optimizing performance in every aspect of an individual's life."

—Victoria D. Stennes, Managing Director, In-Flight Customer Services, Delta Air Lines

"This program has changed my life. Thanks, Jack."

—Bob Glowaki, Resident Vice-President, Merrill Lynch

"*The Corporate Athlete* has enabled me to perform to the highest levels of my abilities."

—Greg Jones, Vice President, California, State Farm Insurance Companies

"As an NFL quarterback, I often only have seconds to make critical decisions — and those decisions could win or lose games. The training system found in *The Corporate Athlete* has helped me mentally and emotionally to make more game-winning decisions than ever."

—Jim Harbaugh, NFL Pro Bowl quarterback, San Diego Chargers

"These days everybody is running ninety miles per hour—uphill. *The Corporate Athlete* gives you the competitive edge and allows you to maintain it"

—Luke Rohrbaugh, Senior Vice President, Prudential Securities

THE CORPORATE ATHLETE

How to Achieve Maximal Performance in Business and Life

JACK L. GROPPEL, Ph.D.

WITH

BOB ANDELMAN

John Wiley & Sons, Inc.

New York • Chichester • Weinheim • Brisbane • Singapore • Toronto

To my parents,
Howard and Pauline Groppel

This book is printed on acid-free paper.

Copyright © 2000 by Jack L. Groppel, Ph.D. All rights reserved

Published by John Wiley & Sons, Inc.
Published simultaneously in Canada

Credits appear on page 285 and constitute an extension of this copyright page

No part of this publication may be reproduced, stored in a retrieval system, or trans-
mitted in any form or by any means, electronic, mechanical, photocopying, recording,
scanning, or otherwise, except as permitted under Sections 107 or 108 of the 1976
United States Copyright Act, without either the prior written permission of the Publisher, or authorization through payment of the appropriate per-copy fee to the Copyright Clearance Center, 222 Rosewood Drive, Danvers, MA 01923, (978) 750-8400, fax
(978) 750-4744. Requests to the Publisher for permission should be addressed to the
Permissions Department, John Wiley & Sons, Inc., 605 Third Avenue, New York, NY
10158-0012, (212) 850-6011, fax (212) 850-6008, E-mail: PERMREQ@WILEY.COM.

The information contained in this book is not intended to serve as a replacement
for professional medical advice. Any use of the information in this book is at
the reader's discretion. The author and the publisher specifically disclaim any
and all liability arising directly or indirectly from the use or application of any information contained in this book. A health care professional should be
consulted regarding your specific situation.

Library of Congress Cataloging-in-Publication Data

Groppel, Jack L.
The corporate athlete : how to achieve maximal performance in business
and life / Jack L. Groppel with Bob Andelman.
p.   cm.
Includes index.
ISBN 0-471-35369-8 (alk. paper)
1. Success in business—Health aspects.   2. Executives—Health and
hygiene.   3. Businesspersons—Health and hygiene.   4. Performance—
Health aspects.   5. Physical fitness.   6. Nutrition.   7. Job
stress.   I. Andelman, Bob.   II. Title.
HF5386.G778   2000
650.1—DC21   99-32357

Printed in the United States of America

10 9 8 7 6

Contents

PART III: THE JOY OF EXERCISE

PART IV: THE CORPORATE ATHLETE SPIRIT

PART V: THE 21-DAY CORPORATE ATHLETE PROGRAM

PART VI: MANAGERIAL FITNESS

Foreword

I'm very excited about Jack Groppel's new book, *The Corporate Athlete*. Jack and I go back a long way, nearly two decades. We first connected through the world of tennis. The common bond was sport science. Jack was searching for new research-based technologies that could enhance the competitive performance of tennis players from a physical perspective—biomechanics and exercise physiology. I had an identical quest, except my search was from a mental perspective—sport psychology. Over time, we developed a deep appreciation for the interconnectedness of all the sport sciences.

Exercise physiologists and sport psychologists rarely share a similar vision of the world. By the mid-1980s, however, a mutual dream began to take form—a fully integrated, holistic, state-of-the-art performance training center. Within seven years, that dream became a reality. At our offices on nine acres on beautiful Lake Nona in Orlando, Florida, exercise physiologists, biomechanists, clinical psychologists, sport psychologists, orthopedic specialists, and rehabilitation and massage therapists work holistically to enhance human performance in high-stress applications. The company was founded by Jack, renowned fitness trainer Pat Etcheberry, and myself, and we named it LGE Performance Systems. Training there today are world-class athletes from a wide diversity of sports, pilots, surgeons, FBI SWAT teams, educators, and business executives from every sector of Corporate America. We call our business clients "Corporate Athletes" and nearly twenty thousand will go through our Mentally Tough Corporate Program this year.

This program is precisely the focus of Jack's book. Jack has done a masterful job of illuminating how the mind, body, and spirit interact in the crucible of corporate high performance. He zeros in specifically on the powerful roles that nutrition and exercise play in successfully meeting the never-ending challenges of business today. The latest cutting-edge research findings are distilled into practical, digestible strategies to help Corporate Athletes perform on demand, regardless of circumstances. *The Corporate Athlete* is a must read for anyone searching for real solutions to the relentless pressures of today's corporate life.

James E. Loehr
author of *Mentally Tough* and *Stress for Success*

Acknowledgments

So many people have played an important role in my life as I developed the concepts within this book, starting with my parents, Howard and Pauline Groppel. Dad, thanks for guiding me in discipline, perseverance, and drive, as well as a tremendous love of nature and the outdoors. Mom, thanks for teaching me by example the true meaning of deep, family love.

I also want to acknowledge the support of my sister, Ruthann, and her family, as well as my lifelong friend Bill Wicks, and his family.

I sincerely thank my business partners, Jim Loehr, the creative genius behind the Mentally Tough program, and Pat Etcheberry, who has no peers in the fitness training industry. Jim, thanks for your support, guidance, understanding, and for being such a great friend. Pat, thank you for your tremendous friendship and support, as well as for showing me that world-class training is as much a psychological art as it is a physical effort.

The entire staff of our firm, LGE Performance Systems, has my gratitude and appreciation for its belief and dedication to our cause. In particular I'd like to single out David Striegel, Brian Wallace, and Steve Gray for their individual contributions to *The Corporate Athlete*. And special thanks to Ginny Chambers, Susana Oates, and Sandra Hahn for your help in organizing not only this manuscript but also my entire life while I'm on the road. I'd literally be lost without you.

Thanks also to my coauthor, Bob Andelman, for your creativity and contributions in writing and developing the manuscript for this book. I would like to extend my gratitude to my literary agent, Joel Fishman, for his perserverance and dedication. I also want to extend thanks to my editor, Tom Miller, for his insight and vision in pulling together the manuscript into book form. To ESHA Research, I thank you for your continued support of my work and for the use of your outstanding software in nutrition analysis.

And to Meredith Luce, the dietitian I worked with on the nutrition section of this book, thank you for all your hard work. I'd also like to acknowledge the input of Rick Nelson, Randy Gerber, Kevin J. Corcoran, Tom Grantham, Rich Franchella, and Clarence "Pooh Bear" Williams in the research for this book.

I am fortunate to have had two astounding mentors in my life, Chuck

Dillman and Bob Singer, who each taught me that the science of human performance is more than just manipulating data. People such as Paul Roetert, Tim Heckler, Vic Braden, Dennis Van der Meer, Stan Smith, the late Arthur Ashe, Tom Gullikson and his late brother, Tim, David Loveless, and Jodie Abendroth represent special associations that enrich my daily life.

I wish to express special thanks to Becky Johnson, Caroline Rivera, and to Warren and Kitty Jamison, who helped so diligently in the organization of the original "Anti-Diet" concept. And to four megaperformers who have, over the past several years, personally demonstrated to me how kindness, humility, and love of family can play an irrefutable role in a successful life: Zig Ziglar, George and Barbara Bush, and Colin Powell.

And finally, to the thousands of world-class athletes and Corporate Athletes with whom I have had the great fortune to work, you have impacted me greatly and I thank you for your time and ongoing contribution to this work.

Jack Groppel

There are several people whose contributions I'd also like to acknowledge, starting with Jack Groppel, who made a believer out of me, too.

Everyone I met at LGE, starting with Jim Loehr and Pat Etcheberry, was extremely gracious, knowledgeable, and helpful in guiding me through sometimes unfamiliar terrain. I'm grateful to all of you. It was also a pleasure interviewing the professional and Corporate Athletes profiled herein. They were extremely generous with their time, sharing personal experiences and opinions.

A few other thank-yous: to our editor, Tom Miller; to my agent, Joel Fishman of Bedford Book Works; and to my overworked and much-appreciated tape transcriber, Becky James.

Jack talks a great deal about mentors, so I'd like to say a word about one of mine, who passed away as we were finishing *The Corporate Athlete.* Fred Arnott was a high-school teacher of mine back in North Brunswick, New Jersey. He was the kind of guy who spent extra time and energy in nurturing young people, in both their studies—he taught art—and in grasping the bigger picture of life itself. Many kids who connected with nothing else in school found a connection through him. I have such great memories of Fred—his love of jazz, his wacky sense of humor, and, most of all, his intense humanity. I have been fortunate to have had many mentors over the years, but none greater or more beloved than that crazy old art teacher.

I'd also like to acknowledge my 2½-year-old daughter, Rachel, who learned how to use a computer during this book's evolution. So if you spot any typos, know that she did the best she could to catch them all.

Bob Andelman

Introduction

Executives and employees in the new millennium can protect their health and happiness and continue to perform at high levels only by doing what athletes do—train. You must become a Corporate Athlete, which means adapting the training mentality of elite, high-performance athletes.

Issues of fitness, nutrition, mental toughness, sleep, recovery, rituals, balance, attitude, spirituality, and emotional skill are fundamentals in the training; successful competitors in sports learn to embrace stress, not run or hide from it. In fact, they use stress to become stronger, faster, more focused, and powerful.

The Corporate Athlete is the first book that applies an underlying total health program to specific, practical business situations. It specifically applies the health and fitness components of the Mentally Tough training program to the busy, overworked businessperson. This is a sound program that will benefit anybody looking for peak job performance and improved health in his or her daily life.

This is *not* a quick fix. You will not get an instant solution to your high-stress career, mediocre diet, and low-energy lifestyle overnight. You *will* learn how somebody just as busy as you has been able to turn his or her career and life around following this commonsense program.

As you'll discover later, it takes twenty-one days to break habits, ninety days to change behaviors. What will you do better and differently because of Mentally Tough training?

- Have as much energy at eight o'clock tonight for your family as you had at eight o'clock this morning for the office.
- Be on when you need to be on.
- Respond to change, adversity, and crisis more constructively.
- Display more positive attitude and confidence.
- Perform more consistently toward the upper range of your talent and skill.

Compared to professional athletes, Corporate Athletes are under more pressure with higher consequences for failure, more demands on their time, and no off-season.

And that's not all. Training as an elite Corporate Athlete helps slow down the aging process. Proper exercise, nutrition, and mental toughness extend an employee's productive life span by reducing the risk of developing chronic diseases such as heart disease, diabetes, and cancer. Adequate sleep heads the list of the basic forms of recovery; adequate nutrition comes second. Longer, happier, more productive lives represent a rich payoff for everyone.

The program in this book is based on scientific research and proven results from the field of sport science. It specifically targets the busy businessperson—the Corporate Athlete—at every level of the organization. Executives and professionals are ravenous for this information and are scooping it up in droves. Why? Because there are few, if any, solid nutrition programs designed for executives and professionals and none that includes the performance-enhancing edge *The Corporate Athlete* packs.

"Corporate Athlete" is a term I use because to perform at high levels, a corporate executive needs as much stamina as a professional athlete needs in competitive sports. Consider the demands that today's business climate makes on Corporate Athletes: they must perform at highly competent levels under intense pressure for ten or more hours a day, often six days a week. They are expected to continue this extraordinary output over a career span of four decades.

How does that make you feel? Most people respond by saying that it makes them feel exhausted or even depressed. But that only goes to show that you need this technology as much as an athlete in sport. You do not have the leisure of an extended off-season, and you cannot pick and choose the days or the weeks when you are willing to put yourself on the line and compete. That is why we say you are the athlete of all athletes, and that is why you need the information in this program.

At LGE's Orlando campus we have trained professional athletes such as tennis players Jim Courier, Pete Sampras, Monica Seles, Aranxta Sánchez-Vicario, Jennifer Capriati, and Chanda Rubin; golfers Ernie Els, Nick Faldo, Helen Alfredsson, Se Ri Pak, Kelly Leadbetter, and Mike Hulbert; Olympic gymnast Wendy Bruce; and hockey players Eric Lindros, Ken Daneyko, Mike Dunham, Mike Richter, and Petr Sykora; NFL quarterback Jim Harbaugh, 1998 AFC Defensive Player of the Year Charles Woodsen, and fullback Clarence "Pooh Bear" Williams; and 1998 Indianapolis 500 winner Eddie Cheever.

In March 1989 the U.S. Tennis Association sent me to meet with Michael Chang and his parents in Palm Springs, California. I asked Michael how much running he did. He said he ran thirty to forty minutes, steady state, every day.

Here was the fastest person in tennis and he was doing *linear* training. In other words, he wasn't alternating between stress and recovery—oscillating, in a word—although tennis is purely an interval sport. I suggested that Michael change his routine, and we developed a periodization training schedule for him. In June of that year he won the French Open.

What about you? Do you fly through the day, all stress, all the time? Or do you, like the world's smartest and best-trained athletes, allow yourself time to recover and strengthen from the stress hits? You have at least the same stress demands as they do—probably more! That's why we teach the same Mentally Tough skills to thousands of Corporate Athletes from *Fortune* 1,000 companies such as Morgan Stanley Dean Witter, Estee Lauder, Merrill Lynch, Bristol Myers Squibb, Prudential Securities, and the State Farm Insurance Companies.

The Five Keys to Success

The lifestyle principles of *The Corporate Athlete* that professional athletes and thousands of corporate clients have learned from us are:

1. Motivate yourself and others—what works for you will work for those around you.

2. Train yourself mentally and physically—concentrate on growing 1 percent better each day.

3. Hone your performance skills—savor the moment and love the battle.

4. Observe recovery time—development throughout life depends on the amount of recovery you get.

5. Cultivate spirituality—value every second of every day.

For decades, people have given lip service to the roles of fitness, nutrition, and attitude in their everyday lives—not only at work, but at home as well. All Corporate Athletes are aware of their importance. Awareness does not need to be improved. What needs to be improved is committing to correcting the problem. The issue is awareness vs. commitment.

My Story

My undergraduate degree from the University of Illinois (UI) was in wildlife biology from the College of Agriculture. My only job offer was with a well-known pork production company. One of my job tasks would have included cleaning manure from the pens. *Sooooo* . . . I entered graduate school with every intention of pursuing a masters in population genetics at UI's Department of Dairy Science. Had I pursued that life, I might be counting wolves in Wyoming and probably loving the outdoors. Fortunately, my sister, Ruthann, and the girl I was dating at the time talked me into looking at physical education.

I got straight A's for the first time ever in my life and continued for the next five years, earning a masters and a Ph.D. in exercise physiology.

While I was working toward my Ph.D., I was eating *constantly*. I would exercise, but then I'd head straight to the nearest snack machine to unwind with a bag of chips and a bottle of pop. Several nights a week, I'd join my friends at a bar for a few beers. Despite maintaining my exercise regimen, I put on weight—eventually getting thirty pounds heavier than I am now.

After graduating from Florida State University, I returned to Illinois and became, at twenty-six, the youngest NCAA Division I tennis coach in the nation at the time. But I didn't like how I looked, so I began modifying the way I took care of myself. I'd like to say I was trying to set a good example for my players, but mostly I was trying to deal with my own problem.

In 1981 I was conducting a sports medicine clinic at Hilton Head Island. Former Wimbledon champion Stan Smith was also on the program. He was speaking to the group, and someone stood up and asked, "How are you transitioning your life as an athlete to your new career as a businessman?" Smith talked about how his life as an athlete had prepared him for the competition of business, how he loved negotiation, and how he loved speaking in public as compared to playing a tennis match.

All of a sudden, it hit me—*there is a great athlete in all of us.* That day, I changed the focus of my career and began studying great performers. In the early '80s, a corporate executive heard me put on a tennis coaches' course and he asked me if I could do the same talk for his people that I just gave on performance, on getting fit, on taking care of yourself, on figuring out what is right in your life. I did.

I was already working with Jim Loehr, one of my partners at LGE. We worked one-on-one with several athletes, and in collaboration with the U.S. Tennis Association. Jim had also been conducting Mentally Tough training for businesspeople. We often talked about combining the training of the mind and the body, the physical and the mental, and we opened our firm in the fall of 1991, developing the Mentally Tough training program for Corporate Athletes. The program also applies to medical professions, educators, law enforcement, entertainers, spouses, and children.

Maximizing Executive Performance

There is a great athlete in all of us—mentally, physically, emotionally, and spiritually. *The Corporate Athlete* is about bringing it out of you.

This book is about improving your corporate life every day without sacrificing performance. Other books are of a broader nature, with little or no emphasis for executives and professionals. *The Corporate Athlete* will help you live longer and healthier, but it is primarily about enhancing your performance, making you a better worker or manager and therefore more successful. This is not about sacrifice. It's about making you better right now. You will see, through specific situations, how aspects of *The Corporate Athlete* will benefit you directly, on a day-to-day basis.

The Corporate Athlete is designed to help busy people adapt to a lifestyle change. It concludes with a twenty-one-day training program that encourages and charts progress. It rewards you with daily and weekly benchmarks.

The Corporate Athlete is not like anything a businessperson has ever gone on before, and yet it makes total sense. Other programs cut calories so people lose weight. *For a time.* But none of them supports a quality, long-term, achievable lifestyle. None of them tells you how to achieve peak health and job performance. The others would lead you to believe their plans are for a lifetime, but as a practical matter, nobody can adhere to them. They're too strict! This plan is much simpler: describe the constraints in your job and in your life, and a program will be constructed around it that you can stick with. If you proceed with alert determination, you will succeed.

You will become self-actualized or truly fulfilled only when your needs become your wants. You have needs: nutrition, exercise, spirituality, self-esteem, to love and be loved, safety, and security. For example, you already know that you need to eat well and exercise. When you *want* to eat well and exercise and then make them happen because you want to—not because you need to—you will start down the path to fulfillment. That is when you will handle problems better than anyone else. That is when your performance will go through the roof.

Part I

WINNING THE DAILY MARATHON: MOTIVATION AND PERFORMANCE

1

You Are a
Corporate Athlete

*The business of the future must accommodate an incredible
acceleration of change. In the next millennium, change in
business will be synonymous with progress.*

—Hotelier Steve Wynn

Corporate Athlete Principle 1:

If you want to improve your business
performance, go into training.

Poor morale, low motivation, burnout, skyrocketing employee health care costs, staggering reeducation and retraining costs from high employee turnover are just a few of the areas positively affected by training to be a Corporate Athlete. The ultimate benefits—improved employee health and happiness—in turn not only help the bottom line, they also drive the competitive edge.

The Corporate Athlete is any individual who wants to achieve maximum performance. Whether it's negotiating a sale or developing a customer service program, Corporate Athletes constantly need to be at their best. You must handle pressures at work, perform on demand regardless of the circumstances, access your talent and skills when you need them most, manage your time efficiently, and set realistic goals and expectations for yourself. Basically, when you have to be "on," you must access empowering emotions because—and this is a cold, cruel fact of life—nobody cares what's going on in your life that is preventing you from being on and performing at your highest level.

Corporate Athletes search for balance their entire lifetime. But what is it? Define it for yourself and then make it—whatever *it* is—happen! Of

9

course, you already know it's not that easy. Is it family time, exercise, eating better, time for personal spirituality, time for recreation, to have fun—what is it? For each of us, it's different. And this is a big part of what every Corporate Athlete must do—define a personal mission.

This book details ways of improving your health and happiness, with the underlying goal of improving your performance, both at the office and in your life in general.

You're just starting this program, so let me guess what you are like now. You wake up in the morning between five-thirty and six-thirty, get the kids ready for school, get yourself ready for work, and off you go. Not too much stress in traffic, because you had a good night's sleep, but let's say you get to work at eight in the morning, and from eight until noon, absolute nonstop stress, linear stress. Then comes your first little blip in recovery: lunchtime. But you eat in a hurry because you have to be back in fifteen minutes. So you look at your sandwich and, in one bite, pulverize it. Then back to work at twelve-fifteen, and from twelve-fifteen until six in the evening, nonstop performance stress. Then comes your second blip in recovery, walking to the parking lot—alone at last with your thoughts!—getting in your car, and then traffic. Unbelievable stress from traffic going home. Then comes your third and final blip of recovery in the day: you pull in the driveway at home, and then family stress is created by being home.

Before taking an entirely *different* look at that, let's quantify where you are right now by taking a quiz.

Are You a Corporate Athlete?
Take the Quiz

You bought this book; chances are you either know or suspect that you are a Corporate Athlete. But if you're not sure, take the following quiz. And no fair looking at the answers of the person in the airplane seat next to you.

On a scale of 1 to 10, 10 being the highest, answer the following questions:
Do you characterize yourself as productive?   _____
Do you view yourself as healthy?   _____
Do you view yourself as joyful?   _____
Can you change the way you feel into a positive emotional
    state whenever you choose?   _____
How well do you prepare for the big events in your business
    life?   _____
Do you consider yourself spiritual in nature?   _____

Do you get balance in your life?   _____
Are your performance skills at work as good as they can be?   _____
Are your skills with your family as good as they can be?   _____
Do you mentally, emotionally and physically train as well as
   you could?   _____
Are you as motivated to do things for yourself as you
   could be?   _____
Is it easy for you to find the energy to do the things you
   must do?   _____
What is your perception of how well you keep up with your
   workload?   _____
Is it easy for you to eat healthfully about every 2 to 2½ hours
   throughout your workday?   _____
On average, do you have lots of high-quality sleep at night?   _____
Do you eat well?   _____
Do you have a positive attitude toward the company you
   work for?   _____
Do you intentionally minimize your intake of sugar and fat?   _____
Is it easy for you to get quality time for . . .
Family?   _____
Nutrition?   _____
Exercise?   _____
Recovery?   _____

   Subtotal: _____

For the following multiple-choice questions, choose the most appropriate response:
How many glasses of water or juice do you drink each day? (Coffee
   and sodas don't count.)
      A. 0   C. 3 to 6
      B. 1 to 2   D. 7 or more   _____
How many hours do you exercise weekly?
      A. 0   C. 2½ to 5
      B. 1 to 2½   D. More than 5   _____
How many sick days have you had in the past 12 months?
      A. 5 or more   C. 1 to 2 days
      B. 3 to 4 days   D. 0   _____
How many abdominal curls do you perform per day?
      A. 0   C. 51 to 100
      B. 25 to 50   D. More than 100   _____
How many minutes do you spend stretching each day?
      A. 0   C. 15 or less
      B. 5 or less   D. more than 15

How many servings of fruit, vegetables, or whole grains do you have each day? (1 serving = ½ cup by volume)

    A. 0 to 2　　　　　　　　　C. 7 to 10

    B. 3 to 6　　　　　　　　　D. 11 or more　　　_____

What is the average number of hours of sleep you get per night?

    A. fewer than 5　　　　　　C. 6 to 7

    B. 5 to 6　　　　　　　　　D. 7 to 9　　　　　_____

How often do you estimate that you laugh at work in one day?

    A. Never　　　　　　　　　C. Occasionally

    B. Seldom　　　　　　　　　D. Frequently　　　_____

How many cups of coffee, tea, or other caffeinated drinks do you consume in a day?

    A. More than 3 or　　　　　C. 1 to 2 cups or
       equivalent　　　　　　　　equivalent

    B. 2 to 3 cups or equivalent　D. 0　　　　　　　_____

What is the extent to which you feel challenged and excited about your work?

    A. Nonexistent　　　　　　C. Moderately

    B. A little　　　　　　　　　D. Very　　　　　　_____

Take 0 points for every "A" answer, 3 points for every "B" answer, 6 points for every "C" answer, and 10 points for every "D" answer.

Multiple-Choice Subtotal:_____

Overall Total:_____

Answer these nonscored questions as they pertain to you:

Could you "peak" for presentations or meetings better than you do
   now?

How good would you be if every time you had to be "on" you had
   incredible energy and felt great?

What needs to happen to connect you to living your life better?

What must happen for you to make a personal commitment to being
   an elite performer in business and in life?

What are the three major priorities in your life?

1. _____

2. _____

3. _____

Scoring Key
270 to 320—Ultimate Corporate Athlete
235 to 269—Elite Corporate Athlete
210 to 234—Corporate Athlete mentality but can still improve
180 to 209—Surviving in the Corporate Culture but in need of
            improvement
160 to 179—Barely surviving
 22 to 159—Red Alert!

Motivation Through Positive Attitude

At Johnson Controls Automotive Systems Group in Plymouth and Holland, Michigan, management has always believed that healthy people are more productive. That's why the company built a world-class fitness and medical center and why it puts its leadership development people through our Mentally Tough program.

"We are strong believers in positive attitude," says Director of Leadership Development Rodger Price. "People aren't going to follow someone who isn't excited about leading. So if you're going to lead people, you have to act."

That's exactly what we teach: If you want to be upbeat, *act* upbeat. Before you know it, you will *be* upbeat. Being able to change your physiological chemistry, and thus your emotional state, on command is the definition of what it means to access an empowering emotion on demand. When things are tough, or when you just don't feel like being there, but you must perform, you can still access powerful, positive emotions.

"The revelation for us was, *Guess what!* It works!" Price says. "You can certainly see the application in a one-on-one sport such as tennis. If you worry about a match and you act nervous, it is a spiral downward. But if you want to be somebody who is confident, start acting confident."

Training for Success

Do you think professional athletes fuel their bodies with fast food? Would they be able to exercise or practice once a month and still have the energy to perform at championship levels during competition? Of course not. Corporate Athletes are no different, except that the demands are greater for you. You must perform daily at high levels at work and at home. And because your corporate career lasts longer than the professional athlete's, you must train every day, like professional athletes, with a long-term program that includes nutrition, exercise, and recovery. Remember, athletes train constantly to perform in one race, game, or match. Corporate Athletes usually perform *all* the time and rarely train. If we are to keep improving year after year, this pattern will have to change.

Employees can protect their health and happiness and continue to perform at high levels under great pressure by doing what athletes do:

T est yourself and then give yourself the time to improve.
R ecovery, to get stronger emotionally, mentally, spiritually, and physically.
A ffirm your attitude on an ongoing basis.
I ntensify your effort with intervals interspersed.
N ourish your body, mind, and spirit.

Today's employees must become Corporate Athletes, which means adapting the training mentality of elite, high-performance athletes. Rituals, balance, attitude, emotional skills, mental preparation, teamwork, recovery, fitness, nutrition, and sleep are fundamentals in the training process. Successful competitors in sports learn to embrace stress, not run or hide from it. In fact, they use stress (physical, mental, and emotional) to become stronger, faster, more focused, and more powerful. Compared to professional athletes in sports, Corporate Athletes are under more pressure, with higher consequences for failure, more demands on their time, and with no off-season. Short-term corporate solutions to day-to-day problems are often directly opposite to solutions derived from a long-term perspective. The long-term perspective means designing more adaptive work cultures that support employee health, quality of life, and personal renewal. To meet the challenge of today's workplace, employees must be stronger emotionally, more flexible, more stress-resilient, and mentally tougher than ever.

It's Never Too Late

I don't care where you are in life or where you are in your career, the human system will do whatever you train it to do. If you train and if you practice mentally, emotionally, physically, and spiritually, there is all the evidence in the world to support the fact that you will continue growing throughout life.

Corporate Athlete Action Items

- Reenergize yourself at various times of the day by walking up three or four flights of stairs or by going for a short walk outside at various periods during the day.
- Do at least one thing today to improve the balance in your life, be it with family, exercise, good nutrition, prayer, meditation, or anything else that provides you with a feeling of balance.
- Review the Corporate Athlete quiz again to see where you can improve by 1 percent today. Write it down, and try to do better by just a little. No drastic changes yet.

2

Commit to Yourself: Find the Corporate Athlete Within

*You will find rest from vain fancies if you perform
every act in life as though it were your last.*

—MARCUS AURELIUS ANTONINUS

CORPORATE ATHLETE PRINCIPLE 2:

Take ownership and responsibility for who you are.

If you are overweight, you must own it. Don't just say, "I know I'm overweight." Own it—be responsible for it.

Why do we work so hard in business? Why do we kill ourselves at work with long hours and punishing workloads? Oh, we complain about it all, but we still end up doing it. Our jobs depend on it. We set aside time—personal time—to get the work done.

Yet, we don't work to take care of ourselves. We set aside time to get a work project done, but we won't set aside time to take care of ourselves. What is it about exercise, nutrition, and spirituality that we will actually avoid them at all costs or sacrifice them so we can do more work?

At a recent corporate training program I heard the CEO make a presentation about what demands the next millennium would bring. He said the following would have to occur: Decisions must be made faster; there must be more streamlined thinking; improved vertical communication along with improved personal responsibility and accountability; improved use of e-mail and voice mail; improved processing systems; improved information sources and outsourcing; the devotion of time to cross-functional activities; and the empowerment of individuals at all levels of the corporation. There will be increasing requests for everyone to step up and do more.

When Martina Navratilova hit the tennis scene, Chris Evert suddenly found herself no longer dominating the women's game. Evert made a huge commitment to herself to improve, to get fit, and to take control of her destiny. Because of Evert's commitment to herself, she raised the level of her competitive abilities and created one of the greatest rivalries in tennis history.

You are the only person who puts yourself on the line, takes it on the chin, and sacrifices yourself to perform for the company. That means that in our business lives we must stop doing things that are not bottom-line-oriented. But why can't we do the same for ourselves? Why don't we stop doing things that are not bottom-line-oriented for ourselves physically, emotionally, mentally, and spiritually?

The Corporate Athlete Within

Most Corporate Athletes are aware of the importance of eating and exercise, but they don't know how to commit to these things over the long run. Once you discover the athlete within, you can train yourself to find the time, handle the pressure, get out of a slump, and work out a program. Only you know what you are in control of and what you are not. And only you can tap the energy of your personal desires, build your self-image, and unearth the stick-to-itiveness you need to make a healthy choice with life-changing results.

How can you become a person of action? Have you recently examined your life, mentally, emotionally, spiritually, and physically? What must you do to commit to taking action in your life?

Here's one idea: Learn to anticipate the *benefits* of your decisions. Then face the reality of your condition. There is always fear of some sort: fear of not losing weight, fear of confrontations, even fear of cold-calling. But you must let go of your fear.

Hitting 110 Percent: Performance and Recovery

Everything is going great for Bob Glowaki and his family. Maybe *too* great. One son just graduated from chiropractic school. Another is getting a degree in film production from the University of Delaware. The third is getting his master's degree in communications. And his daughter is a senior in high school. On the professional side things are pretty swell, too. He raised profitability at his eleven Merrill Lynch offices in Illinois and Iowa to ninth best in the corporation and was named Manager of the Year in

1998. The downside to all this was that Glowaki, who is in his twenty-fourth year with Merrill Lynch, was promoted to resident vice president and relocated to Chicago. His daughter didn't want to move in the midst of her senior year. Who could blame her?

Glowaki took the promotion, of course, along with the increased responsibility. And thus began the greatest challenge of his career, living in Chicago during part of the week, Peoria part of the week, and on the road the rest, all the while shifting out of one job and into another, learning new faces, and trying to maintain some semblance of a family life. Glowaki is living in hotel rooms and trying hard to eat well, exercise, and manage stress.

He copes in creative ways. He takes somebody to lunch every day so he's never lonely. "One of my sons told me to buy a basket of fruit and keep it in my room," he says. "'Every time you're tempted to get a burger,' he told me, 'grab an apple.'"

Eating well was less of an issue than making time for exercise. "I started writing time in my appointment book to do my workouts," he says. "Now I get on a treadmill—somewhere!—for twenty minutes, three times a week. I also started running in the evenings because it relieved stress. Exercise didn't disrupt my life at all; it *organized* my life. I'm getting a lot more done with a lot less effort."

But with so much running around, such long hours, he also makes time for recovery. "I say to my wife, 'I'm going to stay home today. It's a beautiful day.' To which she says, 'You're going to lose your job.' And I tell her, 'No, it'll make me *better* at my job.' Sometimes it's a nice, sunny day and I'll just go home and clean my pool. Recovery is a big part of what we do."

Speaking of this, Glowaki says that his transformation into a great Corporate Athlete has been healthy for his marriage of thirty years, too.

"My wife's in great shape," he says. "When I started on this, it was great for her because she always exercised and ate the right stuff. When I became 110 percent, it was great for our relationship."

Improving Health and Happiness

You know what I hear more than anything else from my corporate clients? "I know exercise is important, but I just don't have time." That is what everybody says. Well, by the time you finish reading this book, you'll realize not only that you have the time, you'll *find* the time.

It is a matter of understanding your priorities. What are your values? What is important to you?

The goal for you as a great Corporate Athlete is to have a lifestyle that enables you to access every ounce of your talent and skill to the point that the only limitation you have in your life *is* your talent and skill. What we find is that the limiting factor for most Corporate Athletes is how they live their life. They do not live their life to the point that they can even get close to accessing their talent and their skill.

We at LGE believe that health and happiness are the foundations of everything we do. You must get those parts of your life going in the right direction before you can truly find out how good you can be. Can you increase productivity? Absolutely—*if* you focus on your health and happiness first.

Productivity is usually pretty good already for the people who come to us, but they also believe they can do more. For example, a financial consultant we worked with was on pace to make $750,000 a year—the most he had ever made—and within two years, he'd probably earn $1 million annually. He was doing great professionally. Could he do better? Yes, but not without improving his health and his happiness.

The 360 Process Marathon

Human Resources within Morgan Stanley Dean Witter is an umbrella that encompasses benefits, compensation, training, and professional development. During September, October, and November of each year, the entire corporation tackles several enormous tasks simultaneously, closing its books, budgeting, and business planning for the next year, and conducting its 360-degree performance evaluation process.

"The 360 is incredibly intense," says Claudine McIntee, vice president of training and development within Human Resources.

LGE has conducted Mentally Tough seminars for a number of divisions at Morgan Stanley Dean Witter in recent years, and McIntee approached us about customizing a program specifically to help people in human resources get through their year-end process.

"Year-end" is a term that might as well mean going to war for the stress it implies. "We are always coaching and counseling all of our in-house clients," McIntee says. "It made me wonder what we were doing for ourselves to make sure that *we* were at the top of our game for the year-end process."

These three months would be easier to accommodate if employees literally trained the other nine months in preparation for the fourth quarter. Instead of just waiting for it to happen, I suggested that they should be training like any other professional athlete getting ready for a big annual competitive event when they must be *on, on, on!*

The 360 review is an internal feedback and evaluation system that more and more corporations, from General Electric to The Home Depot, are implementing. Its results are immensely valuable, but for the human resources people at ground zero, it's an enormous amount of work from summer to virtually the New Year.

"There are extremely high expectations if you say that you work at this firm," McIntee says. "People here demand nothing but excellence from themselves and others, and we put in a lot of hours. During the year-end process, colleagues are in the office at six-thirty in the morning and sometimes don't leave until one the next morning, plus weekends. Our hope is that we get people to look at a corporate environment in a different way and not to take themselves so seriously. You really do have to have a sense of humor, and sometimes you just have to go with the flow. Some days you almost want to say, 'Someone put me out of my misery, because I am going to lose my mind.' After a while it becomes comical because that is how exhausted we get."

Don't Wait to SEE

It's unfortunate—but true—that so many people wait for Significant Emotional Events (SEE!) to occur in order to make positive changes in their lives.

Other reasons why people might get motivated include peer groups involved in physical activities. If you have an office where coworkers tend to play softball, most likely you would be inclined to do that.

Once you get into regularity and you know what daily exercise feels like, you will do everything not to miss doing it.

Research shows that there is a dropout rate of about 50 percent within three to six months after most people initiate some kind of formal, healthy lifestyle program, so even if you are in the committed state, you still will need constant reinforcement. Try not to find excuses why you don't have the time or why it hurts too much. Look for ways to make your experience more interesting and more reinforcing so you stay with it.

If all that fails, consider your *workout* periods as time to concentrate on *work* without the usual interruptions. Wouldn't *that* be an efficient use of your time?

Many Corporate Athletes don't understand that they can take control of themselves and manage their time better. Once you understand what you can do well and what you need to improve in, your life will become your own, and your new journey will begin.

Corporate Athlete Action Items

- Identify what will connect you to living your life better.
- Have you had any SEEs (Significant Emotional Events) that have changed the course of your life? What are they?
- Identify what must happen for you personally to make the commitment to be an elite Corporate Athlete.
- Identify anywhere in your twenty-four-hour day where you could expand the day to include what you need to do—exercise, time with family, prayer, meditation, or eating better. If you still can't see how you can expand your day, keep reading. I'll show you the way.

3

Put Stress to Work for You

When I work I relax; doing nothing makes me tired.
—PABLO PICASSO

CORPORATE ATHLETE PRINCIPLE 3:

Quit trying to reduce your stress. Instead, increase
your capacity for stress! To do this, you must
increase the frequency of recovery.

Most people equate the word "stress" with something that needs to be avoided. And while it's almost impossible to define stress in a manner that would meet the needs of all of us to whom the term applies, there are times when we all need a certain amount of emotional, mental, and physical stimulation in life to counterbalance boredom and tedium.

In this chapter I'll review stress concepts. If you're interested in learning even more about stress, I encourage you to read my partner Jim Loehr's book *Stress for Success*.

"Mental toughness" refers to a dynamic state of being in which the tough person meets stress with a flexible and responsive attitude characterized by strength and resiliency. Being Mentally Tough means that if you are in a performance mode you can access the Ideal Performance State even under the most difficult circumstances.

Ideal Performance State (IPS) is the period during which you will perform at the peak of your mental and emotional ability. It is the most effective and reliable mental, emotional, and physical state for performing at your highest level. Corporate Athletes experience a specific group of positive feelings and emotions when they are in IPS—they feel challenged, energized, and confident with a sense of joy, fun, and fulfillment. Someone in business may speak of "being on a roll" when talking about how they felt when in IPS. In sports the popular term is "in the zone."

It's not stress that's detrimental to health, but rather the inability to control stress.

"You have to push your body real hard for a period," says two-time French Open tennis champion Jim Courier, a client of ours at LGE, "and then you have to ease back on it and give it a little bit of time to recover and get stronger. Then you push it hard again and start over."

We Corporate Athletes allow ourselves time to practice when we want to improve a golf swing, learn a new computer program, or teach our children how to ride a bicycle. And we know what happens when we practice too much or don't practice enough—we deteriorate. Understanding the principles of stress and recovery, along with training that specifically fits your needs (not your *materialistic* wants), will help you understand the method behind this training program.

"In the corporate world, the attitude of most people I know has always been to find ways of reducing stress," says Rodger Price of Johnson Controls. "I may try to reduce my stress at certain times, but we're living beings and we depend on stress. That was a new concept for me. Now I say, 'Bring it on!' I can manage it."

I will teach you how to let stress do its job, emphasizing the nutritional and physiological components of this phenomenon. Corporate America has been sold a bill of goods about stress, that stress is a career-destroying monster. Not true! Avoiding stress reduces functional capacity, but seeking stress in the correct manner helps you reach your highest potential.

You Are What You Train to Be

Your response to stress will depend entirely on how you are exposed to stress.

One of my partners, exercise physiology guru Pat Etcheberry, is a very playful guy. Every athlete who comes down to our Orlando campus hears from Pat that there are alligators and wild boar running through the woods all around us. Then he sends them out jogging. On a dirt road behind our property, Pat and an assistant get ahead of the athletes in the bushes, crouching real low, aiming a videocamera at the joggers. When several NFL offensive linemen he was training came upon them, Pat started shaking a sapling and making sounds like a wild boar. You should see the video! They probably hit personal bests in the forty-yard dash.

Two weeks later, five members of the FBI's elite hostage rescue team were on hand for our Mentally Tough program. As he had with the NFL players, Pat sent the FBI agents off into the woods. But when they heard Pat and his assistant rustling in the brush, their response was much different. They not only stood their ground, they also crouched for action. Pat's assistant panicked. "What if they brought their guns?" he said. He and Pat stood up fast.

Exposure to stress will increase your functional capacity. In fact, stress is the stimulus for all growth.

How you train with exercise will train your physiological response to emotional stress. *So don't exercise to get healthier*—exercise to increase your capacity for stress. Exercise to get stronger emotionally and physically; then you'll get healthier in spite of yourself.

Stress and Recovery

If there is a better way of doing his job, or if someone has an idea for improving his personal life, Rick Brown is interested in hearing about it.

A forty-year-old vice president at First Union Mortgage Corporation in Jacksonville, Florida, Brown is an avid consumer of self-help books, ranging from Stephen Covey's *The 7 Habits of Highly Effective People* to Kenneth Blanchard's *The One-Minute Manager.*

Like many people, Brown wants to get through his day without being beaten down by the many stress hits his job inflicts. "Our occupation would be considered pretty high-stress on occasion, certainly," he says. "Making sure that you are not getting things blown out of proportion is crucial. It is real easy when the stress levels rise to get overemotional and let some frustration turn into hostility or an inappropriate response."

Brown's key takeaways as a trained Corporate Athlete involve time management: planning his schedule better, looking ahead, visualizing the day or week ahead, and making appointments for personal recovery time.

"I was real guilty of taking on-the-job frustration home with me," he says, "not learning to let go and kind of shutting down emotionally at the end of the day. I used to get preoccupied worrying about things that I really had no control over."

It's all part of managing the stress that is thrown his way. Instead of looking for relief, Brown now welcomes the stress in his life, tackles it, recovers, and awaits the next hit.

Choose Health and Happiness

Once you reach a certain level of performance based on your innate talent and all the skills you developed throughout your life, how in the world do you keep improving? This is the basic underlying question for all Corporate Athletes, because once you wrap up one year's tremendous performance on December 31, the year starts all over again on January 1. You're only as good as yesterday, not last year. The question we must ask ourselves is this: How can the best of the best, the elite of the elite, continue improving their performance once their talent and skills are already pushed to the limits? The answer is that they must keep looking forward.

You *choose* to be a great performer within your talent and your skill. You must train to bring your talent and skill to life on demand. It's the attitude you bring to the table that determines where you go from here. Don't be just a spectator in your own life. A spectator watches your family grow up, watches your business pass you by. Participate in your own life.

What was found from the laboratory of world-class sports was what we at LGE call the performance triad. It is a triangle that has at its pinnacle performance/productivity, with the baseline (or the foundation) being health and happiness. Our premise is: *Once you are the best, the only way to keep improving your performance day after day is to improve your health and your happiness.* If you improve the legs of the triangle, you improve the strength of your overall performance.

As soon as you say you are the best—whether it is in sports or business—you no longer are. You should never think you are so good that there is no room for improvement, because there always is. You should think you are *good.* You should have very positive feelings. You might think you are the best from a confidence standpoint when making a presentation, but then steadily keep growing and improving.

We have known for years that the mind influences the body. For example, how do you know if people at the office are having a bad day? Body language. If their heads are slumped over, or if their spines are not erect as they walk, you can tell they're having a bad day. It's the mind influencing the body.

But we also know that the body can influence the mind. It manifests in how you carry yourself, how you think and act, even the articulation of speech.

When you're trying to influence someone, whether in sales or simply making a presentation, 93 percent of the influencing process is your body's physical presence, your physiology, and your articulation. The words you use are only 7 percent of the influencing process.

The way you breathe, your posture, how you walk, and your facial expressions determine the state you are in. If you don't believe this, smile for about thirty seconds and see how you feel. Then create a frown and turn the corners of your mouth downward to the point where you really have the appearance of being sad or virtually angry. I guarantee that within a few seconds you will start feeling that way. Now smile again and notice the change.

At the 1991 U.S. Open tennis tournament, Jimmy Connors was playing Aaron Krickstein in the fourth round and was losing badly in the fifth set. Connors was pulled wide and could not return Krickstein's shot. As Connors' momentum carried him into the railing, he looked at the gentleman sitting in the front row (I was in the third row, so I easily heard this comment) and said, "I've got him right where I want him!" Even though Connors was in a losing situation and was struggling, he still found humor.

I believe that we have to look at our lives and our jobs in the same way. When we are born, we are not given a road map on how to find our way. It is only through trials and tribulations that we get stronger. It is how we handle those problems that determines if we will be healthy and happy.

It is not the problem itself that causes our misery, it's how we perceive the problem and how we respond. We do not have to be at the mercy of our emotions. If we are negative or have a bad attitude, this sets up our entire physiology for a negative reaction, not the positive response that is appropriate and adaptive. Ralph Waldo Emerson said, "The ancestor of every action is thought." How you perceive a situation and the processing of that thought will determine your response.

Great success is inseparable from having great amounts of energy and vitality. If you want to produce the desired result, you must drive your emotional state and control your emotional response. No matter how bad it gets, you can always control your state. I believe that the megaperformer of the future will be Corporate Athletes who, when they get into a high negative energy state will realize that this is not conducive to great performance and will utilize all the strategies presented here to access a positive emotional state.

Recovery does not necessarily mean that you must relax. Recovery could involve paperwork, phone calls, etc. When and how to rest are vital to our well-being. The key to life is balancing stress and recovery. Without recovery, all stress eventually becomes excessive stress. Pure positive energy (or fun) is the single best measure of balance between stress and recovery.

Acclimate to what you must do, and learn on your own to balance your time. No one will baby you in Corporate America. No one else will tell you when to go home from work.

Some Corporate Athletes we talk to about spreading a Mentally Tough attitude through their organizations say, "I can't do this because I don't get any support from up above." That is a total cop-out. If management doesn't buy into this, it doesn't mean anything. Cultures don't change unless individuals change, and that is true of society. It starts with you and how you decide to act for yourself.

There Is No Finish Line

Bea Cassou, thirty-seven, is a managing director in corporate finance at Morgan Stanley Dean Witter. She works with media and entertainment companies such as Walt Disney, cable companies such as Cablevision Systems, and broadcasting companies such as CBS when they need money, both debt and equity, and also on merger and acquisition transactions.

"We struggle daily with issues of how to maintain the energy to do what we do at the pace that we do it for a long period of time," she says. "I have been doing this for twelve years. You can always sprint, but it is hard to do the marathon all day long."

What's life like in the Morgan Stanley Dean Witter fast lane? "It is like athletics," says Cassou. "Stress is our practice, our training, our improvement. We put pressure or stress on ourselves so we get to be better athletes, better tennis players. It's the same in banking, the same in the corporate environment. You put more stress on yourself so you are more productive, more effective, so you do better and better. If you reframe the way you look at it, you feel better about it, but you also understand that there are limits."

The term "Corporate Athlete" is a natural one at Morgan Stanley Dean Witter. "We use that term a lot, 'athlete,'" Cassou says. "In situations of recruiting, of promotion, of compensation, or when we are discussing people, we often ask, 'Is this person an athlete?' To be an athlete is a high compliment around here, because it means this person is someone who works extremely hard, pulls a lot of weight, does the heavy lifting themselves. This is the person who makes it happen, who does the work, who gets out in the front line. This is the 'athlete' rather than 'This is the relationship guy.'"

Stress has a very negative connotation, but it is something that people like Bea Cassou are learning not only to live but also to grow with every day. "You put yourself in stressful situations," she says, "and your whole life becomes stressful because you put many stressful situations in your life. Looking at it as something that is not negative but life-enhancing was a new approach for me. Developing tools to deal with stress was my most important takeaway—planning times to rest, planning time to recover from the stress. The analogy I use is working out every single day. You can't exercise the muscles that you toned up yesterday; you have to let them rebuild before you have a heavy workout again."

It's all about oscillating, moving between situations, giving yourself a break from stressors when necessary. Oscillation doesn't necessarily change your workday, but it does change the way you live your overall life. Rather than constantly running from a very intensive workday to dinner, trying to pack in as much as we can, say, "I am going to go home and rest," or anything that is a release from the stress we have. Although it doesn't reduce the stress, it does increase the release, forming an overall better balance in life, so we can do this longer and grow more.

Cassou now plans stress recovery time in her otherwise insane schedule rather than assume it will happen any other way. "In Manhattan, where I work, you tend to pile things on, layers upon layers of often stressful activity," she says. "Now I look at my day today, or the week ahead, think about what the demands will be, and say, 'Okay, when am I going to rest? When am I going to heal from this stress? When am I going to sit back and take a breath?' Because once I do, then I can go conquer the next set of tasks. Don't let days and weeks and years pass, trying to pull yourself across the finish line. There is none, of course."

Exercise Is Stress and Recovery

While exercise is physical stress, it is also mental and emotional recovery. The thing about the body and understanding stress is that your body can't tell the difference between the physical stress of exercise and the mental stress of the office. Stress is stress. If you don't believe that, look at what happens to heart rate under physical stress of exercise; it goes up. But under the mental stress from the office, your heart rate goes up also, and so does blood pressure, as does the sweating response you feel in your hands. But the key point of exercise is that while you are getting that physical stress—that training stress, we call it—your mind is getting mental and emotional recovery.

The Entertainer

Jeff Sklar is typical of the thousands of men and women we work with on the corporate side. A partner and vice president of institutional sales at Gruntal & Co., a private partnership investment bank in Manhattan, Sklar is a person who has never waited for the world to collapse before he recognized the need to do something.

"I'm a relationship guy, a client guy," Sklar says. "I represent the firm, entertaining our largest money management clients at least three nights a week, often on weekends. I take them out to dinners and sporting events."

What a delicious job! Great food, fascinating people, exhilarating entertainment—and it pays well. What could be wrong with that? Well, there's the stress. And the great opportunity to quickly get overweight.

What a corporate athlete like Sklar needed was a way of raising his energy level in a positive, constructive way, on an ongoing basis. But he also needed to get recovery.

We helped Sklar access energy when he needed it—in part through better nutrition, but also by learning to pull back when he didn't need it, enabling him to do a better job recovering. We did this by developing an overall program of exercise, nutrition, and mental training.

"Sometimes you trade on your strength to the point where you don't realize how inefficiently you're using it," Sklar says in retrospect. "I never realized how much I could accomplish if I marshaled my energy more effectively. Doing so has enabled me to give 150 percent.

"Now I think like a sprinter, not like a marathoner," he adds, "and that has been powerful to me in every aspect of my life."

That's very much like life. Life itself is a marathon, but you've got to develop the attitude of a sprinter: Sprint like crazy, then get *recovery*. Sprint like crazy and get *balance*.

The Magic of Interval Training

There are two hormones in the system that help us perform. One group of hormones is called catecholamines (pronounced *ka-te-ko-le-meens*). When the fight response occurs, your body becomes flooded with them. They are responsible for the fight response. The other hormone is cortisol. Massive amounts of cortisol occur during the fear or flight response. I'm sure you have heard of the fight or flight response. Exercise helps your body increase its capacity for catecholamines. It increases catecholamine response. It decreases resting levels of catecholamines and increases catecholamine recovery. Isn't that how you would want to respond to stress mentally and emotionally? Get a quick spike of catecholamines? A higher spike and a faster recovery? Yet at the same time, exercise trains your body to decrease its output of cortisol, and it increases the output of endorphins, those naturally occurring hormones that give us the feeling of a sedative. We call it the most powerful drug known to humankind, and it is in your body. So you see, exercise helps you recover mentally.

But how should you exercise properly? When doing your aerobic training, we no longer want you to do flat-line training. All of us have grown up with the thought that when we exercise we should get our heart rate into the target heart rate range and then just simply keep it there for twenty or thirty minutes and we get a good level of aerobic fitness. That would improve the heart-lung function, but the problem is that nothing in nature occurs in a flat line.

We have already talked about how we are creatures of oscillation. So if you want to put stress to work for you, what I want you to do is start doing interval training. If you exercise the way I will train you later in this book, you will train your body's physical response to emotional stress.

Rise Up, Fall Back, and Live to Rise Again

Dale Carnegie told the story of two men who were out chopping wood. One man worked hard all day, took no breaks, and stopped only briefly, for lunch. The other chopper took several breaks during the day and a short nap at lunch. At the end of the day, the woodsman who had taken no breaks was quite disturbed to see that the other woodsman had cut more wood than he. He said, "I don't understand. Every time I looked around, you were sitting down, yet you cut more wood than I did." His associate said, "Did you notice that while I was sitting down, I was sharpening my ax?"

One thing we recommend at LGE is to practice an "IPS look" during your recovery phase. If you're walking, keep your head up, shoulders level, and arms loosely held at the sides—the walk of the confident prizefighter. Don't swagger or walk cockily; walk with confidence.

We all work at intervals. Remember, the heart beats in cycles, the brain works in cycles. We even sleep in cycles. If we exercise in cycles also, it trains our physiology to get in the same status as we are mentally, as our heart beats, as our muscles contract.

Many corporate executives love to exercise. They exercise in the morning, at lunchtime, or in the late afternoon. Research shows that if you really want to reduce the levels of stress in your life, the best time to exercise is late in the afternoon. That helps you accommodate the stress you have been through for the day, releases the endorphins, gets you into a calm yet energized state, and prepares you for the evening with your family. But the key point is this: If you cannot exercise then, at least get some exercise when you can. Many Corporate Athletes plan their exercise in the morning because they are still totally in control of their time.

Bad News on the Line

At a multibillion-dollar company, I was doing a one-day program for its eight top executives. When I spoke about stress and recovery, the chief executive officer of the company stopped me in midstream. "I want to create a situation for my people," he said. Then he looked at his seven charges and said: "Here it is: You are going in to make a major presentation on a multimillion-dollar project. You must be at your best. Just as you walk into the reception area of the office of the decision-maker you are going to be selling, the person's assistant tells you that you just got a call from me, and it is an emergency, you have to call the office. Now, you know this is not going to be a good-news phone call. But you make the call, and you hear the bad news, and it *is* bad news, and you hang up. I want to know what you are going to do. Are you going to go right into that meeting immediately after receiving bad news?"

Everyone unanimously said no.

"What will you do?" the CEO asked. "You can't say to the assistant that you are leaving for a while."

Suddenly someone suggested, "But I could say that I am going to go use the rest room. No one would ever question me doing that."

The CEO endorsed that approach, to which I added an idea of my own: Take a hike instead of actually going to the rest room (unless, of course, the bad news you received forced you to go). Go up two or three flights of steps, literally changing your heart rate and chemistry. That should take fewer than five minutes. *Then*—and only then—go into the negotiation. The key thing is, when you are going into recovery, you don't want to dwell on the negative news from the phone call. Get over the negative news, then go into recovery, then go into your meeting.

Recovery Time Increases Productivity

After a year as an up-and-coming account executive with the Clinique cosmetics company, Shelly Bishop, thirty-five, found herself in a difficult situation, at odds with a supervisor.

"I'd taken as much as I could," she says. "The stress level with my boss was a daily hurdle and I was unable to focus on my real job responsibilities—which were motivating my Clinique consultants and driving my retail business. Things like staying up until all hours of the morning (many days in a row), working on projects that she would create on a whim, faxing them back to her only to have her tear them apart in two minutes and want them completely redone. This despite my real job requirements calling for me to be on my feet, in stores, from early morning until evening."

Clinique had literally taken over her life. She was single at the time, living in a two-bedroom apartment in Greenville, South Carolina, and Clinique—a line of five hundred different products—followed her from the front door and on into the kitchen, the den, her home office, and her bedroom. She had tons of mail from various Clinique offices and retailers, stacks of reports that she had no idea how to read or what they meant, stock control books, and faxes were everywhere. It was really out of control.

She got physically sick and could not get well, so she took a leave of absence.

When she returned to work, the boss was gone but her home was still all work, all the time. Her mom—a professional secretary—helped Bishop go through everything in her home office, taming the paper tiger. "I had to get my home life straightened out, and I had to make the commitment to myself that Clinique was Clinique and Shelly's life was Shelly's life, and they weren't going to go back and forth," she says.

It's hard having an office in your home. Everything that had to do with Clinique had to stay in her office, which meant that she could no longer bring work into the den and watch TV. She had to sit in her office and do it because that was where she did Clinique, and the den was her personal enjoyment space.

"I'm now married and expecting a child, but my husband, Christian, and I still have conversations about *our* home vs. *my* home office," Bishop says. "Sometimes he tells me, 'Okay, Clinique's time is over, it's my time.' And I'll still say, 'Okay, but just one more thing, just one more thing.' You can't ever walk away from it. Still, I learned the hard way that I can't keep going and going. I've got to have recovery time."

Bishop has incredible results to show for her new discipline. At Clinique's annual sales meeting in 1998, she was recognized as one of the top account executives in the company.

Office Oscillation Strategies

Anyone who took an introductory psychology course has heard the name Abraham Maslow, who developed the hierarchy of human needs. On the foundation are physiological needs: food, water, sleep. What we found in our research is that the most basic human need is the need to expend energy to move, to be stimulated, to be aroused, and then to recover energy through food, water, and sleep.

Oscillation applies to the way you run your business life, too.

When Origins Natural Resources, a division of Estee Lauder, conducts product knowledge, sales training, and company philosophy education programs, oscillation is always a part of the program.

"If you've been lecturing—or listening—from 9:30 A.M. to 4:00 P.M., you're not going to be as successful as if you had stopped the lecture and done some movement or activity to reinforce the knowledge and the learning," says Stacy Panagakis, executive director of education worldwide for the cosmetics company. "Within the education department, we talk as a group about how important it is to have short intervals of lecture, combined with movement or activities to solidify the knowledge. It helps increase retention and understanding of what we are teaching."

Origins' philosophy is: "Beauty begins with your well-being." "We believe beauty is as important on the inside as on the outside," Panagakis says. "You must take care of yourself. At our annual national sales meetings we get up in the morning and power-walk as a group. We have Yoga instructors come in. We try to reinforce well-being as a company."

Another component of the Origins approach is the chair massage offered to its retail customers and, on Fridays, to its employees at corporate offices. It consists of a fifteen-minute shoulders-and-neck massage, soothing what Panagakis calls "the telephone muscles."

Behavior modification is the key to improving your corporate life. Whether you are a leader in business today, a middle manager, or someone climbing the corporate ladder, you must get control of your lifestyle. Schedule recovery. This becomes a very important part of life and the only way that stress truly becomes your friend.

Corporate Athlete Action Items

- Get some form of exercise today.
- Plan ahead when you will get your exercise time into your day.
- Improve your mental capacity tonight by helping your child with calculus homework, solving a crossword puzzle, or learning new words of a foreign language.
- Whether it's physical, emotional, mental, or spiritual, challenge yourself in each area at least once today.

4

Preparing for the Big Game

When the One Great Scorer comes to write against your name,
He marks not that you won or lost, but how you played the game.

—GRANTLAND RICE

CORPORATE ATHLETE PRINCIPLE 4:

If you're going to be more productive, if you're going to be a better performer, you need more energy.

When I say men and women need more energy in a corporate presentation, people look at me and respond like Scotty, the chief engineer on the original *Star Trek:* "You cannot squeeze blood out of a turnip! I'm giving all I've got; I don't have anything left to give!" Well, I disagree 100 percent. I'm going to teach you where you can find more energy, and describe the choices you can make to recover energy from stress within any twenty-four-hour cycle. It's all about recovery.

Everyone is a performer, whether it's Pete Sampras, Elizabeth Dole, or you. And when it comes time to do the job, you'd better be good and you'd better be on. Making sure you know *that* is what success is all about. To get you moving in the direction of success, you must face the truth about yourself. Self-examination is vitally important, and it must be cold-blooded and honest.

If you ever lost a sale, didn't receive an expected promotion, or gave a poorly received presentation, you must look at how your performance was received. The perception of who you are out in the marketplace, as well as your own perception of yourself, are prime determining factors in your ability to achieve success. Like it or not, perception is reality.

When we emotionally lose control, there is no chance for high performance.

What is your reflexive response when you receive a stress hit? Are you critical? Do you hold contempt? Are you vengeful? Do you withdraw emotionally? Are you defensive? If any of these is the case, you must face the truth for yourself.

Jana Novotna was ranked among the top tennis players in the world for many years. She probably received the most publicity when she was beating Steffi Graf 5–2 in the third set of a Wimbledon finals in 1993. On the precipice of big success, Novotna went through a total collapse and lost the final. The same thing happened to her in a couple of other tournaments, and she was beginning to wear the label of a great player who couldn't win the big ones.

Is it possible that you, like Jana Novotna, have incredible talent and skill *but,* when it gets to crunch time, you realize that you're just not able to perform at the highest level of your ability? If that is the case, you, just like Novotna, must train and expose yourself to stress so that your response to stress becomes the highest level possible. Unless you get your life wired right it will be impossible to bring your talent and skill to life every time the demand presents itself.

There is a happy ending to the Jana Novotna story, by the way. She did reach her dream and won a Wimbledon singles championship in 1998, achieving a major life goal—and only after enduring incredible stress.

Great Moments in Top Performance

When we examine the megaperformers in business today, we find that they are readily able to access the positive emotions responsible for high performance.

Do you think Michael Eisner always gets enough sleep before going to work? Do you think Bill Gates never gets stuck in traffic before going to a big meeting? Do you believe that Leonard Lauder, directing a multi-billion-dollar enterprise, *ever* works without stress? To these great executives, the fact that they did not sleep well at night, were stuck in traffic, arrived late for a meeting, or even ate something that disagreed with their stomach had nothing to do with pulling off a great performance. Early in their careers, they all learned one of the cruelest and coldest facts about corporate life: No one cares whether you slept last night or had a fight with your spouse this morning; you still have to perform, and perform well.

Was this ability to perform on demand a learned skill? I find that it is 100 percent learned. Regardless of the competitive arena—business, sports, or life—the megaperformers learn how to access the Ideal

Performance State whenever and wherever they need it. Today we know that possessing talent and skill are not enough; you also must learn how to bring the full force of all your talents and skills to life when you need them.

No Boundaries, No Limits

We don't know the boundaries of human performance. In a physical sense, who is to say that a human being won't ever high-jump over ten feet? It will happen one day. Don't ever limit yourself physically, mentally, emotionally, or spiritually in any way. And especially do not let the drudgeries of everyday stuff get in your way.

Team sports have an off-season, often three or four months long. It is a perfect time for the players in those sports to get needed recovery from a tough schedule. You don't get three or four months off to recuperate from *your* competitive life, do you?

Athletes, if they are not on a team, can pick and choose their schedule of competition. Tennis players such as Pete Sampras or golfers such as Nick Faldo, two of our clients, can call their agents and say, "Tell that tournament in the third week of October that I want to play." But you? Fat chance. Try telling your boss, "Liz, third week in October, I plan to work." You'll do that exactly *once!* You can't afford to mess around with your career that way. Your career is performance on demand, and it is showtime every day.

My job is to help you understand how, when you need to be on, you can get into an emotional state that you will perform at the highest level possible. Yet when you are not "on," you must take care of the most important person in your life—you. That's why you are the athlete of all athletes.

Control Your Energy

As a speaker on the Peter Lowe International motivational seminar circuit, a program that packs thousands of people into arenas across the country, I have had the opportunity to get to know one of the most energetic, electric women I've ever met in my life, Jodie Abendroth. For the past six years she has been Lowe's director of operations, meaning that she is responsible for overseeing every major and minor detail before, during and after each seminar event, of which there are twenty-five to thirty annually.

"I used to be in a high-energy, high-stress state at all times," she says. "We put on these awesome events featuring President George Bush; his wife, Barbara; Colin Powell; Christopher Reeve—and while it was going on, I'd be so pumped up, I'd be high-fiving the janitor of the arena. When it was over, however, I'd go back to the hotel and literally get sick. I'd throw up. I'd get headaches. I wouldn't be able to go out and celebrate with my team."

Abendroth was a perfect candidate for LGE's Mentally Tough program. We showed her how to more effectively control her energy. Now when she has to be "on," she has mechanisms for taking care of herself along the way.

"I used to not eat, I'd actually forget to eat because I just didn't seem to have time," she says. "Now I go to the green room where we meet and greet guests and get some food and water. My team and I take laughter breaks. And I pray all the time. During an event, I'll oscillate the stress by leaving the energy of the show for a while. I'll go outside the building and walk. This way, when I have to be on, I'm ready to go."

Postevent illness is a thing of the past. "Instead of being sick," Abendroth says, "I actually feel energized. The events are no longer a continuous, moderate level of stress; rather they are extended highs and lows."

Before she learned to take care of herself with oscillation and recovery breaks, Abendroth's marriage ended and this mother of a three-year-old was often depressed. "I'm never like that anymore," she says. "Food, exercise, water, laughing, and praying inserted into my daily lifestyle at just the right times give me great recovery."

One factor that gives Abendroth's job its unique stresses is that when she's not onsite at a Peter Lowe event—which typically take place in twenty-thousand-seat NBA and NHL arenas—she works from home alone. Those are two very different operating environments. She's learned to take advantage of her home environment, where she is her own boss, and to walk away from her desk when the stress builds.

Abendroth starts her day at 4:30 A.M. with an aerobic workout at the gym. Breakfast is at 6:00 A.M., followed by prayer and a few moments of mentally organizing the day to come. From then on crisis management lies ahead.

Mindful Performance

During the U.S. Open tennis tournament in 1983, Tom Gullikson played the no. 9 seed, Chip Hooper. Gullikson played a phenomenal match—despite deafening noises overhead from jets taking off and landing at nearby LaGuardia Airport—and won in four sets. I shook his hand immediately after the match and said to him, "I don't know how you do it with all those planes going over!" Tom's response: "What planes?"

Is there any reason you can't stay just as focused and in control when everything around you is spinning out of control?

Perfect Practice Makes Perfect

Zig Ziglar is one of the funniest, yet most genuine human beings on the face of the planet, a man who gives incredible meaning to the things he says.

Over dinner one evening, Zig told me that when he got started, he would tape the first ten minutes of his talk and later play it back to hear for himself what he actually said. He found that he often hadn't said anything—at least from his perspective. Oh, he knew that he had entertained people, but he convinced himself that he hadn't given them what he intended. This from one of the greatest personal motivators of the twentieth century!

Another thing he told me is that he rehearses every talk he gives even if it is the same talk he has given before. Now, here is a man who is self-actualized—he truly has it all together emotionally, mentally, spiritually, and physically. And Zig still rehearses before every time he goes onstage. That says a lot about any individual's desire to grow, learn, and improve.

Corporate Athlete Action Items

- List any times in your professional career when you have been "in the zone." How did it feel, and what were you able to accomplish at that time?
- List any times in your professional life when you have been so overwhelmed that you got sick or felt guilty about various issues. What caused these feelings, and what could you have done differently at that time to improve your performance and your feelings?
- Identify what you could do today to get better prepared for an upcoming big event. Start practicing your ideas to improve today.

Part II

MASTERING THE SECRETS OF PERFORMANCE NUTRITION

5

Eat to Recover

The first wealth is health.
—Ralph Waldo Emerson

Corporate Athlete Principle 5:

Nutrition may well be the single most important limiting factor preventing Corporate Athletes from achieving their maximum potential.

How do you regard the food you eat? Primarily as a source of pleasure? As a reward? As solace when you're unhappy? As a source of emotional satisfaction in hostile or unprofitable situations? As a means of recovering not only expended energy but also expended minerals and vitamins?

Unfortunately, many Corporate Athletes don't realize their potential because they have not been exposed to the relationship between performance and nutrition. This proved equally true more than twenty years ago in the field of sports nutrition.

Sports nutrition is a relatively young field. New and emerging facts appear constantly that assist nutritionists/dietitians and sport scientists in advising athletes about their nutritional intake. One thing is clear: Sports nutrition is not a quick fix; it is a lifestyle that yields high returns in performance. Athletes place great demands on their bodies. They must commit to getting it right. Of the thousands of world-class athletes I have worked with nutritionally, the one who stands above others is French Open champion Aranxta Sanchez Vicario. Like all the others, she found that nutrition needed to be a lifestyle and that there were no magic foods.

This chapter is based on scientific findings, personal experience, and consultations with world-class professional and Corporate Athletes. From all this, one recurring truth emerges: Nutrition is job no. 1 to maximize performance.

Set a World-Class Training Table

Today's athletic training table contains foods such as vegetables, fruits, and whole grains along with low-fat meats such as fish, turkey, and chicken. The diet that helps a great athlete perform at a very high level is the same diet you should have to stay healthy and perform well in life. It includes moderate to high amounts of complex carbohydrates from fruits, vegetables, and whole grains; moderate amounts of protein, largely from fish and grains but also from meat; and low amounts of fat—as much as possible of the unsaturated kind found in plants and fish. That's what I recommend you eat every day. Complex carbohydrates sustain the high energy level that maximum performance requires, although it's also vital to meet your protein and fat requirements.

Studying the world's greatest athletes and examining their nutritional needs for top performance brought me to a very interesting conclusion: What works for them in competition is exactly what you need to perform, mentally, at high levels and also to maintain optimum health. What the professional athlete in sport requires, you, as a Corporate Athlete in business, also require to sustain maximum performance over your long workdays, week after week, year after year.

Eat Anything You Want

A successful PGA Tour golfer followed our advice to lose forty pounds in six months and regain his competitive form.

The first time we met, I said, "What do you like to eat?"

"Frozen yogurt," he replied, "and steak."

"All right," I told him. "You can have them."

The golfer was stunned.

"You're kidding!" he said. "Every other consultant I have ever worked with told me I couldn't eat those things anymore!"

As you might guess, as soon as I told him he could still consume his favorite foods, I had him hooked. Then we figured out *how much* frozen yogurt and steak he could have—what limits he could live with, in other words.

I teach choice. After learning the Corporate Athlete program, every meal is a matter of choice. I use a person's favorite foods as a basis and fit it into his or her overall plan, and off we go. When you work with people based on what they like, they stick with the program better than they would with any other possible tactic.

I tell people I am not responsible for them winning or losing. What I'm going to do is give you the best information and research I know.

However, the decision to make the right choices and compete at the highest level is up to you. You must own your decisions. You must be responsible for what you do.

The Seven Nutritional Secrets of the Corporate Athlete

1. Weight doesn't matter. My experience in working with thousands of executives over many years, coupled with ongoing analysis of scientific studies, establish this principle beyond doubt. No controllable factor plays a more powerful role in boosting business stamina, productivity, and creativity than lowering the amount of fat, within reason, and increasing your body's lean muscle mass by improving your lifestyle.

2. Don't punish yourself. It's not all carrots and "rabbit food." Corporate Athletes never let themselves feel deprived; when they want a thick steak, a luscious dessert, or a candy bar, they indulge themselves. They don't feel guilty about it either, because most of the time they eat smart, light, low-fat, and nutritious.

If you look on food as a pure source of simple and well-deserved pleasure, don't be put off. Most slim people enjoy food as much as heavier people do. The difference isn't in lost dining pleasure, it's in training your mind, body, and palate to enjoy nonfattening and nutritious foods. I believe nutrition is recovery; it should be fun.

3. Eat right and avoid hunger pangs. Instead of skipping meals, Corporate Athletes eat more often—we call it strategic snacking. They know which foods are high in calories and fat, so they consume fewer of them; they know which are low in calories and fat, so they consume more of them.

4. Exercise more to prevent muscle loss. If you eat fewer calories of fat and get more exercise, you'll become leaner, more energetic, and healthier even as the years roll by. You can't slow the passage of time, but you can do a lot to shield yourself from time's attacks on your stamina. By reducing your fat intake, you automatically reduce your overall caloric intake and thereby control your weight.

5. Train yourself to change the saturated-fat food preferences you acquired as a child. Our ability to use technology to synthesize and preserve food has victimized us. Ancient humans developed a taste for fruits, berries, and the leaner game meats; today people develop a taste for chips, chocolate, and char-broiled steak. Even though many executives dine frequently in upscale restaurants, some of them have never completely shaken the food preferences they acquired before age twelve. I'm not saying they wish for a hamburger washed down with a cola drink when looking at the menu in a fine restaurant. Nevertheless, their subliminal bias toward high-fat food remains as strong as ever; for proof, look at their waistlines.

As you'll discover later, it takes twenty-one days to break habits, ninety days to change behaviors.

6. Eat to recover. When you physically exert yourself, you become physically fatigued. You must eat well to replenish your energy stores.

When you mentally exert yourself, you become mentally fatigued. Although you don't need as many calories to replenish the muscle tissue as when you've exercised, you still need high-quality nutrition to perform protein synthesis in the brain and generate recovery in the brain.

One of the most important concepts for new Corporate Athletes to build into their lives is recovery. Your body craves fuel. If you don't have the right amount of energy, through the right foods, you won't sleep well and then you've really got problems. Recovery is essential to the Mentally Tough program. Recovery means recapturing energy. Adequate sleep heads the list of the basic forms of recovery; adequate nutrition comes second.

Corporate Athletes train themselves to enjoy eating in terms of recovery rather than in terms of calorie counting, food exchanges, and the other useless mumbo jumbo put out by the weight-loss industry. *Eating should be fun,* so train yourself to take care of your nutritional needs first. Developing this habit is half the battle to reaching the body size you desire.

7. Allow for backsliding. If you've spent your entire life on diets or off diets, the law of diminishing returns applies. Early in the program you'll feel great and incredibly energized. But, as with life, there are days when things just don't go right. Don't panic; just get back on track as soon as possible. Go back to the basics and you'll be fine. It takes time to change habits and behaviors.

Nutrition and Performance

I know numerous business superstars who have horrendous eating habits but still perform at a high level because of their genius in business. And yet as they reach the twilight of their career, every one of these Corporate Athletes realizes the effect of poor nutrition and often complains, "Had I known how much nutrition affects my day-to-day performance, I would have changed my habits long ago."

For Corporate Athletes to excel to their physical, mental, and emotional potential, a diet must be rich in a variety of carbohydrates and protein but low in fat. Current research shows a link between the fuel you choose and the outcome of physical performance. Studies looking at different nutrient distributions in the diet reveal that carbohydrates are the no. 1 fuel source and should constitute at least half of the diet. Protein intake should approximate 15 to 25 percent of the calories eaten daily. Fat, calorically dense, carries the risk of contributing to heart disease, and hence it is recommended that fat not constitute more than 20 to 30 percent—definitely more toward the 20 percent, not the 30 percent—of the diet. Of course, slight variations in the distribution of nutrients will exist based on the individual Corporate Athlete.

The Three-Meals-a-Day Mind-set

Most of us get locked into the three-meals-a-day mind-set. It's no wonder. After all, it's traditional to eat breakfast, lunch, and dinner. Somewhere, we were told if we ate less (in amount, duration, and frequency) we would lose weight. Today, nutritional science gives us insight into these concepts.

We now know the physiological effects of eating (or not eating) three meals a day. Skipping breakfast and eating nothing before noon means your brain is starved of its principal fuel (glucose) until lunchtime. Clearly, you'll be at your productive peak only for a time after lunch—and then only if you don't eat a large, fat-heavy, drowsiness-producing meal.

The day gets off to a far better start if you eat breakfast early in the morning. On the three-meal plan, you will have a rise in blood sugar, but by late morning your blood sugar will drop back so much that you will be definitely in a depressed blood-sugar state. The same occurs in the late afternoon.

Both slumps can be headed off, since the brain works on glucose as well as on oxygen. One simple way to head off blood-sugar troughs is to eat a small snack in the midmorning and another in the midafternoon. This serves to stabilize your blood-sugar levels, enabling you to be more cognitive throughout the day.

Setting Yourself Up for a Productive Day

The setup is called breakfast. Break the fast imposed by sleep, and refuel your mind and body. It's not a new concept. The term "breakfast" dates from the fifteenth century, and the concept probably became well established during or even before the earliest civilizations. It's hard to imagine a gang of pyramid-builders setting out on empty stomachs to pull huge blocks of granite across the Egyptian desert.

The body wants to be energized when it awakens. Research shows that most people reach their highest level of mental energy within six hours of waking up. A protein breakfast won't necessarily make you more alert; a carbohydrate breakfast won't necessarily make you calmer. However, eating something for breakfast is essential to give your blood glucose levels a jump start.

We know that food helps wake us up. After sleeping, your body's glycogen supplies are at their lowest level, and the physical processes need a kick start. The brain works on two things: oxygen and glucose. With little oxygen, you die. With little glucose, you sleep. With little glycogen available for conversion into glucose and no breakfast, you tend to function cognitively way below your best.

People who perform below their potential all morning are likely to say: "I don't have time to eat breakfast." Missing breakfast is often a characteristic of someone who flails away frantically, working hard without accomplishing much. You can change that.

Follow the Mediterranean Eating Style

On the Greek island of Crete, people kept to the traditional Mediterranean diet well into the 1960s. They ate heaps of fruits, grains, and vegetables laced with olive oil and some fish and poultry—and they ate very little red meat. They used so much olive oil that fat provided 40 percent of their calories. Americans are dying on diets averaging the same 40 percent of calories from fat, but the Cretan death rate from coronary heart disease was only 5 percent of ours. In the middle of this century, Cretans and other Greeks were living longer than any other population in the world. As more and more of them abandoned the traditional Mediterranean diet in the succeeding decades, their death rates rose significantly.

What did the long-lived Cretans and Greeks traditionally eat? Daily, they ate pasta, rice, and other grains, breads, potatoes, a variety of vegetables and fruits, beans and other legumes, nuts, olive oil, cheese, and yogurt. A few times each week they ate fish, poultry, eggs, and sweets. They ate red meat only a few times a month.

In the 1960s many Cretans were still farmers who burned much of the fat they consumed through hard work. Another key element in producing the healthy effects of Mediterranean lifestyles was the absence of butter and mayonnaise, with their high content of saturated fats. The olive oil, used instead, is rich in monounsaturated fats, which research points to as the healthiest kind of fat.

In 1960 researchers learned the Mediterranean diet had slashed the rate of heart disease among Mediterranean peoples in half, as compared to their predicted rate based on their cholesterol level. That this is primarily due to the diet was proven by a recent French study of six hundred heart-attack survivors. Half of them followed the Mediterranean diet; the other half ate the diet recommended by the U.S. government and the American Heart Association. After two years, the Mediterranean group had only eight new heart attacks compared to thirty-three in the other group.

The Effects of Carbohydrates

Are carbohydrates unnecessary, as some protein enthusiasts claim? Dr. William Kraemer, director of Ball State University's Human Performance Laboratory and past president of the National Strength and Conditioning Association, says it's like saying a strong forehand isn't necessary in tennis. A player who hits all aces and backhands and only a few forehands can do well with a weak forehand. The body is an amazing machine; in six to eight weeks it can adapt to whatever diet you force it to use.

Some people, eating 65 percent carbohydrates, become water-sensitive. They start to have problems because more carbohydrates drag more water into their cells. This, in addition to the insulin response to the rise in glucose, can also cause an increase in body fat. Sometimes people even gain weight on 65 percent carbohydrates, but in reality they're only getting more thoroughly hydrated.

On the other hand, a high-protein diet may bring a lot of fat with it, create increased stress on the kidneys, and cause calcium depletion in your body. Anyone adopting such a diet needs to remain alert to the dangers involved in consuming large amounts of fat—including rapid weight gain, high cholesterol levels, and heart disease.

The Food-Mood Connection

The latest research into the food-mood connection is tantalizing but inconsistent and incomplete. We may be close to knowing exactly how we can powerfully influence—or even control—how we feel through what, how much, and when we eat. Or maybe not.

Many people have long known how certain eating or imbibing behaviors affect them. Here are several examples:

1. Someone eats a big meal on his day off and says, "I'm going to watch the football game," but before the first quarter ends, he's sound asleep.

2. Working late to prepare for an especially heavy day makes a sales manager eat late. More drinks than she really needs accompany the late

dinner. After the alarm pounds her awake the next morning, she's in no mood for breakfast, and she begins her especially heavy workday in a sugar coma—hung over, tired, and depressed. As a result, she fails to perform at her highest potential.

3. For breakfast, a hungry person eats a stack of syrup-soaked pancakes washed down with coffee—heading for the old caffeine jolt, plus diuretic action with a sugar spike on the way. He gets the jolt after an hour and feels alert but dry-mouthed, hyper, and a bit shaky. Two hours later, his alertness fades into weariness. He's drinking a lot of water without fully slaking his thirst, and he feels like he's gone four rounds with a hard puncher.

4. A Corporate Athlete gets home late, eats a healthy food—swordfish—but since it's all protein, he can't fall asleep.

5. A manager eats pure carbohydrate at lunch—a salad and pasta—and falls asleep by midafternoon.

6. A corporate executive doesn't eat strategically, skips lunch, and goes into a depressed blood-sugar state in the late afternoon.

7. Coffee and colas are consumed throughout the day and then the sales representative feels irritable and nervous all day long. This could also result in at least the *feeling* of an accelerated or irregular heartbeat.

8. A marketing manager eats high-fat foods constantly with few fruits and vegetables, causing constipation and irritability. You do *not* want to be around this person.

9. Chocolate is a woman's midmorning snack, and she crashes by late morning.

10. A man consumes nothing but energy bars and sports drinks during the day and becomes very weak physically, mentally and emotionally. Yes, it is true that we can influence our mood and performance potential by what, when, and how much we eat and drink. But, regrettably, what we learn by trial and error tends toward how to avoid damage to our performance potential rather than how to enhance it.

Several studies show that meals rich in carbohydrates and low in protein have a mild sedative effect. The largest study, conducted by Harvard University and other institutions, discovered—so far inexplicably—that women felt sleepier, and men more relaxed, after eating a carbohydrate-rich meal as compared to one rich in protein.

Research also suggests that frequent small meals sustain alertness far better than fewer and heavier meals. In particular, a heavy lunch has been shown to increase errors on tasks requiring close attention, while a light lunch reduces them. A nutritious late-afternoon snack also decreases errors.

Avoid Simple Sugars

Try to avoid refined carbohydrates. A refined carbohydrate is a food that has been processed until it has virtually no nutrients left. For example, a single slice of white bread is about sixty-five calories—slightly more than whole wheat—but it supplies only a fourth as much fiber and almost no vitamins or minerals; in two words: little nutrition. Although white bread will create glycogen, it's a nutritionally non-dense food when compared with vegetables and fresh fruits, which have fewer calories but are very high in nutrition.

We should consume only small amounts of simple sugars each day. In my experience, only 23 percent of corporate executives have two or fewer servings of sugar a day—as in cookies, chocolate, or sugar spooned into coffee. Most of my other audiences are more on the chocoholic side, averaging well over two servings of sugar a day. This can have an immediate effect on performance.

This is a very controversial topic depending on what source you use in evaluating the role of simple sugar in your diet. The first point of contention is that the body only uses carbohydrates for energy when they are broken down into simple sugars. Complex carbohydrates must therefore be broken down into simple sugars in the digestive system so they can be utilized.

If you need to increase your carbohydrate intake, consider these ideas:

- Think vegetarian. Every food group in the vegetarian world contains carbohydrates.
- Plan meals and snacks around nutritious, carbohydrate-rich foods: whole grain breads, breakfast cereals (rice, oatmeal, barley, and other grains), pasta, noodles, tortillas, fruits (fresh and dried), starchy vegetables (e.g., potatoes, corn, and yams), dairy products (e.g., yogurt), legumes (e.g., beans, soy-based products, and garbanzos).
- Let complex carbohydrate foods take up half to three-quarters of your plate.
- Eat regularly scheduled and strategically planned snacks.
- Increase the number of times you eat in a day rather than overloading at the three standard times of meals.

- Have carbohydrate-rich, protein-dense foods on hand for snacking and in the event circumstances prevent eating a meal (e.g., when traveling).

Fueling with Fiber

You should consume moderate to high amounts of fiber every day. Corporate America is fast becoming very good about this. Nearly half of the executives who attend my corporate conferences report intentionally eating food that is high in fiber. That's much greater than among some of the other audiences I work with.

At the other end of the spectrum, some people get so carried away with fiber that they take fiber supplements. You do not need them. I agree with Bill Cosby. He says, "Fiber? It just helps move things along!"

Fiber can be water-soluble or water-insoluble. Neither kind provides energy, but both have other important functions.

Insoluble fiber is nondigestible and acts like a sponge, absorbing water to help waste products pass easily and swiftly through the colon. It is the best cure or prevention for constipation. Most studies have confirmed that a high-fiber diet can prevent disease and a low-fiber diet has the opposite effect.

If you eat a diet that's at least 50 percent complex carbohydrates you will get enough fiber. Fruits and whole-grain foods are high in fiber. Apple skins and the chaff of grain have fiber. Insoluble fiber is found in the rind of some fruits—in the membrane of oranges, for example.

Water-soluble fiber, found in oat bran, barley, and fruit pectin, helps reduce cholesterol levels, primarily by reducing low-density lipoproteins (LDL—the "bad" cholesterol). However, researchers debate exactly how much water-soluble fiber is required to achieve this effect, and many suggest that the benefit comes as much from the reduction in fat consumption that occurs in a high-fiber diet as from the action of the fiber itself. Until this is clarified, the best course is to eat a high-fiber diet, soluble and insoluble.

As for what research says about fiber intake, some studies also suggest that soluble fiber helps control diabetes by improving your control of blood sugar. Current research is attempting to confirm theories that a high-fiber diet reduces the risk of breast cancer. Eating high-fiber foods also helps reduce obesity because these foods take longer to chew and provide a filled-up feeling without adding lots of calories.

To guarantee that your fiber intake is adequate, eat a variety of foods. Whenever you have a choice, buy or order the least-processed alternative. Raw fruits, vegetables, and whole grains are best.

Avoid getting all your fiber at one sitting because this can have unpleasant side effects, including bowel upsets. Instead, try to eat foods that are high in both kinds of fiber at every meal. A high-fiber diet increases your need for water, so be sure to accompany it with a high fluid intake.

Protein—If You Prefer to Eat Meatless

Can you imagine prehistoric humans worrying about food combinations as they foraged through the grasslands? They ate what and when they could. And if you eat sensibly, you can, too. Contrary to what we used to hear, it's not necessary to combine grains and legumes in the same meal to acquire usable protein. Eat common foods such as whole-grain breads, potatoes, and corn to meet your daily requirement for protein. Fruit is a poor source of protein, as are alcohol and sugar. Here are some excellent vegetable sources of protein:

Source	Protein (grams)
One-Cup Servings	
Barley	5.0
Beans, black	15.2
Beans, kidney	15.0
Beans, lima	14.7
Beans, pinto	14.0
Beans, white	17.5
Broccoli	6.0
Corn	6.0
Lentils	18.0
Spinach	6.0
Rice, brown	5.0
Rice, white	4.0
Soy milk	7.0
Spaghetti	5.0
Single-Vegetable Servings	
Potato (including skin)	5.0
Sweet potato (including skin)	1.7
Other Nonmeat Sources of Protein	
Skim milk (8-oz. glass)	8.0
Two-Ounce Servings	
Almonds	10.0
Macadamia nuts	4.0
Peanuts	13.0
Pecans	4.0
Soy protein isolate	46.0
Walnuts	12.0

The Body Produces All the Cholesterol It Needs

Low-density lipoproteins (LDLs) are the "bad" cholesterol responsible for the blood-flow-reducing buildup along arterial walls. High-density lipoproteins (HDLs) are the "good" cholesterol. Body fat is composed mainly of triglycerides, which are the fatty acids found in the body and in food. The most common fatty acids are saturated, unsaturated, omega, and transfatty acids.

Cholesterol is essential to health, but your body makes all it needs. This means that when you eat more of it, you risk running into a dangerous oversupply. You should consume no more than 300 milligrams of cholesterol a day.

Dietary cholesterol is very different from blood serum cholesterol, and some research shows that dietary cholesterol is not something to concern yourself with. However, this research is not yet definitive, so I recommend that you keep control of your dietary cholesterol intake.

Achieve a low consumption of dietary cholesterol each day. If you were a pure vegetarian—no milk, no eggs, no meat or animal products—you would not get any cholesterol in your diet. Cholesterol is found only in animal products.

Saturated fats, such as those in meats, solidify at room temperature. Saturated fats aren't good at all. They cause a significant increase in LDL and triglycerides.

Monounsaturated fats, found in olive oil, are excellent. Using olive oil for cooking is a tremendous health builder. Monounsaturated fats cause a significant increase in HDL and a moderate decrease in LDL and triglycerides.

Omega-3 fats, found in seafood, reduce the risk of blood clots that could trigger a heart attack by blocking a coronary artery. You can easily obtain all the benefit that omega-3 fats provide from food. You shouldn't need a supplement. Taking omega-3 pills is a waste of money, which research has established.

Hydrogenated oils are treated vegetable oils that your body responds to exactly the same as for saturated fat. Don't be fooled by the words "vegetable" or "soybean" and so on. If "hydrogenated" or "partially hydrogenated" precedes the item, the word "hydrogenated" means it's bad.

Protein

Protein is very inefficient. It can be used as an energy source, but in extremely small amounts. Some research has shown that protein may contribute 2 to 5 percent of the total energy needed to perform.

Protein must be consumed daily because not only is it essential for tissue maintenance, it also helps in producing antibodies, hormones, and enzymes. Proteins are usually made up of twelve to twenty amino acids that are important for daily performance. The highest levels of protein are needed during major periods of growth and during intense strength and endurance performance.

A diet supplying 15 to 25 percent of the calories from protein should meet all of a Corporate Athlete's needs. These protein guidelines assume that you are consuming enough calories. When you eat enough to fulfill your caloric requirement, you will likely take in more than enough protein. To achieve the total protein daily intake as 15 to 25 percent of your diet, you can choose from many animal or vegetable food sources. Chicken, turkey, fish, beans, and nuts are a few that provide substantial sources.

Vegetable protein sources in combination can provide adequate amounts of amino acids. For example, eating lentil soup and wheat bread, pinto beans and brown rice, or baked beans and cornbread combine amino acids to achieve the needs of most Corporate Athletes. Most semivegetarian diets (which occasionally include some animal products) are nutritionally adequate due to the high nutrient density of eggs, milk, and cheese. However, a strict vegetarian (including no animal, dairy, or egg products) must preplan his or her diet, because diets without meat often have inadequate amounts of calcium, iron, riboflavin, zinc, vitamin B_{12}, and vitamin D. If this applies to you, see the section on supplements in chapter 10.

There are potential problems with extremely high protein diets as well. Chronic fatigue due to the low-muscle glycogen stores can occur with intakes of large amounts of protein at the expense of carbohydrates. Also, additional protein can render incomplete or slow replacement of muscle glycogen.

Additional protein can increase the body's water requirement and may contribute to dehydration. The metabolism of protein requires more body water than carbohydrates and even fat.

Remember: Excess protein is converted into fat, and protein takes longer to digest if it is used as a prechallenge meal.

Fats

Fats give food taste and, historically, have been considered a significant fuel source for the human body. It's true that they are a considerable source of fuel because they contain more than twice as much energy per gram as either proteins or carbohydrates, but fats are very inefficient. In fact, they should be considered a secondary source of energy.

Fats can be found in the form of solids (animal fat and lard) or liquids (oils) and can be saturated (solid at room temperature) or unsaturated (liquid at room temperature). Saturated fats include any animal fat, egg yolks, butter, most desserts, creams, etc., while unsaturated fats are basically found in pure vegetable oils. Two types of unsaturated fats have been identified: polyunsaturated and monounsaturated. Consumption of both can lower LDL cholesterol (the bad kind) and triglycerides. The best type of oils to consume are flaxseed, canola, and olive.

If you consume a high-fat diet, you will have more fat to use during exercise. This, however, will lower how much carbohydrate you can store. And although the amount of storage space you have for fat is unlimited, fat cannot be your only fuel source because muscle cannot function well with fat as the primary fuel source. Muscle, even at rest, needs energy. And the most efficient energy is carbohydrate. The role of fat in your system is to spare limited carbohydrate reserves during an endurance phase of exercise or competition but *not* to replace them.

Dietary fat is, however, still important to have in your daily menu. Fat serves as a storage depot and transporter for the fat-soluble vitamins A, D, E, and K. Fat provides an essential fatty acid for the body, linoleic acid, which is necessary for growth and reproduction while also protecting us from excessive water loss and damage from the sun's radiation. But the most recent research indicates that a high-fat diet will significantly impair performance.

Keep in mind the following tips about fat:

- Keep your fat intake to 20 to 30 percent (preferably closer to 20%) of total calorie intake by focusing on leaner and low-fat foods.
- Choose lighter cooking methods such as baking, steaming, and broiling/grilling.
- Be fat-savvy and read food labels. Try for foods that have no more than 3 grams of fat per 100 calories.

Performance and the Prechallenge Meal

Can you imagine former Denver Broncos quarterback John Elway, on the way to the Super Bowl, saying, "Let's grab a double cheeseburger"? Of course not! So why do Corporate Athletes routinely eat that way on the way to a sales call?

Especially important to business performance is the prechallenge meal—what you eat before making a crucial sales presentation, giving a speech, or entering into an important negotiation. Depending on what you select, that meal can either *enable* you to reach IPS, or it may *prevent* you from doing so. However, the prechallenge meal works best as high-performance fuel when poured into a body long nourished wisely and well. The prechallenge meal isn't a miracle cleansing agent any more than a tankful of high-octane fuel will clear a clogged engine on race day.

A diet that enables a great athlete to perform at a very high level is the same kind of diet that you, as a Corporate Athlete, should eat to stay healthy and to perform at a very high level in business and in life.

A well-planned prechallenge meal accomplishes a number of goals. Not only does it prevent you from experiencing low blood sugar (hypoglycemia), it also provides your muscles with needed energy so you won't run out of steam. When you have low blood sugar, you could experience the following symptoms: You could feel light-headed and/or dizzy, become fatigued quickly, have blurred vision, or lack the ability to concentrate. All these symptoms can have a detrimental effect on your performance.

The purpose of the prechallenge meal is to top off your fuel tank. Traditionally, steak and eggs were served at the football training table during breakfast on game day. Here is what science tells us about that famous tradition: Let's say the game started at noon and breakfast was at 9:00 A.M. The boys ate the steak and eggs at 9:00 A.M. as they prepared for the big game. The game began at noon, and at about 2:00 P.M the steak and eggs were leaving the stomach and had produced virtually no energy.

That's because in a steak-and-eggs meal, there is about 2 percent carbohydrate. High-fat, high-protein foods will stay in the stomach up to five hours.

The result: The players received very little energy, and it was like putting a brick in the midsection of their bodies. Today's prechallenge table consists of vegetables, fruits, whole grain breads, pastas, rice, and low-fat meats—all foods that are easily digestible and loaded with energy.

You should eat a small meal one to two hours before performing, whether it's a major negotiation, making a major sales presentation, or going into an important team meeting with your department. You should *eat what you like to eat*. For example, some people cannot tolerate fruit juices before a major business event, while others can. In a psychological vein, it truly is important to feel good about what you consume before you put yourself on the line.

The Corporate Athlete's Nutritional Needs

Your nutritional recovery needs should look like this at most meals:

2 servings	complex carbohydrates
1–2 servings	protein
0.5–1 serving	fat

All of us have seen ratios like these (often in the form of percentages) for years, but what do they mean? How do you know if what you're now eating comes close? The key is that you maintain a well-balanced nutritional program so you have the right mix of protein, carbohydrates, and fat. But these numbers will help:

> 1 gram of protein = 4 calories
> 1 gram of carbohydrate = 4 calories
> 1 gram of fat = 9 calories
> 1 gram of alcohol = 7 calories

It doesn't take a mental giant to see that you can eat twice as much protein and carbohydrate as fat. In fact, the key to great nutrition is consuming high-quality foods and limiting your fat intake.

Let's assume that you need 2,000 calories a day. Some people need a little less and some a little more, depending on how active they are and what their body composition is; we'll get to that later in the book. What we're aiming for, then, is

½ of your intake is carbohydrates = 1,000 calories (divided by 4) = 250 grams
¼ to ⅓ of your intake is protein = 600 calories (divided by 4) = 150 grams
⅕ to ¼ of your intake is fat = 400 calories (divided by 9) = 44.4 grams

View nutrition as recovery. Eat to recapture your energy, and eat to fuel your body so you can be on when you need to be on.

Corporate Athlete Action Items

- Eat breakfast.
- Keep your saturated-fat intake low.
- Putting together energy-yielding meals that are low in fat but high in flavor can be easy if you follow these guidelines:
  - At each meal think in terms of at least two servings of bread, cereal, or pasta such as a bowl of cereal and a bagel at breakfast.
  - At each meal, always include a serving of fruit or juice, such as a bunch of grapes for dessert at lunch.
  - At each meal, try to eat at least one serving of a protein food such as vegetarian chili topped with shredded, low-fat cheese.
  - Have whole-grain breads and cereals, pasta, fresh vegetables, and fruit fill at least half of your plate.
  - Minimize sugar intake during your workday.

6

Liquid Recovery

To succeed you must add water to your wine,
until there is no more wine.

—JULES RENARD

CORPORATE ATHLETE PRINCIPLE 6:

Drink the right fluids—plenty of them—
to maximize your recovery.

Although some research exists supporting the use of caffeine, and although our culture teaches us to virtually exist on caffeine, we recommend that you minimize your intake of beverages that contain caffeine. Examples are Coca-Cola, Pepsi-Cola, coffee, Mountain Dew, Dr Pepper, and tea. These beverages will have a dehydrating effect, causing you to urinate more quickly and lose more fluids. Drink water instead!

Many people rely on coffee to get them going in the morning or to pick them up during the workday. Most realize that they are asking a drug to achieve what only adequate sleep can accomplish. They probably also know that substituting caffeine for sleep month after month will make them look older fast. They know all this, yet even in this youth-oriented culture of ours, they continue a practice that speeds the aging process while helping to prevent them from reaching their greatest potential.

Where do you start to break an excessive reliance on the caffeine jolt? If you're one of those night owls who believes that you function best on considerably fewer than eight hours of sleep combined with a caffeine jump start, or if you feel that it's stylish or cute to fumble until midmorning, the first step is to rid yourself of those delusions. Success at this task depends on reorganizing your life to get adequate sleep.

If you can't live without the late-night shows, program your VCR and watch them a day late, at dinnertime. Can't fall asleep early? Join a health club and recover from the mental stresses of the day through exercise. The healthy, pleasant feeling of fatigue you'll get with the proper amount of exercise will make it much easier to fall asleep promptly.

Do whatever it takes, but get enough sleep so you wake up in the morning feeling rested and eager for the day. With adequate exercise and rest, your craving for caffeine will diminish or even vanish.

Alcohol

The good news about beer: There's no fat. The bad news is that beer has 62 percent wasted (nutritionless) calories. Of all the alcoholic drinks, beer is the healthiest nutritionally because it's 36 percent carbohydrates.

Red wine, fat-free and with 10 percent carbohydrates, was briefly touted as a miracle weapon against heart disease. This happened after researchers noted that French people, who typically drink red wine with their meals, have a remarkably lower heart disease rate than Americans in spite of eating a diet even heavier in saturated fats. Subsequent studies revealed that the French diet has only recently moved into the high-saturated-fat range, meaning millions of today's French adults grew up eating a far healthier diet than they do today. As a result, their heart disease rates are creeping up as their levels of artery-clogging begin to match ours. In other words, it may not have been the wine but the diet.

Some research suggests that one or two drinks a day might benefit your health, but more stress the liver and open the door to a host of other problems.

On the basis of present-day research, it might not be hogwash to assert that one drink a day provides health benefits. However, compelling evidence exists to prove this contention: Consistently drinking more than three ounces of alcohol a day decreases performance and longevity.

Research has shown that performance decreases after ingestion of alcohol. Alcohol may compromise physical and mental performance by decreasing the release of glucose from the liver. Also, this will cause a decrease in blood glucose and possibly lead to hypoglycemia.

Alcohol consumption in the evening can lead to a state of dehydration the next day if adequate fluid replacement does not occur.

Have You Had Your Water Today?

Our bodies are made mostly of water, which we constantly use in a number of ways, of which perspiration and excretion are merely the most obvious. You must replenish your water-based system frequently by drinking sixty-four ounces (eight glasses) of water every day. Sodas don't count. Coffee and tea are diuretics; they cause you to lose more water. Rather than helping you meet your body's daily water requirement, coffee and tea have the opposite effect.

Only about 9 percent of the professionals in corporate America drink more than seven glasses of water a day. The consumption of water is critical for both body and cerebral functions.

The biggest complaint I get is, "Wait a minute, I'll be going to the bathroom all day." My answer is, "That's okay, it won't take long."

Even if you keep a glass of water on your bedside table, you're still somewhat dehydrated when you wake up after a good night's sleep. Many of us have trained our bodies to accept this situation, and in any case, the feeling of thirst is not a reliable indicator of mild dehydration.

As soon as you get up, drink a full eight-ounce glass of cool water. It's so easy, and it does so much to prime your body to shift into high gear. There's another advantage to drinking a glass of water first thing in the morning: It gets you off to a flying start toward fulfilling your body's need for eight glasses a day. If you shortchange your body on water, you shortchange yourself on stamina.

Keep in mind that our bodies are more than half water. It's constantly being consumed in countless ways, among them digestion, body cooling, blood replacement, elimination of wastes, and lubrication of the joints. In fact, all of our cell processes and organ functions depend on water. If you force your body to function without giving it enough water, it can't perform to its highest potential.

The Issue of Thirst

Can you dehydrate just living a normal day? Absolutely. Although your water loss isn't as noticeable as that of a sweaty athlete, you're losing water constantly through a variety of normal body processes; you perspire to some degree even in an air-conditioned building. But even without that, you lose water constantly through the pores of your skin. Your body also uses water for numerous lubrication, digestion, elimination, and replacement activities that are constantly going on. In fact, it's not practical to try to list all the body's needs for water; suffice it to say that nothing works without water.

Even though it's so vital to our very existence, we tend to ignore our water needs until, going without, we become quite uncomfortable. Don't take feeling thirsty merely as a signal that you need a drink of water right now; take it as a signal that your water replacement habits need some serious work. You should never get thirsty.

Remember that you can easily satisfy your thirst before your body's needs for water are satisfied. Schedule your water intake; don't merely react to a thirsty feeling.

The diuretic action of coffee and tea makes you lose more water than you gain by drinking them. Many soft drinks also contain caffeine, and between the diuretic effect and the stress put on your system to cope with their sugar content, it's questionable whether you have a net gain of moisture from drinking one.

Alcohol is even more of a diuretic, since it must be broken down by the liver and kidneys—a process that consumes considerable amounts of water. If the stomach doesn't have water available, your kidneys will pull it out of your body's cells. The "cotton mouth" you get the morning after the big party is due to dehydration. It's not a joking matter when you realize that you've just struck a blow to the health of every cell in your body.

For satisfying your body's unceasing need for water, nothing is better than just plain water, preferably cool rather than ice-cold.

How do you know if you're drinking enough water? You'll know you're drinking enough if you drink eight glasses a day.

Corporate Athlete Action Items

- Add lemon, lime, or orange slices to your water to give it some zing.
- Bottled water may taste better to you than tap water. Go for it.
- Many people drink more water if it is cool.
- Carry a plastic eight-ounce bottle with you to refill as needed.
- Minimize your intake of alcohol for the next week to no more than one drink per day. And no, you cannot save up for the weekend and have six or seven drinks on Saturday.
- Minimize your intake of caffeine. The ideal is to have none, but if you must, try to have no more than the equivalent of two five-ounce cups of coffee a day.
- Get in the habit of taking a bottle of water into every meeting you have at work.

7

"Diet" Is a Four-Letter Word

More die . . . of too much food than of too little.
—John Kenneth Galbraith

Corporate Athlete Principle 7:

Weight doesn't matter. It's the amount of body fat you're carrying that should be your concern.

Knowing how to improve your ratio of lean body mass to fat is the first step toward accessing IPS regularly and achieving permanent weight loss. The second step is developing sufficient motivation to carry you through to your goal.

For women, having 27 percent or more of body fat is a good marker for being overfat; for men the number is 20 percent.

Obesity is defined as storing excess fat as a reserve. Few sources give an exact body fat percentage at which we can say someone is obese, but a woman with more than 32 percent and a man with more than 25 percent body fat would be approaching obesity.

Regardless of your current ratio of body fat to lean body mass, you should give high priority to reaching the ideal ratios. Ideally, a woman's body fat will be under 22 percent and a man's under 17 percent. However, you must have some fat, both on your body and in your diet. Women should never allow their body fat to go below 12 percent; men should avoid dropping below 5 percent. Although there are cases of athletes of both genders being under those minimums, they should be the exception, not the rule.

Getting a Grip on Your Body Image

Don't think in terms of weight loss. Focus on the ratio between lean body mass and body fat—the most important issue in improving health and boosting performance. Weight is simply an unreliable indicator of either health or performance potential. Losing weight without exercise eliminates more muscle tissue than fat.

If you are seriously overweight or aren't already a regular exerciser, get your doctor's approval before starting any exercise program. Once you've done so, find a convenient health club or gym where you feel comfortable. Use it three times a week for strength-building workouts. Many health clubs also provide facilities for aerobic exercise and endurance training. If your club can't help with the endurance element of your program, organize your routine around some activity you enjoy: tennis, racquetball, rollerblading, biking, hiking, walking, swimming, or whatever fits your schedule.

Spot reducing and body contouring are exciting concepts to many of us. The problem is, the desired results don't occur, and more stress is created. However, exercise has a wonderful ability to reshape your self-image. In the first place, it will give you an attractive, more toned look, which is rightly prized. Regular exercisers tend to move more gracefully, carry themselves straighter, and project more energy.

People who participate in sports, particularly women, tend to appreciate their body shapes more than sedentary people do, whether or not they approach the model thinness that society holds up as perfection.

As noted by researchers, regular exercise also helps establish a positive family environment. Exercising together not only helps keep the family close, its members also have less time or inclination to indulge in activities harmful to health.

Give Your Body What It Needs

The same sacrifices and training go into developing a career as a tennis player as they would for someone who wants to get to a very high level of whatever field he or she is in. For example, for someone to become CEO of a corporation, sacrifices need to be made.

The difference, as Shawn Foltz will attest, is that no one starts on a serious CEO career path at age eleven, as she did with championship tennis at that age. Foltz, now thirty-one and a Ph.D. in counseling psychology, was once the no. 1 female junior doubles tennis player in the United States, one of the top three in singles, the no. 1 collegiate tennis player in the United States in 1989, and even a model and an actress in a movie, but that wasn't good enough for some of the people around her. She developed an eating disorder after constantly being told that she would be a better tennis player only if she lost weight.

"I had just lost a tennis match in Louisville, Kentucky, and my mom, my dad, my brother, myself, and my coach went to a restaurant," Foltz recalls. "My coach asked me what I was going to get, and I said, 'Oh, a hamburger!' He said, 'No, you are not. You are getting a salad with no dressing. You are too fat. You can't move around the court. You will never do anything in your life if you don't lose weight.' And so, like everything else in my life, I wanted to do that really well, and I almost died." She was told not to eat, so eventually she didn't eat anything.

I met Foltz after this nonsense had been going on for several years.

"Dr. Jack," she said, "I don't know what to do. I *crave* a hamburger! I really want a hamburger."

I said, "Well, go eat a hamburger."

That was like blasphemy to her ears, based on what those closest to her had been spouting.

"I can't," she said. "It's bad for me! It is protein, it uses up all the blood that needs to go to my muscles in order for me to do *dah da dah da dah. . . .*"

All I could do was tell her a basic fact. "If your body is craving something, you have to eat it."

Fortunately, she did, and that simple advice was a first baby step toward recovery. Today, Shawn Foltz listens to her body. No more diets. If she gains weight, she will exercise and cut back a little bit, but she never again will stop eating what her body craves.

The Problem with Measuring Weight

Junk your bathroom scales. Heave them out. They're worse than useless.

Let's say that Joe, a professional athlete, packs more than two hundred pounds on his under-six-foot frame. He has the "not an ounce fat" look. Yet on some life insurance charts, he's overweight for his height. In reality he's in top shape, and his ratio of 10 percent fat to 90 percent lean body mass makes a mockery of the charts.

Robert, a professional accountant who avoids physical exercise, is the same age, height, and weight as Joe, but Robert's corpulent body is 30 percent fat and only 70 percent lean body mass. Compared to athlete Joe, accountant Robert has to lift three times as much fat every time he stands up. He has to do it with 20 percent less lean muscle mass by volume, and with only a fraction of Joe's muscle power. No wonder Robert tires quickly.

After an ordinary day in the office, Robert goes home feeling exhausted; after an ordinary day of competition or physical training, Joe is full of energy and ready to enjoy his off hours to the fullest. No wonder accountant Robert buys any diet book promising rapid weight loss without effort; no wonder he talks a good story about losing weight but never does; and no wonder walking a long way utterly exhausts him.

So throw your bathroom scales away because muscle weighs more than fat. Scales are dangerous since it's so seductively easy to think, "Numbers don't lie." Even though following the Corporate Athlete program for several weeks makes you slimmer, stronger, and more energetic, unless your weight is down you can become discouraged. Some people lock onto the weight thing. In the absence of a better reading on the scale, they fail to appreciate the enormously more important fact of steadily growing leaner, healthier, and more capable.

Measure Yourself, Don't Weigh Yourself

Your body fat can be measured in many ways. Many universities and hospitals throughout the world have underwater weighing machines. You put on a swimsuit and are submerged while breathing through an apparatus. After you exhale as much as you can, your body is weighed and the device measures your density relative to the density of water. It can tell you within 1 percent what your body fat percentage is.

Some doctors, hospital staffs, and university researchers use skinfold calipers to measure the thickness of the fat underneath the skin. Mathematical equations convert the caliper reading to body fat percentage, yielding a result within 2 percent of the reading obtained by the water immersion method. At LGE, we use body plethysmography (a Bod Pod) or air displacement to measure body density.

You can also use inexpensive plastic skin-fold calipers to measure yourself. Researchers find that plastic skin-fold calipers are adequate for personal assessment. Although they are still in development, these devices are better than relying on your bathroom scale.

I prefer that you get your body fat measured, because it is the best way to determine your health, but the next best way to determine your level of "fatness" is the Body Mass Index (BMI). Unless you are incredibly athletic and are very muscular, the BMI is an adequate method of evaluating your physical health because it is an indicator of the relationship between weight and height. Your BMI is calculated by this formula:

$$Body\ mass\ index = weight/height^2$$
(Weight is in kilograms and height is in meters, squared.)

Classification	Men	Women
Normal	24–27	23–26
Moderately obese	28–31	27–32
Severely obese	>31	>32

Example: A man is 6 ft. tall and weighs 185 lbs.

6 ft. = 72 in.

There are 2.54 cm in 1 in.

72 in. × 2.54 in. = 182.9 cm

There are 100 cm in 1 m

182.9 ÷ 100 = 1.83 m

There are 2.2 lbs. in 1 kg

185 lbs. ÷ 2.2 lbs. = 84.1 kg

Body mass index = 84.1 kg ÷ 1.83^{2}m

BMI = 25.1

How Long Does It Take to Get There?

No simple, hard-and-fast rule can cover how much time it takes to reach the ideal ratio of body fat to lean body mass. Consider these two individuals: first, a twenty-four-year-old moderately active woman in good health with 27 percent body fat; second, a fifty-six-year-old sedentary man in poor health whose body fat is 35 percent. How rapidly each person changes depends on age, gender, activity level, and body fat percentage. Therefore each person has different needs to consider before setting goals for improved health and nutrition.

Those who set out to increase the level of exercise in their lives should obtain a doctor's approval first, but this is especially important for anyone who has any heart or circulatory ailment, a serious chronic condition, is more than thirty years old, or is more than 5 percentage points over ideal body fat.

Regardless of how much body fat you need to lose and how much muscle you need to increase, please remember: It's going to take time! Unfortunately, people get warped in their thinking about how fast they can make these changes in their body's composition.

Metabolic Syndrome

There is considerable evidence that the pattern of body fat distribution is an even more important predictor of the health risks of being overfat. Fat distributed in the abdomen (male pattern obesity or the "apple" shape) is associated with a greater risk of high blood pressure, diabetes, heart disease, and premature death when compared to those who are just as fat but distribute it below the waist (female pattern obesity or the "pear" shape).

We recommend you use the waist-to-hip ratio as a simple means of determining your body fat pattern. To do this, simply divide your waist circumference (narrowest part about two to three inches above the umbilicus) by the circumference at your hips (usually the largest circumference is around the buttocks). This ratio should be below .95 for men and .86 for women. If your number is greater than this, we recommend that you have your blood pressure, lipids (triglycerides and HDLs), and glucose level checked to see if you are at an increased risk of metabolic problems such as insulin resistance syndrome and/or coronary artery disease. Our research has found that a cross-training program of both aerobic and resistance exercise with good nutrition is the best way to prevent this syndrome.

Waist-to-Hip Circumference Ratio (WHR) Norms for Men and Women

			Risk		
	Age	*Low*	*Moderate*	*High*	*Very High*
Men	20–29	<0.83	0.83–0.88	0.89–0.94	>0.94
	30–39	<0.84	0.84–0.91	0.92–0.96	>0.96
	40–49	<0.88	0.88–0.95	0.96–1.00	>1.00
	50–59	<0.90	0.90–0.96	0.97–1.02	>1.02
	60–69	<0.91	0.91–0.98	0.99–1.03	>1.03
Women	20–29	<0.71	0.71–0.77	0.78–0.82	>0.82
	30–39	<0.72	0.72–0.78	0.79–0.84	>0.84
	40–49	<0.73	0.73–0.79	0.80–0.87	>0.87
	50–59	<0.74	0.74–0.81	0.82–0.88	>0.88
	60–69	<0.76	0.76–0.83	0.84–0.90	>0.90

Healthy Fat

Monounsaturated fats, especially olive oil, are excellent nutritionally, being great sources of the fat your body needs. Monounsaturated fats cause a significant increase in HDL (good cholesterol) and a moderate decrease in LDL (bad cholesterol) and triglycerides.

Eating one or two servings of any cold-water fish weekly is associated with lower risk of heart disease, certainly a matter that should concern every Corporate Athlete. Research indicates that the higher the fat content of the fish, the greater the cardiovascular benefit. Fish with moderate to high fat content include freshwater bass, bluefish, carp, catfish, halibut, herring, mackerel, mullet, ocean perch, orange roughy, pompano, rainbow trout, salmon, sardines, shad, and smelt.

Trim and discard any visible fat and the liver of the fish, and don't eat the skin because pollutants or contaminants tend to be concentrated in those areas. The omega-3 fats that provide the greatest cardiovascular benefits are found throughout the flesh of cooked seafood and are retained well in most canned fish.

Know What Is in the Food You Eat

Many people claim that they can't lose weight no matter how they eat. Aside from exercising far less than they think they do, these people generally defeat their weight-loss efforts with easily overlooked habits, such as ignoring the fat and calorie content of salad dressings; loading their baked potatoes with fat-heavy butter, sour cream, or bacon bits; and disregarding the empty calories of soft and hard drinks.

Tasty salad dressings with zero fat are in the supermarkets now, and alternatives are available for the other overlooked sources of fat just mentioned. Everyone who is serious about losing weight should make healthy changes in all these areas.

There is very little nutrition in dressing—I've searched, because I like it! I always order dressing on the side, or if I can't get it that way, I push it to the side of the plate. I dab my fork in it and leave most of the dressing on the plate, but I still get enough for taste. I encourage you to try it.

Lose Weight without Dieting

If State Farm's insurance operation in California were a stand-alone company, its operations would rank it the sixth-largest insurance company in the United States. Greg Jones is its chief executive officer; he is personally responsible for ten thousand employees.

As you might imagine, it's an incredibly demanding job, one that makes it difficult for him to manage his diet and exercise as well as he'd like.

"I've never been seriously overweight, but I have struggled with really high cholesterol," says this former college basketball player. "My doctor said I was going to have to go on some pills, and I resisted that. My problem was that I ate really bad stuff. I wasn't conscientious about it at all. I wanted to lose weight but I didn't know how to do it."

Jones, forty-nine, began following the tenets of the Corporate Athlete Strategic Eating Guide and achieved the results he sought. "It was a commonsense approach that had more to do with being knowledgeable about what I eat than going on a diet or counting fat grams," he says. "The next thing I knew, I lost more weight than I planned—twenty-five pounds in a year."

He eventually found a lower overall, sustainable weight than he had been at in years. "More important," he adds, "is that my cholesterol came down more than a hundred points. My doctor couldn't believe it."

Jones, a husband and a father of two, says the biggest change in his behavior was that he paid more attention to everything he ate. "I never before would have looked at a box to see how much saturated fat was in it," he says. "Wouldn't have read it; didn't care. Now if something has a high degree of saturated fat, I avoid it. And the more I avoid it, the less I miss it."

Some key changes:

- Jones eats oatmeal every day.
- His wife prepares healthier foods at home.
- Instead of eating red meat daily, a habit borne of his midwestern upbringing, Jones might have a cheeseburger once every two or three months.
- Exercise is still a challenge, but he takes pains to at least walk daily.

"I don't diet," Jones says. "I just eat differently. It's been two years now, and I feel like I could maintain this lifestyle for as long as I wish."

Train Your Body by Eating Often

Skipping meals and fasting for extended periods train your body to store fat against the next shortage of food. Here's how it works: When you fast, lipogenesis enzymes, already programmed to absorb fat, have nothing to work on. The body says, "I'm starving, so I must protect myself to survive. I'll store fat like crazy when I can." As a result, it creates more enzymes, which create more fat when food becomes available. The quickest way to build a potbelly is to eat only one meal a day because you keep your body on famine alert.

If weight loss is your aim, minimize the lipogenesis enzyme action by never allowing yourself to get hungry. Take care to always have a good breakfast, enjoy a low-fat midmorning snack, and eat a nutritious lunch. Then have a nonfat snack in midafternoon so you don't go to the dinner table feeling ravenous. The body now says, "What, more food already? I'll boost my metabolism to get rid of it." The opposite course—skipping breakfast, skimping on lunch, and eating heavily in the evening—works against weight loss.

Two Ways of Training Your Metabolism by Eating

Winning the fight against your body's fear of famine (without dying in the process via anorexia nervosa) is possible if your goal is to improve your ratio of fat to lean body mass. Here are two tactics to make this easier:

1. Keep your caloric intake consistent from day to day. Avoid repeatedly making wide swings in your daily caloric intake. If your reducing plan calls for 2,000 calories a day, work at staying as close to that number as you can. Especially avoid deliberate wide swings—eating, for example, 2,800 calories one day and 1,500 the next "to make up for it." How does the body react to wide swings? First, it gleefully stores fat on the 2,800-calorie day, and then on the 1,500-calorie day it slows its metabolism so it won't have to use its reserves of fat to continue normal functions. Then, with the famine-avoidance training you've just given it, your body can probably manage to continue storing a little fat when you return to your normal reducing diet of 2,000 calories a day. This explanation simplifies a very complex process, but the essential message is accurate: Constant changes in the volume of food intake work against weight loss; consistency in the amount of food intake makes a reducing plan more effective.

2. **Eat several small meals a day.** Consume four to six small meals instead of two or three large ones. By never getting too hungry, you dull your body's fear of famine and keep your metabolism at a high, fat-burning level.

Corporate Athlete Action Items

- Never consider yourself on a diet.
- Determine your BMI and your waist-to-hip ratio.
- If at all possible, get your body fat measured.
- Begin by setting goals you can reach. Start slowly and work your way into sports gradually. Just as you need to progressively work your way toward a higher level of activity over a period of weeks, so you need to begin each exercise session by warming up for a few minutes.
- Be sure to do some form of exercise each day, understanding the roll of recovery. One way to do this is to follow an aerobic day with a strength training day or to just do some stretching on a total recovery day. Remember, the stress of exercise is the stimulus for growth, but you grow (get stronger or gain stamina) during your recovery time.
- Reverse the effects of poor nutrition and couch-potato syndrome and improve the quality of your life and health.

8

The Corporate Athlete Strategic Eating Guide

Taste is the only morality. Tell me what you like,
and I'll tell you what you are.

—JOHN RUSKIN

CORPORATE ATHLETE PRINCIPLE 8:

Take the time to figure out a menu for your life.

Tremendous strides in medical technology, nutritional research, and exercise research during the past twenty years promised substantial increases in longevity. This expectation, torpedoed by junk food and fast food, sank without a trace in an ocean of fat.

This eating guide is designed to direct your eating strategy so *you are always in control* even when Grandma serves up her famous three-cheese lasagna or everyone in your department seems to have a birthday all in the same month! The idea is that you don't lose your head when it comes to what goes in your mouth. People go off diets or overturn their healthy eating plans by detaching their brains from their bodies when it comes to food. Because of habit, circumstance, and mood, people often reach for the wrong foods.

This Corporate Athlete strategic eating guide, developed in collaboration with Meredith Luce, M.S., R.D., L.D./N., and a clinical dietitian specializing in sports nutrition, will empower you to be in control when it comes to all situations involving food. Consider this your consciousness-raising eating guide to seeking the Ideal Performance State.

The Ten Steps to Eating When You Need
to Perform at Your Best

If you put diesel fuel in a Ferrari every day except race day, and on race day you put high octane in it, it still won't work well. The carburetor will be all gunked up. And the same thing can happen to you and your engine.

Here are ten basic guidelines:

1. Start developing your best pre-event meal long before the need.   The important thing is what works for you. So find out through trial and error well before your gigantic, once-in-a-lifetime, do-or-die event. In particular, if you drink coffee or tea, find out what those stimulants do for you. Keep in mind that the effect you experience in low-tension situations will probably be magnified when tension is high.

2. Eat smart for at least several days before a big event.   Don't fall into the trap of thinking that you can be careless about eating right up to showtime, and then fix it all with a "magic bullet" meal. It doesn't work that way. To ensure maximum performance, come to your pre-event meal with your blood sugar holding steady. That means eating small, sensible meals five or six times a day in the week preceding the event.

3. Never eat a big pre-event meal.   Big meals burden your body and blood supply with a heavy digestive demand that reduces your alertness and saps your energy.

4. Avoid alcohol.   Alcohol is a powerful drug whose power to impair judgment and reduce alertness, even when consumed in small quantities, has been well documented. Alcohol's effect on you is impossible to predict with certainty in the context of your performance at an important event. One little drink taken for whatever reason will often have the opposite effect of what you intend.

5. Avoid high-fat foods.   If you want to protect your performance potential, avoid fat-heavy foods before an event. Fatty foods linger in the stomach, providing little energy, and demand so much digestive effort that your alertness may be reduced.

6. For an energizing effect, eat a light, low-fat meal that's half or a little more than half carbohydrate, with protein making up the balance.   This will increase the supply of endorphins in your brain, making it easier for you to access the Ideal Performance State with all its attendant feelings of confidence and challenge.

7. Want to boost your alertness? Eat more protein.   When you need to "get up" and want to boost your alertness, eat protein. If mood control isn't your main concern, eat for sustained energy. For an event you expect will go on for a long time, increase the carbohydrate portion of your preperformance meal. For shorter performances, increase the protein. If hot temperatures are expected, eat a little less; if you anticipate cold, eat a little more. However, don't let a hot day keep you from fortifying your body with at least a minimum of sustainable energy.

8. Nervous? For a calming effect, eat a meal that is purely carbohydrate—no protein. Eating only carbohydrates will send more tryptophan to the brain, where it will tend to increase the supply of serotonin, a natural calming chemical. Eating even a small amount of protein blocks the calming effect.

9. Your best pre-event meal includes foods that you enjoy. As long as it's not loaded with fat or calories, be generous to yourself. Enjoy a favorite food before you perform. Eating what you like can have a tremendous, positive effect.

10. Foods are like drugs—they can powerfully influence your mood. You'll find that your best pre-event meal can set you up to give your best performance, add to your confidence, and keep you alert and energetic. The rest is up to you.

Personalize Your Eating Plan

One of the keys is personalizing your eating. Choose foods that you like. Yes, *eating should be fun*—not painful, laborious, or guilt-ridden. It should not be used as reward but as an important mechanism of recovery. Just as there is an Ideal Performance State, so there is an Ideal *Recovery* State (IRS). For maximum performance, take care of the recovery needs first—that is, foods and liquids should be consumed to enable you to recover the nutrients you have expended since your last fueling stop. Corporate Athletes train themselves to enjoy eating in terms of recovery rather than in terms of calorie-counting, food exchanges, and other useless mumbo jumbo put out by the weight-loss industry.

Strategic eating is about balance. A balanced diet involves the correct ratio of protein, fat, and carbohydrate. The foundation of a balanced nutrition program is to highlight nutritionally dense foods and not calorically dense foods. Nutritionally dense foods are not necessarily high in calories but are very high in nutritional content of vitamins and minerals. Examples include broccoli, apples, and lean protein sources. Calorically dense foods are high in calories but not very high in nutritional content. Examples include chocolate, sugar, white bread, and butter.

Train yourself to take care of your nutritional needs first. Developing this habit is half the battle to reaching the body size you desire or to the performance state you seek. Eating without regard to what your body needs can cause disaster, so learn how to eat to replace the nutrients your body has consumed.

It's time to talk about what goes on the plate. The Mentally Tough program advocates that Corporate Athletes eat three meals per day with two organized snacks. Eating on schedule allows the body to keep its energy high. Remember, food is fuel; by eating periodically throughout the day you give your body organized fueling points to better meet your energy needs.

Simply defined, a meal must have at least three parts. Those parts should come from three different food groups. For example, a bowl of minestrone soup (vegetables and grain groups), a pumpernickel roll (bread group), and low-fat yogurt for dessert (dairy group). By including at least three different food groups you not only make the eating experience more rewarding, you also present your body with a broader spectrum of nutrients.

Strategic eating blends the head and the mouth to put you in control to achieve your ideal performance state.

Do It Yourself

Putting meals together yourself (versus someone else doing the cooking) is a great advantage for following the Corporate Athlete's plan and achieving the Ideal Performance State because *you* are in control. *You* control which foods you buy. *You* control how they are prepared. *You* control how much you serve. But to prepare healthful meals, you must have supplies on hand. A bare cupboard is a guaranteed call to 1-800-PIZZA. There are certain staples that every home should have to pull together a meal without a great deal of time and effort.

But buyer, beware! Based on total value of grocery store sales, the five top foods in the United States are (1) Coke, (2) Pepsi, (3) Kraft processed cheese, (4) Campbell's soup, and (5) Budweiser beer. It's no wonder obesity is such a problem in the United States. In 1980, one out of four people was obese; now it's one out of three!

Having good foods available is half the battle. The correct supplies allow for sumptuous dining in short order. Use this list to check the adequacy of your refrigerator and cupboards:

Stocking the Refrigerator and the Kitchen Shelves

Breads, Cereals, Grains and Pasta Group		
Barley	Couscous	Graham rackers
Cornmeal	Dry pasta (including orzo)	Low-fat crackers
Cornstarch	Frozen waffles	Nutrigrain bars

continued

Oatmeal
Rice

Rice cakes
Soft corn tortillas

Unbleached flour
Variety of breads
(e.g., bagels, whole
wheat bread, pita)

Vegetable Group

Broccoli and onions
Carrots (including minis)
Cauliflower
Celery
Corn
Cucumbers

Frozen spinach
Green beans
Lettuce
Onions
Peas (fresh or frozen)
Peppers

Potatoes
Squash
Sweet potatoes
Tomatoes
Yellow squash
Zucchini

Fruit Group

Apples
Applesauce
Bananas
Dried fruit (e.g., apricots,
raisins)

Fresh or frozen berries
Fresh lemons
Grapefruit or other citrus
Grapes

Orange juice
Oranges
Pears
Tangerines

Protein Group

Canned beans (e.g., kidney,
garbanzo, pinto)
Chicken breast
Cold-water seafood

Lean ground beef
Low-fat deli cuts (e.g.,
turkey, roast beef)
Peanut butter (low/
reduced sugar)

Raw almonds
Tuna canned in water

Dairy Group

Low-fat cheese (e.g., Swiss,
cheddar)
Low-fat cottage cheese

Low-fat yogurt
Nonfat instant dry milk
powder

1% or skim milk
Parmesan cheese

Other: Condiments, Herbs/Spices, Sweeteners, Beverages

Bottled water
Brown sugar
Chutneys
Cooking oil spray
Fresh cilantro and basil
Fresh garlic
Fresh ginger root
Ground cinnamon
Herbs and spices
Honey

Horseradish
Ketchup
Light mayonnaise
Light salad dressing
Light soy sauce
Light teriyaki sauce
Low-fat cream cheese
Low-fat/no-fat sour
cream
Low/reduced sodium
chicken broth

Low/reduced sugar jams
and jellies
Margarine
Mrs. Dash seasoning
Mustard
Nutmeg
Olive oil
Oregano
Peppercorns
Salsa
Thyme

Plan Your Meals Three Days at a Time

To keep your taste buds entertained and to present your body with the widest variety of nutrients, you need to plan ahead. Strategic eating involves forethought. Strategic eating uses your head.

With your taste buds piqued and pencil and paper at the ready, let's plan a menu. Take three days at a time only. List the words:

Breakfast #1 _____

Lunch #1 _____

Dinner #1 _____

Breakfast #2 _____

Lunch #2 _____

Dinner #2 _____

Breakfast #3 _____

Lunch #3 _____

Dinner #3 _____

Next to Breakfast #1 write: cereal and fruit (you choose what type of cereal and what kind of fruit)

Next to Breakfast #2 write: bagel and low-fat cream cheese

Next to Breakfast #3 write: scrambled egg whites and rye toast (or other bread)

Now fill in lunch for all three days. Let's say:

Lunch #1: veggie pouch and low-fat cheese

Lunch #2: chicken and rice soup with peanut butter and low-fat crackers

Lunch #3: canned spring-water-packed tuna on sourdough roll

Of course, planned meals are not always guaranteed meals, because even though you planned to bring a sandwich for lunch #3, the office gang wants to go to Bennigan's. That's why we call it a planned menu. And that's where the 80-20 rule of business applies to your nutritional needs. Instead of 80 percent of your business coming from 20 percent of your clients, look at it this way: Eat really well 80 percent of the time and then you can stray from the "ideal" 20 percent of the time.

As far as dinner is concerned, take into consideration who else is eating and where you'll be. Dinner #1 might be listed as "out with friends" or might have to be something light after an evening exercise class. Regardless, write it down so that when you go to the grocery store you can purchase it and have it available, if not for meal #1 then perhaps for meal #4.

Corporate Athlete eating principles encourage variety. Dinner #2 shouldn't be a reheated Dinner #1. If you're having a turkey sandwich for lunch, then don't have grilled chicken at dinner. Instead, choose a pasta with a light vegetable/tomato sauce, or go for a fish dinner.

When it comes to planning meals there are questions of availability to consider—how much time and money you have available and whether the foods you desire are available. But the most important question should be one of responsibility—that is, responsibility to your mouth. Simply, what are you in the mood for? What do you want to eat? You may feel like something with a lot of crunch or something with a lot of spice. Perhaps you want to keep it simple and quick and go for a healthy liquid meal. Whatever it is, the decision should be a matter of personal taste. Asking yourself what kind of food you are in the mood for is vital to successfully giving yourself a balanced diet.

Let's say that you and your friends decide to go to Denny's for lunch. They all order burgers and fries, but you decide to be good and order the spinach salad with low-calorie dressing. Two hours later you justify the dark fudge ice cream because you were such a good eater at lunch. We call this displaced eating. You displaced your true food preference, creating a void. So after not satisfying your food need, you overcompensated with a worse choice! When you deny yourself in one place, you end up having to satisfy yourself someplace else. Ask yourself what you really feel like eating.

Occasional indulgences are part of the Corporate Athlete's eating strategy. But don't abuse your right to eat. Eating one piece of cake is fine, half the cake is not.

Something Was Missing

Reeves Callaway is an unusual guy. The founder of Callaway Cars in Old Lyme, Connecticut, has a lot of elements that would make people say, "That's a cool guy." He builds some of the fastest automobiles in the world. He has a stack of résumés from young men and women who would kill to work for him. And yet?

"I was putting off the things I should be doing," he says. "You can paint a good picture of me as an accomplished man, but something was missing. I wasn't feeling very strong, very directed, or enthusiastic about what my next step might be."

The conundrum facing Callaway is one familiar to many successful, self-motivated men and women in our society, and it goes like this: Even as we work hard enough to achieve our dreams and the dreams of others, very few of us have the vision to take care of ourselves along the way. We are much more focused by the nature of our accomplishments.

That's what happened to Callaway. Not long after he turned fifty, this divorced father of two told his father, Ely Callaway, founder of the Callaway Golf Company, that something was missing in his life. Ely told his son about our work with professional golfers, and it wasn't long before Reeves was at our Orlando campus in search of inspiration and strategies to make the required changes in his life.

"I felt like I was out of shape. I'm 6-3 and I weighed 210—about 20 pounds overweight. I was once a good athlete but had let that drift. I didn't know anything about nutrition."

Callaway no longer hits the icebox for a quart of rum-raisin ice cream. "And I don't eat eggs for breakfast," he says. "Butter is off the list. But that's what I was asking for. I'm not a fanatic. I'm sitting at my desk right now with a bag of carrots, grapes, and a Clif Bar. My weight is down; my energy is up."

The Good Taste Meal Planning Primer

Personalizing your eating is the key to the Corporate Athlete eating strategy. Short on menu ideas? Get started with some of the ideas that Meredith H. Luce, M.S., R.D., L.D./N., and I put together:

Breakfast Planning Tips

Start the day with a nutritious breakfast. Research indicates that breakfast skippers struggle more with weight than do breakfast eaters. Eating first thing in the morning gives your metabolism a jump start, like putting gas in your car. Remember, food is fuel.

Think in terms of whole foods; fruit has more fiber than fruit juice.

Always include whole grain breads or cereals (carbohydrates, starches); they are your main source of energy.

Choose some kind of protein-rich food. Protein foods include 1 cup of low-fat milk, ¼ cup of low-fat cheese, 1 cup of fat-free or low-fat yogurt, ¼ cup of egg substitute, and 2 tablespoons of peanut butter.

Watch those fats. They include: butter, margarine, oil, cream, half and half, and cream cheese. A little is okay for taste, but a lot goes to your waist.

Three Planned Breakfasts

Each breakfast is equal to about 350 calories.

> 1) 1 bagel
>   1 tablespoon peanut butter
>   1 apple, sliced

2) ½ cup scrambled egg substitute prepared with cooking oil
    spray
    ½ cup grits
    1 slice whole wheat toast
    1 tablespoon all-fruit preserves
    ½ cup orange juice

3) 1½ cups Cheerios
    1 cup skim milk
    1 banana

Lunch Planning Tips

Avoid skipping lunch—it only sets you up for overeating later.

Try making your lunch at home. Brown-bagging keeps food costs
down. Besides, you'll have lunch available when you're hungry.

If a microwave is handy, try a frozen low-fat meal such as Healthy
Choice or Lean Cuisine.

Anything fried should signal a red light.

At restaurants, request condiments on the side.

Think green. Vegetables rate high on the nutrient and fiber list. For
that matter, think orange, red, yellow.

Three Planned Lunches

Lunch will provide the energy you need to get you through the day. Each
lunch is equal to about 400 calories.

1) 2 slices rye with mustard
    3 ounces lean luncheon meat
    Add tomato slices and leafy lettuce
    ½ cup juice packed pineapple chunks

2) 1 cup vegetable soup (Healthy Choice or Campbell's Healthy Re-
    quest)
    1 slice cheese toast (1 slice fat free cheese on 1 slice whole wheat
    toast)
    6 carrot sticks
    2 Fig Newtons
    1 cup skim milk

3) 2 slices pumpernickel bread
    ½ cup water packed tuna or 98 percent fat-free chunk chicken

Mix with celery, pickle relish, and fat-free or reduced-fat mayonnaise or fat-free sour cream or fat-free yogurt
Serve with lettuce leaves and tomato slices
1 cup sliced cucumber
1½ cups mixed fruit

Dinner Planning Tips

Plan ahead by taking something out of the freezer and put it in the refrigerator the night before you want to have it.

Watch portion sizes, as this is the time of day we tend to overeat and the time of day when we need the least amount of fuel. Three to four ounces is an appropriate portion size for a serving. An easy way to estimate portion size is to remember it should be no bigger than the size of your hand.

Remember the three-fourths rule: Carbs first for three-fourths of the plate, including grains, veggies, fruits. Then the remaining fourth for a protein.

For a sweet treat, pile fresh, low-fat whipped cream on angel food cake.

Eight Planned Dinners

A little meal planning goes a long way. Having the ingredients on hand and a menu in mind make it easy. Watch the portion sizes.

1) ½ chicken breast without skin
   Add a little BBQ sauce for taste, or marinate in a fat-free Italian dressing. Bake or grill.
   ½ medium baked potato topped with salsa or fat-free sour cream
   ½ cup steamed broccoli
   ½ cup steamed carrots
   1 fresh apple

2) 1 cup spaghetti noodles
   ¼ cup pesto sauce
   2 cups tossed salad
   2 tablespoons reduced fat Italian dressing
   ½ cup fruit sorbet

3) 3–4 ounces broiled fish
   ½ cup rice pilaf
   1 cup steamed vegetables
   ½ cup fat free frozen yogurt

4) 8 ounce veal cutlet (not breaded)
    1 cup carrots
    1 cup corn
    1 cup fresh fruit

5) 6 ounces turkey (skinless)
    1 cup boiled new potatoes
    2 cups peas

6) 1 complete chicken breast (skinless)
    1 cup corn
    1 cup green beans
    1 cup grapes

7) 6 ounces steak (sirloin)
    2 cups mixed vegetables (corn, carrots, peppers, onions)

8) 3 cups beef stew, with onions, carrots, and potatoes
    1 cup rice

Strategic Snacking

We've already made the point that eating fuels your body and keeps your energy level at a peak. Since we advocate eating three meals per day, the other two or three eating events will be called strategic snacks.

A strategic snack uses your head first and your mouth second. A snack without strategy or forethought will not provide the long-lasting energy you need. Most people think of a snack as a single food item such as a candy bar or a piece of fruit. Both of these items are carbohydrate-dense and will indeed boost your blood sugar levels but in fact will bring you down sooner. In other words, you get the sugar kick, but the hormone insulin rushes out into the bloodstream and ushers the excess sugar in the blood into the liver and muscles. A feeling of lethargy results. With a strategic snack—not only strategic in choice of foodstuff but also in timing—you get a slower rise in blood sugar with a long-lasting result. The reason? Strategic snacks combine carbohydrates and protein.

Several studies show that meals or snacks high in carbohydrates but low in protein have a mild sedative effect compared to a more balanced combination of carbohydrates and protein. Eaten by itself, carbohydrate stimulates the production of the calming hormone serotonin. But when carbohydrates are eaten in combination with protein, the protein prevents the production of serotonin and stimulates the development of the energizing hormones dopamine and norepinephrine. Energizing hormones keep us revved and alert, promoting the Ideal Performance State.

Guide to the Ideal Performance State and the Ideal Recovery State

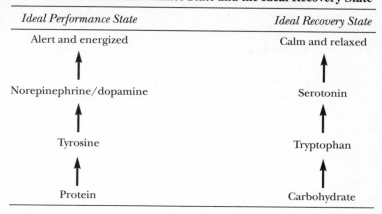

Ideal Performance State	*Ideal Recovery State*
Alert and energized	Calm and relaxed
↑	↑
Norepinephrine/dopamine	Serotonin
↑	↑
Tyrosine	Tryptophan
↑	↑
Protein	Carbohydrate

Enjoy and experiment with your own favorite strategic snacks.

Strategic Snacks

Milk Group
- Low-fat cheese cube with pretzels or low-fat crackers
- Low-fat cheese slices or spreads on low-fat crackers or rice cakes
- Low-fat cottage cheese and fresh fruit
- Dips made of low-fat cheese, cottage cheese, buttermilk, sour cream, or yogurt, with crackers or raw vegetables
- Fruit smoothie and pretzels or other bread group

Fruit and Vegetable Group
- Fresh fruit and yogurt, cheese, or lean deli cuts
- Orange slices and yogurt, cottage cheese, or muffin
- Canned fruit chunks or slices—pineapple, pear, mandarin orange, etc., and cottage cheese
- Fruit and cheese kabobs—alternate fruit and cheese cubes
- Applesauce and low-fat muffin or whole grain bread
- Raw vegetables—celery sticks, carrot sticks or curls, cherry tomatoes, cauliflowerettes, broccoli, cucumber coins, served plain or with low-fat cheese dip
- Raisins and other dried fruits and nuts or seeds (a.k.a. trail mix)
- Dried apricots and raw almonds
- Apples with peanut butter, or banana with peanut butter
- Ants on logs—celery filled with peanut butter and dotted with raisins
- Celery sticks or cucumber boats stuffed with cottage cheese, cheese spread, tuna salad, or egg salad (all low-fat)

Protein Group
- Cold meat cubes, rolls, sticks, or slices and fresh fruit
- Hard-boiled eggs and tomato juice
- Nuts, sesame seeds, toasted sunflower seeds, and dried fruit
- Peanut butter—in sandwiches, on crackers, for a vegetable dip
- Pretzel kabobs—alternate cheese cubes
- Treasure logs—roll thin meat slice with low-fat cheese or low-fat cheese spread
- Tuna fish on crackers, in sandwiches

Bread and Cereal Group
- Crackers—wheat, graham, or enriched, with cheese, spreads, dips
- Cornbread and tomato juice
- Fruit bread with applesauce and 1 percent or skim milk
- Nut breads with low-fat cream cheese and/or glass of 1 percent or skim milk
- Zucchini, carrot, pumpkin breads with apple butter or peanut butter or low-fat cream cheese
- Breadsticks and cottage cheese
- Muffins with low sugar spread or low-fat cream cheese
- Low-fat granola or crunchy mix—unsugared cereal (Cheerios, Chex, etc.) mixed with raisins, peanuts, sunflower seeds, etc.
- Peanut butter crackers with 1 percent or skim milk
- Graham crackers with 1 percent or skim milk

The Glycemic Index of Foods

In the past, we have been told to consume carbohydrates (basically any carbohydrate) for energy. But times are not the same. How much of a jolt of energy you get depends not on whether the carbohydrate is simple (a sugar) or complex (starch) but on its glycemic response.

The glycemic response of a food refers to its ability to raise blood sugar levels. This response is determined by several factors—how much food is eaten, its fat content or the amount of fat eaten with it, the fiber content, and the food's preparation. For example, honey on rye toast has a lower glycemic response than pure honey alone.

The glycemic index (GI) is a ranking of a food's glycemic response compared to a certain reference food. For our purposes, the reference food is glucose (sugar), and its GI equals 100. A GI greater than 60 is considered to be high, 40 to 60 is moderate, while a GI of less than 40 is considered a low glycemic response.

For many of us, we associate insulin with diabetes. But contemporary nutritional science demands that we pay close attention to the issues behind what and when we eat, the type of food we consume, the speed of that food's ability to increase blood sugar, the subsequent response of insulin, and finally, the role of insulin in either burning that blood sugar or storing it as fat.

The primary job of insulin is to increase the use of glucose by the body. That, initially, decreases how the body uses fat. At the same time, insulin also promotes the development of fatty acids. This is what happens: Insulin first sends glucose to the liver. Once the liver's glycogen level reaches a 5 to 6 percent concentration (not too much, is it?), the storage of glycogen stops there. If you exercise after eating a meal, some glucose is transported to the muscle, but your muscles can store only about a 2 percent concentration of glycogen (again, not too much). If the storage depots are full, all extra glucose will be converted to fat.

Insulin also facilitates the transport of amino acids to the cells after proteins are broken down. When associated with growth hormones, insulin increases the capability of amino acids to penetrate the cells. Insulin also inhibits the breakdown of proteins within the cells, especially muscle cells. Therefore, amino acids are released from these cells less frequently. So insulin promotes the formation of protein within cells but prevents protein breakdown inside the cells.

When insulin is absent in the bloodstream (which occurs normally between meals if you do not snack), large quantities of fatty acids are released into the blood. This, in turn, causes the conversion of some fat into cholesterol. When this happens, your cholesterol levels can rise dramatically. This high concentration of cholesterol, which can become extreme in cases of diabetes mellitus, may lead to the development of atherosclerosis, the clogging of the arteries.

There are three fundamental reasons why you should not allow your blood sugar concentration to rise too high:

1. Glucose causes great pressure in the fluid around cells, which can cause cellular dehydration if glucose levels get too high.

2. Excessive amounts of blood sugar can cause a loss of glucose in the urine.

3. Since too much blood glucose can cause a loss of glucose in the urine, pressure is created within the kidneys. This, in turn, can cause the depletion of essential body fluids and electrolytes.

To understand how various foods can stimulate rises in blood glucose, we need to discuss the factors determining the glycemic index:

- The type of sugar—fructose (fruit sugar) has the lowest GI for all sugars.
- Fiber content—soluble fiber makes for a lower GI than insoluble fiber.
- Protein and fat generally indicate a lower GI.
- Compact versus crumbly—compact foods tend to have a higher GI than crumbly foods (e.g., pasta has a higher GI than bread).
- Resistance to digestion (e.g., whole grain breads have a higher GI than breads made from refined flour).
- Amylose (sugar) versus amylopectin-starch (fiber)—sugary foods have a higher GI than fibrous and starchy foods.

For a complete list of foods and their glycemic ranking, see J. Brand Miller and Kaye Foster-Powell's "International Tables of Glycemic Index," originally published in 1995 in the *American Journal of Clinical Nutrition*, vol. 62, pp. 871s–893s.

Nutrition Labeling Savvy

Now let's talk about one of the best things for consumers to come out of government in a long time: nutrition labeling. This initiative was spearheaded by Phil Sokolof of Omaha, the man who, a few years ago, took on McDonald's and other fast-food chains with full-page ads saying they were poisoning America. With that fight won, Phil moved on to food labeling.

The new nutrition labeling act turns a pitiless spotlight on how bad some foods are for you. Not surprisingly, the food industry is doing its best to minimize the damage and still stay within the law. Their main tool of deception is "serving size." By cutting serving sizes in half, they cut the Percent Daily Value in half—the number they believe most label checkers look at. Candy bars are a good example. Some of them claim that each bar contains two or more servings, even though they know most people eat the whole bar at one time. A small, 8-ounce can of pork and beans claims two servings, so they can legally assert that one serving supplies only 490 milligrams of sodium, which is 21 percent of your RDA. But if you put away the whole can, you consume 42 percent of your daily allotment of salt.

The key element is serving size. The Percent Daily Value on the label shows what you get by eating one serving of the food in question, but if you ordinarily eat two or three servings of the food at a time, double or triple the Percent Daily Value.

Corporate Athlete Action Items

- Begin the habit of strategic eating today.
- Follow the 80/20 rule of eating. That means that 80 percent of the time you eat impeccably well and 20 percent of the time you can stray a little. Eat even better if it's possible.
- Prepare a good day of nutrition for the next twenty-four-hour period.
- At a restaurant, try ordering without a menu only healthful items.
- Prepare your snacks at least one day ahead.
- If you take your lunch to work, plan and prepare it well ahead of time.

9

On the Road Again

It is the rough road that leads to the heights of greatness.
—LUCIUS ANNAEUS SENECA

CORPORATE ATHLETE PRINCIPLE 9:

There's no reason to eat poorly—even when you're running like mad.

At your desk, in the car, at home, on a transcontinental flight, or in a hotel, I will show you how to set a healthy table. This chapter includes tips for ordering in restaurants, fast-food establishments, and convenience stores that will help make healthy choices easier.

Most of the time the Corporate Athlete is too busy for leisurely meals. For some of us, nutrition comes from fast-food outlets and airplane meals. Even when you're not traveling, you and your spouse eat out almost every night.

Eating on the Run

Everyone reading this book has at one time or another—and probably often—had to hurry up and eat or go without. Whether it's between sales calls, between meetings, or between appointments, there always seems to be a problem with eating, especially at midday.

When you're on the road in your rental car rushing hurriedly from one meeting to the next, there are times when you need to eat, and eat fast. And although this philosophy of eating fast does not fit into the Corporate Athlete's regimen, I recognize that there are times when you absolutely have to live this lifestyle. Since there's no way around it, here are my recommendations on the quick hits:

86

You don't have to stick to carrots in the salad bar, but you should avoid mayonnaise-soaked dishes. Get into the habit of saying "no cheese" when you order anything they could possibly put cheese on; this simple change could keep thousands of calories a year out of your system. (A single ounce of most hard cheeses has about 100 calories and 10 grams of fat—mostly the saturated kind.) Those unnecessary calories can stay with you as body fat.

So skip the burgers, fish sandwiches, and fries. Anyway, you'd probably rather eat something high in fat at other times, perhaps when you're relaxing with family and friends. There are times when you have no control over what's served, but you do when you're eating on the run. It takes no more than a few seconds to make the healthier choices. *Eating on the run is no longer an excuse to eat poorly.*

There's nothing wrong with eating at fast-food restaurants, unless all you ever eat there is a burger and fries. Most fast-food restaurants have very healthy selections. For example, many have the capability for excellent grilled chicken meals. Burger King has the BK Broiler, McDonald's has the McGrilled Chicken DeLuxe. Hardee's, Wendy's, Carl's Jr., Checkers, Steak-N-Shake, and Taco Bell have their versions of the same meal. Many of these fast-food chains also have very good salad selections (but watch out for the dressing). One very important point in ordering from a fast-food restaurant: Their job is to cater to your taste.

When ordering I always ask the servers to omit the special sauce. However, like everyone else, I like moisture in my sandwich, so I often ask for mustard and sometimes ketchup on my sandwiches. Lettuce, tomatoes, and pickles also add to the moisture and flavor of any sandwich.

At hotels and some fast-food restaurants, pizza is a very popular item. A cheese pizza with nothing else on it is about 27 percent fat—not bad for a fast-food restaurant. A hamburger can be up to 56 percent fat, and that includes the bun.

However, you can do something I find quite tasty. I learned about it by chance while dining at a pizza restaurant with a friend who is lactose-intolerant and can't eat cheese. My friend ordered a small pizza with no cheese, but with extra tomato sauce, mushrooms, and other vegetables. This astounded me. I asked the manager if it was a common request. He said, "It happens occasionally, but not too often."

I decided to order the same thing. Yes, I know: We grow up with certain tastes; the idea of a pizza with no cheese seems incredible. I must tell you, though, it was absolutely terrific. As an extra bonus, it ended up being about 5 to 10 percent fat instead of the 27 to 30 percent fat provided by just the cheeses. (Adding meat to the pizza booms up the fat content even more.)

Many fast-food restaurants have a salad bar (and some even have a pasta bar). Just be wary of the dressing and also of how much butter the pasta in the pasta bar contains. If prepared poorly, a very healthy staple can become unhealthy and loaded with fat.

Packing Your Brown Bag for Work

Eat light, eat often, and eat a variety of nonfat or low-fat foods. When you're at work, often the best way is to brown-bag it so you can control what you eat. Otherwise the route salesperson for the vending machine down the hall has more control over what you snack on than you do. If you depend on him or her, or on the local fast-food restaurant, the odds are you'll consume large amounts of fat and get very little nutrition. If your workday extends from 7:00 A.M. to 7:00 P.M., I recommend never leaving home without a brown bag filled with healthy foods. You may feel less conspicuous by putting the brown bag inside an attaché case or workout bag or by keeping it stashed in your desk.

If the brown-bag concept makes you uncomfortable—an understandable reaction, given the importance of image—there are alternatives. You could, for example, have an extra attaché case for food only. A nylon zipper bag might be a good choice. Or you could bring in a few days' supply of fruit and keep it in a bowl in your office.

A sliced turkey breast sandwich on rye bread with lettuce, tomato, and mustard is an outstanding lunch. Add a couple of pieces of fruit for fueling your Ferrari the right way at midday.

The brown bag should also contain your midmorning snack and your midafternoon snack. In the midmorning you could have fruit: an apple or a peach; a bagel or a whole-wheat roll; trail mix; or cereal in a plastic bag. Any of these would be tremendous. Your midafternoon snack could duplicate the alternatives for the midmorning one, but don't repeat the same snack over and over. These midmorning and midafternoon snacks serve to stabilize your blood sugar, thus keeping you "up" mentally for the next couple of hours.

If you leave with the family on a long trip, take a brown bag with fruit, whole-grain rolls, fat-free pretzels, rice cakes, and so on. It's a great way to teach your children how to eat for health, longevity, and good appearance.

The Business Dinner

Be careful when eating out. Many restaurants have a "healthy menu," but the items they list may not be the best foods for you. Some "healthy" items on menus still are extremely high in fat. The best Corporate Athlete thing to do at any restaurant also impresses the client: *Never open the menu.* Simply decide what you would like to eat beforehand and ask them to fix it. You might decide on grilled chicken breast on a rice pilaf, grilled chicken with pasta, or sliced turkey on whole-wheat bread with lettuce, tomato, and mustard.

If you feel compelled to eat red meat, ask the server if the restaurant has veal, because it's lower in fat than mature beef. If your client orders dessert and you feel compelled to have dessert, ask for fresh berries or fresh fruit. If unavailable, ask for a small piece of angel food cake or a small dish of sherbet.

If your client orders a Caesar salad, you can simply order a lettuce and tomato salad with your dressing on the side. Then minimize the fat from the salad dressing by dipping your fork vertically in the salad dressing (no scooping allowed). This leaves enough dressing on the prongs of the fork to get the taste of the dressing without the high caloric (and usually fat) content of the dressing.

Simply refuse to feel pressure from clients to order a lot of alcohol and red meat. If you want to join them in a drink, order a glass of wine and sip on it the entire evening.

"I Believe, I Believe!!"

Is your career up in the air?

Peter Cathey's is—every day. He is the chief executive officer of a Connecticut-based retail company called World Duty Free Inflight.

When you board an overseas airline flight, the drink and meal service is followed by a retail service during which the flight attendants sell duty-free products on the aircraft. Through the aisles they push a cart that has merchandise supplied by Cathey's company. Flight attendants—more than forty-five thousand of them working for thirty airlines worldwide represent World Duty Free Inflight—are paid a commission on every sale.

Besides the flight attendants, Cathey has five hundred full-time employees spanning the globe from his offices in Ridgefield, Connecticut, to a warehouse in Hong Kong.

Like many business travelers, Cathey did the same things when flying overseas as he did domestically, from drinking alcohol in-flight to eating heavy meals and not altering his sleep patterns. But the difference between the two types of trips is analogous to the difference between a wind sprint and a marathon. So one of the areas we retrained Cathey in was the way he travels. He no longer fears the Jet Lag Reaper.

The change occurred not long ago, after I conducted a Mentally Tough program at Oxford University in England for executives of the Estee Lauder corporation and a few of its selected retail partners. Cathey was in that seminar, and he and I sat together on the flight back to the States. He basically mimicked everything I did on the trip, from eating and drinking to sleeping and stretching.

"I am always amazed that the airlines stuff so much food at you during these flights," he said to me on board. "Dinner service, breakfast service, snacks . . . "

"Peter," I said, "it is not just *what* you eat. There is also an amount issue and the issue of *when* you eat it."

The flight left London at 9:00 A.M. local time. Cathey was already dog tired after a week of training at Oxford and dreading the added strain of flying overseas.

As we ate a plate of pancakes, Cathey said, "Boy, those things are going to lay in your stomach forever."

"No, not really," I said. "These will burn off, trust me. In fact, the pancakes will act like a sedative and allow you to get some good-quality sleep." To his surprise, Cathey fell asleep soon after and slept soundly for almost four hours.

About two hours before landing, I said, "Now, what are you doing today?"

"My wife and two friends are waiting for me to play golf," he said.

"Great," I said. "Stick to eating proteins between now and then."

Before we landed, Cathey had a piece of chicken, a small salad, and a lot of water. This twenty-two-handicap golfer nonetheless got off the plane anticipating a horrible day of golf.

Well, after playing almost par golf for the first eight holes, Cathey's wife and his friends were stunned. "You weren't at a business seminar in London," his wife said. "You were at a golf school! Where the hell did you go?"

The next day, my phone rang. It was Peter Cathey.

"I believe, I believe!!" he said. Later, he told me: "Now if I'm on a night flight or a reasonable night flight, meaning we are fed before eight at night, local time, I might have *one* glass of wine, if that. But then I focus in on water intake and getting on local time."

Traveling Overnight from the United States to European Destinations

If your plane departs the United States at 7:00 P.M., remember that it is at least midnight at your destination. Once the plane's wheels are up, change your watch to the time at your point of arrival. Then psychologically set your mind to that time.

Sleep is important, so what you eat and drink are very important. Alcohol should be kept to a minimum, as it will interrupt your sleep cycle and it will dehydrate you.

To ensure your chances of good sleep, choose a meal based on carbohydrates. Protein will make you alert and will affect your ability to sleep. Also, be sure to drink plenty of water or juices to minimize the effects of dehydration.

For more specific strategies, consider these three approaches:

Scenario 1

You will arrive by air in the morning and immediately go into an important meeting.

When you awaken for breakfast on the plane, be sure to have a little protein. Choosing a whole-grain cereal or a low-fat protein breakfast will be beneficial. If you are already a coffee drinker, you should have some coffee, as your body is used to it. If you're not a coffee drinker, avoid it. For the noncoffee drinker, only consume coffee as a last alternative to overcome any sluggishness you might have. Be aware, however, that it could make you jittery and snappish.

After deplaning, walk briskly to Customs and, whenever possible between there and your final destination, walk around and absorb some sunlight. This will prepare you physically, mentally, and emotionally to maximize your performance.

Scenario 2

You will arrive by air in the morning, get to your hotel, and have four hours before your meeting.

Now you have to answer a question as you awaken on the plane: Did I sleep well and am I ready to start my day, or am I still very tired and need more rest?

If you slept well and feel rested, have a breakfast of whole-grain cereal or a low-fat protein meal. If you did not sleep well and feel fatigued, you may want to have a light carbohydrate meal (e.g., fruit and a bagel). For the rested and wide awake, exercise or go for a walk as soon as you get to your hotel. For the person still requiring more rest, take an hour nap once you get to your hotel, then go for a brisk walk or get some exercise. Getting out into the sunlight will help awaken you as well.

Scenario 3

You will arrive by air a day prior to your important business meeting (e.g., you arrive on a Tuesday morning and the meeting is on Wednesday morning).

The ideal plan would be to follow the sleep and eating patterns mentioned in the first two scenarios. If you are still fatigued upon arriving at the hotel, take a nap, but make sure you start becoming active—don't stay on U.S. time! Try to follow the local schedule as much as possible.

Get outside and walk around. You could even take a short nap in the midafternoon, but then move around by either sightseeing, exercising, or going for a brisk walk. Then get to sleep at a time so you will be rested for the big meeting the next day.

Traveling All Day from Europe to a U.S. Destination

Although issues of nutrition and rest are very personal for each of us, the following general recommendations are based on scientific information.

If you depart Europe in the morning, you will likely arrive at your U.S. destination during the workday. Once the plane's wheels are up as you depart Europe, change your watch so you immediately begin living on the time zone of your point of arrival. You now have two alternatives: You could take a short nap to get on the U.S. time zone as soon as possible, although this is not an easy alternative because you already have had a full night's sleep in your European city. Or: Don't sleep! This will allow you to rest more easily on the night of your arrival in the United States. Most research encourages you to stay awake if possible. Caffeine and alcohol intake should be kept to a minimum to avoid dehydration, and you should drink plenty of water or fruit juice.

If you want to take a nap, lower the window shades so the sun isn't coming through the window, and make use of a sleep mask so you can facilitate your ability to sleep.

Scenario 1

You arrive during the day and must go immediately into an important meeting.

Do everything within your power to be alert and energized upon arriving for your meeting. Your meal or snack prior to arrival should consist of low-fat protein, and you should have consumed plenty of water. In addition, during the last couple hours of the flight, you should get up and walk in the aisles, and do some isometric exercises or some light stretching. Obviously, you can't do a full workout on the plane, but you can "awaken" yourself through some light activity.

"When I am on a long trip, I always stretch on the plane," says Jim Courier. "I usually go to the galley and stretch there, where the flight attendants are. It's a good way to get to know them. It's fun."

As you leave the plane, walk briskly to Customs, and with any spare time you have (e.g., you arrive fifteen minutes prior to your meeting), go for a short walk and try to get into the sunlight.

Scenario 2

You arrive during the day and have about four hours before going into an important meeting.

You should eat on the airplane as described in Scenario 1, but now you should go to the next level. If you brought your workout gear, exercise as soon as you get checked into your hotel.

Courier says, "I always make sure that when I get off the plane, if it is a longer trip, I go out and get a sweat. I feel like I have to do something active to jump-start my body. Even if I arrive late at night, I will go into the hotel gym or whatever and just go jump on a treadmill or on a bike just to break a sweat."

If you didn't bring any exercise clothes, you could still go for a long walk or do some sightseeing, but try to get some activity. Also, try to get into the sunlight, so your body will adapt more quickly.

Scenario 3

You arrive a day before the big meeting (e.g., you arrive on Tuesday and your meeting is on Wednesday).

The key factor in this scenario is to get adjusted to the new time zone upon your arrival. If a nap on the airplane is important for you personally, take the nap as early in the trip as possible. I suggest that you stay awake for the trip. In that way, research says, you will sleep more readily that night and adjust to the new time more easily. On the airplane, be sure to eat low-fat protein meals and drink plenty of water and fruit juices.

"Special Request" Meals When Traveling

Your travel agent can easily put your dietary requirements on computer. Then, each time you make an airline reservation, your reservation automatically requests a special meal. These special meals are often outstanding, since they are not made in normal mass production in advance but are specially made each day for those passengers who request them.

On most airlines you can order the following special meals: Baby, Bland (Low-Sodium), Child, Cold Seafood, Diabetic, Fruit Only, Hindu, Kosher, Low-Fat, Muslim, Toddler, Vegetarian (Lacto), and Vegetarian (Pure). (Please note: The children's meals are not necessarily healthy.)

On a recent trip from Tampa to San Francisco, my travel agent ordered "low-fat" meals for me. Here's the comparison of what I ate vs. the regular meal most other passengers were served:

Tampa to Dallas

Normal Meal	My Low-Fat Meal
Ham and cheese on a sub roll with mayo	Turkey on whole-wheat bread with lettuce
Bag of Fritos	Low-fat tortilla chips
	Apple

Nutrition

Normal Meal	My Low-Fat Meal
432 calories	338 calories
24.6 g protein	14.9 g protein
34 g carbohydrates	58.3 g carbohydrates
22.4 g fat, of which 5.88 g were saturated	6.67 g fat, of which 1.34 g were saturated

Calories from Fat

Normal Meal	My Low-Fat Meal
47 percent	18 percent

Dallas to San Francisco

Normal Meal	My Low-Fat Meal
Meat and cheese tortellini in cream sauce	Salad with low-calorie ranch dressing
Salad with Thousand Island dressing	Chicken breast (3-oz. without skin), with
Large macadamia nut chocholate chip	light tomato sauce
cookie	Wild rice and steamed vegetables (corn, green beans, broccoli, and cauliflower)
	Pita bread
	Fresh fruit (½ apple, ⅓ orange, 2 prunes, and lettuce garnish)

Nutrition

Normal Meal	My Low-Fat Meal
1,192 calories	580 calories
1,577 mg sodium (66% of RDA)	1,278 mg sodium (53% of RDA)
37.9 g protein	40.8 g protein
125 g carbohydrates	97.1 g carbohydrates
61.4 g fat, of which 15.2 g were saturated	5.26 g fat, of which 1.17 g were saturated

Calories from Fat

Normal Meal	My Low-Fat Meal
46 percent	8 percent

If you fly often, you know that the airlines never seem to tire of handing out those little, fat-laden packages of salty peanuts. Without considering the peanuts on the flight, everybody who hadn't special-ordered a low-fat meal got food containing 129 percent of their daily Recommended Daily Allowance (RDA) for sodium in just two meals. For anyone who has high blood pressure, this is not a great idea. A large number of fortysomething and older people have this condition, although many of them don't know it. By contrast, I consumed 73 percent of my sodium RDA. If

I had been concerned about high blood pressure, I also could have ordered low-fat, low-sodium meals and reduced that percentage.

My food contained fewer than 3 grams of saturated fat, compared to the more than 20 grams most passengers ate. They put away more than 1,600 calories (not counting the calories in the alcoholic drinks some of them consumed). I consumed fewer than 1,000 calories.

If the attendant offers you peanuts or pretzels, choose pretzels. You can probably eat twenty times the amount of pretzels without equaling the fat in one small bag of peanuts.

In terms of the overall quality of the eating experience, I believe my low-fat meals were far superior to the regular menu. And they didn't cost any more, either. All it takes to get in on this good deal is a phone call at least twenty-four hours before you fly.

Controlling Dehydration Aloft

Never drink alcohol on airplanes unless a specific celebration overrides your concern about what happens to your body. Alcohol causes your body to dehydrate even more than it ordinarily would in a plane's dry air.

Drink juices and water. Stay away from coffee or tea (again, unless you absolutely must have them) because they are diuretics, which cause you to lose more water than you normally do. Preserve your ability to perform at a high level at your destination; replenish your water instead of losing it by drinking the wrong fluids. Losing significant amounts of water impairs your judgment and makes attaining the Ideal Performance State almost impossible.

Ordering from Room Service

Eating healthy on the road can be tough. To eat healthy when ordering from room service requires more care than ever.

I once flew into a city the evening before I was to give the opening address at a national sales meeting for a multibillion-dollar corporation. I was excited about doing this program and was feeling great. By the time I reached my hotel in a rental car, it was about 8:30 P.M., and I decided to check out the only restaurant still open. What a spread they had set up—their weekly Sunday evening all-the-prime-ribs-you-can-eat buffet. Can you imagine?

If I wasn't into this whole lifestyle change, I would have been in that buffet line in a heartbeat (and possibly would have moved a step closer to losing out on many millions of heartbeats as a result). However, I wanted healthier food.

Back in my room, one of the "healthy items" on the room service menu was grilled chicken breast on a whole wheat sourdough bun. Since I needed to stay awake to do some work, it sounded great, so I called in my order and asked (as usual) what came with it. The response was incredible: French fries—on the "healthy" menu! I told the young lady that I did not want French fries and asked if I could have fruit instead.

"I'm sorry, no substitutions are allowed."

"Just give me the sandwich with no French fries."

Obviously new on the job, she said the French fries came with it.

Instead of arguing, I said, "That's fine." However, I had a taste for some calamari. Although I knew I was getting a little carried away with the amount of protein, I hadn't eaten much protein all day. I had snacked throughout the day on healthy carbohydrates, so I felt like I could stray a little bit. The appetizer list in the room service menu had fried calamari. I asked my room service person if the calamari could be grilled.

"Of course it can be, sir," she replied in her most helpful tone, "whatever you want."

That made me very happy. I ordered grilled calamari as an appetizer with a "healthy item" grilled chicken breast sandwich with French fries.

By the time my meal arrived it was well after 9:00 P.M. and I was starved. Both plates on my tray were covered. Under one cover I saw my wonderful grilled chicken breast sandwich (no mayonnaise) with the fries I never wanted. Then I removed the second cover and found breaded and deep-fried calamari—a nightmare of fat.

Now I had to think. Do I pass on the calamari, or do I say, "The heck with it," and just eat it? I really wanted the calamari, but I also really wanted to eat healthy. So I rationalized: Calamari is not a porous food. It's tough, almost rubberlike in texture, so it shouldn't absorb much fat from the grease it was cooked in. That's all it took. I ate some of the calamari one by one, but only after peeling all the breading off. It sure tasted good, but my fingers were one big glob of grease when I was through. (*That's* why I ate only a few.)

Traveling can often undo good habits. But traveling doesn't have to mean putting your healthful home habits on hold. We recommend a revival of the brown-bag concept. Creative totes of strategically planned snacks will keep the fat intake low, your energy needs at peak and minimize having to pay five dollars for a slice of cold, chewy, and greasy airport pizza!

On the Road and in Hotels

Success is simply a matter of forethought. Deciding what to eat on your trip is just as important as deciding which suit to pack, if not more so. What's the Boy Scout motto? "Be prepared!"

You may find yourself in situations where you don't have immediate access to a snack, such as on the road, in a business meeting, or sightseeing. Carry a few cans of low-sodium vegetable or tomato juice and some peanut butter crackers to maintain your blood sugar. Then you won't get overly hungry and feel tempted by the first available convenience store or fast-food drive-through.

When you are traveling by car, take a cooler of healthy snacks and drinks as well as several plastic bottles of water that can be refilled. Snacks might be fresh fruit, low-fat crackers, or trail mix; see chapter 8, "The Corporate Athlete Strategic Eating Guide," for other ideas.

Most hotels have spa facilities and a pool. Inquire as to what is offered and the times they are available for usage. Work a workout into your travel schedule! Talk about convenience—a health club right near your bedroom. No excuses!

No exercise facilities in-house? Inquire about a scenic but safe walk to take before or after your day of meetings. Just because walking is not your usual sport doesn't mean it can't suffice when traveling—all you need to pack are a pair of sneakers.

When the weather outside is frightful, stay inside and climb the hotel stairs for exercise. Twenty minutes of running up and down four flights can be a great workout.

Corporate Athlete Action Items

- The next time you go to a fast-food restaurant, try to special-order your food.
- The next time you fly, order a low-fat meal—at least twenty-four hours ahead of flight time—and see how you like it.
- Try special-ordering the next time you eat out or when you order room service. You don't have to have your food exactly the way it's described in a menu.
- On your next business trip, call ahead to the hotel at which you will be staying and ask about the availability of exercise equipment and alternative eating options. Then plan ahead to fit these things into your busy schedule.

10

Vitamins, Supplements, and Herbs

*Beholdest the earth blackened; then, when We send
down water upon it, it quivers, and swells, and puts forth herbs
of every joyous kind.*

—Koran, 22:5

Corporate Athlete Principle 10:

It's far better to get your vitamins and minerals from food rather than from pills. But take a supplement as an insurance policy.

This conviction is based on findings that more vitamins and minerals are absorbed when they're obtained from food than when they come from pills. It's unwise to rely on pills for vitamins and minerals instead of eating a nutritiously dense diet.

Vitamins and minerals are called micronutrients, meaning you don't require a lot of them each day, but you definitely need them. They are essential for many bodily functions and processes. Without vitamin C, for example, your body would have trouble fighting infection; without vitamin E, your circulatory system would falter; without calcium, your bones would become brittle; without iron, your body could not produce life-essential hemoglobin in the blood. No matter how well you think you eat, you must be sure (as Mom always said) that you're getting your vitamins and minerals.

Size, genetic individuality, age, gender, and percent of body fat, not to mention the degree of activity, contribute to tolerance of a nutrient. What is safe for one person could be toxic for another. Nutrient recom-

98

mendations in this chapter are designed for healthy people age fifteen and over. These recommendations are not for pregnant women.

How Well Do You Eat?

This is a typical daily diet of a person who thinks she eats well. She is 38 years old; 5 feet, 5 inches tall; weighs 125 pounds, and is moderately active.

Breakfast
1 cup Shredded Wheat cereal with ½ cup low-fat milk
1 banana
2 cups coffee

Lunch
Turkey sandwich on whole-wheat bread
Salad with low-calorie dressing
Iced tea

Dinner
Baked chicken breast (no skin)
Baked potato (plain)
Salad with low-calorie dressing
Frozen yogurt

Here's the analysis of her diet for that day, showing the nutrients she consumed as a percent of her Recommended Daily Allowance (RDA):

Item	Quantity	% RDA
Total calories	1,045.0	50
Carbohydrates*	153.0 g	51
Fiber	16.5 g	79
Calcium	294.0 mg	37
Iron	7.66 mg	51
Zinc	6.01 mg	50

*Of her total carbohydrates, 53.5 g (35%) were from simple sugar.

Look good? Not only is her total calorie intake very low, but also the following nutrients were less than 100 percent of her RDA: vitamins A, B_1, B_2, D, E, pantothenic acid, and the minerals copper and sodium.

She is eating her way into several vitamin and mineral deficiencies. Her low intakes of calcium and iron are particularly dangerous. She needs to add foods rich in calcium and iron, consume seven servings a day of fresh fruits and vegetables, and take a vitamin and mineral supplement.

What's the Latest on Vitamin and Mineral Supplements?

If you eat a high-calorie, well-balanced diet, you do not need a vitamin/ mineral supplement. In practice it's almost impossible to achieve a perfect diet, especially if you travel a lot. I know, because I travel extensively, and I try to eat well.

When I worked with golfer Nick Faldo, I asked him if he took a vitamin supplement. Faldo, who grew up in Europe, where people generally eat a well-rounded diet, said, "You Americans, you think you can take a pill and everything will be okay." Well, if it's possible for you to eat fresh fruits and to get an incredible variety of vegetables and all the grains you're supposed to have, you probably would not need a vitamin supplement. But in our rat-race society, where it's *go, go, go,* it's difficult to get fresh foods all the time. We eat too many overly processed foods or foods that are overcooked or poorly prepared. It's almost impossible as a Corporate Athlete to get the recommended daily vitamin and mineral requirements without taking a supplement.

For thirty days I monitored my dietary intake, recording everything that went into my stomach. After the thirty days, I evaluated each day and found this: I gained weight (trying to eat everything I needed) and I still had a shortage in some vitamins and minerals.

Interestingly, I recently read that 85 percent of all registered dietitians take a vitamin/mineral supplement. After studying this further, I surmised that it's virtually impossible to eat all fresh foods (avoiding processed foods) and get all your basic nutrients.

Can you go a day or two without getting the RDA of vitamins and minerals without incurring problems? Sure, but I don't recommend it. Instead take a multivitamin, multimineral supplement each day. It's an inexpensive insurance policy.

Many people will tell you that it's much better to consume supplements that are made from naturally grown substances. On the surface that seems logical, but it's not necessarily been shown to be true. Historically, research has established that your body doesn't know the difference between an organic vitamin and an inorganic one. There is some evidence that natural forms of vitamin E are more rapidly absorbed. But in many cases, the body absorbs and assimilates synthetics to the same extent that it utilizes vitamins from natural sources. Natural and synthetic forms of vitamin C, for example, have been shown to be equally potent. My feeling is that peer-reviewed journals will report one day on the added benefits of organic, natural vitamin supplements, but until then, the jury is out.

Don't Overdo It

Deficiencies in folic acid and vitamin B_{12} can impair mental and emotional well-being, but there's no evidence that high doses of them help people think faster or feel better. The whole idea of overdosing to extend the benefits of some nutrient or other may spring from an unconscious analogy to stepping on the gas. In reality, a better analogy is to filling up the gas tank: Once it's full, your car can't use more gasoline. It's the same with nutrition: Once you've filled up your daily requirement of all the things you need, consuming more of them can't make you go faster.

Vitamins A, E, D, and K are the four fat-soluble vitamins. If you take megadoses of these, you can create a toxic problem because your body stores these vitamins. Vitamin C and the B-complex vitamins are water-soluble, so if you take too much of them they are flushed away that day.

Don't get carried away, however. If you start taking 5,000 milligrams of vitamin C, some experts theorize that you will just urinate it away and increase the possibility of causing kidney stones.

In sum, it's not as easy to meet the RDAs for all the vitamins and minerals as has often been claimed, so I recommend a supplement but not megadoses.

What's the Story with Antioxidants?

In the normal workings of your metabolism, unstable substances called free radicals are created in your body. The development of the free radicals is compounded as you are exposed to various forms of adverse stimulation. Factors such as smoking (or even exposure to secondary smoke), smog, radiation, ozone exposure, and even physical exercise enhance free radical development.

A free radical has a normal proton nucleus that is supposed to have a pair of electrons orbiting around it, but actually it is missing one electron. This unstable molecule is very dangerous to your system. As soon as it's released among the cells in your body, it aggressively tries to attract an electron from a healthy and stable molecule. Once it grabs an electron, it becomes stable and is no longer a free radical. But the molecule it stole the electron from is now a free radical—and it goes on a rampage to find another electron to become stabilized. The process is ongoing, becoming a chain reaction. Research today estimates that each of your body molecules gets about a hundred thousand hits a day from free radicals trying to steal electrons. It is this constant bombardment of cells that causes potential carcinogenic situations to develop in your body.

Free radicals occur in our basic metabolism. The higher your metabolism, the more free radicals are created. Other toxins, such as pollution, cause free radicals. We either take free radicals in or produce them in the body. Oxidizing free radicals causes them to attack the cells of the body. Scientists theorize that free radicals are partially, and possibly wholly, responsible for the results of aging, such as the changes that take place in cells and the development of heart disease.

It is believed by researchers that during respiration, cells pick off electrons from sugars and add them to oxygen to generate energy. As these reactions take place, electrons sometimes get off course and collide with other molecules, creating free radicals. When exercising, you step up respiration and raise body temperature; both produce more free radicals, causing a fairly chaotic environment at the cellular level.

We can minimize the impact of free radicals with antioxidants. Antioxidants prevent the premature oxidation of free radicals, which means they can't go in and cause problems. Research suggests that low-density lipoprotein (LDL) cholesterol—the kind that clogs arteries—sticks to artery walls when it has been chemically damaged or oxidized by free radicals. It appears that a diet high in olive, canola, or peanut oil and that excludes butter and mayonnaise reduces the tendency of LDL to oxidize. Substituting olive oil, canola oil, or peanut oil for butter and mayonnaise will go far toward minimizing dietary-associated heart problems. Monounsaturated fats also tend to keep blood flowing more smoothly, so it's less likely to block a coronary artery and set off a heart attack.

Nutritional science has discovered a way over the past several years to provide your body with substances that have extra electrons. In that way, bodily cells won't be continually bombarding one another to regain their stability. Four substances in nature have been identified so far to carry out this important mission. Antioxidants, as they are called, include the beta-carotene in vitamin A, vitamin C, and vitamin E, along with the mineral selenium. (There are others, but these are the primary ones.) Each has the potential to add stability to your body's internal environment.

You can get most of your antioxidants from natural sources. Dark-colored fruits and vegetables provide beta-carotene and vitamins C and E. For example, carrots are loaded with vitamin A; oranges with vitamin C; green, leafy vegetables with vitamin E; and Brazil nuts with selenium. However, if these are not reliable sources for you and if you prefer taking supplements, here's what I recommend:

Vitamin A: 10,000 I.U.s (I.U. = International Unit) (Beta-carotene)
Vitamin C: 250 to 500 mg (If you smoke, figure on 25 mg per ciga-

rette to combat the free radicals formed by smoking. If you choose to take more than 250 mg, divide the dosage into 250 mg in the morning and 250 mg in the evening.)

Vitamin E: 200 to 400 I.U.s

Selenium: 70 mcg for adult men and 55 mcg for adult women

For a more accurate and individualized selenium recommendation, multiply your weight in pounds by 0.4 to get your daily allotment in micrograms of this important antioxidant.

High doses of selenium are toxic. Serious problems can result from overdosing, loss of hair and diarrhea being only two. It's virtually impossible to overdose on selenium from food, but it's a real danger when taking supplements.

A Cautionary Word

A general rule on taking supplements: Do not go by the thought that if a little is good, a lot must be better. Even though vitamins and minerals are food supplements, in large doses (megadoses) they can have a harmful pharmacological effect. Err on the side of caution.

Vitamins: Functions and Sources

Space does not permit a compete listing of every function of each vitamin; only the most important or best known are given here:

A

Functions: Important to good vision and reproduction. Deficiencies can cause vision problems, especially night blindness. Helps develop healthy skin, hair, and bones.

Sources: Broccoli, carrots, dark green leafy or yellow-orange-red vegetables; mangoes, papaya, dairy products, eggs, and fish liver oils.

B₁ (Thiamin)

Functions: Promotes the release of energy from carbohydrates and helps to synthesize nerve-regulating substances.

Sources: Whole-grain cereals, legumes, liver, pork, seeds, and brewer's yeast.

B₂ (Riboflavin)

Functions: Needed to release stored energy for use and is required for the function of vitamins B₆ (pyridoxine) and B₃ (niacin). Essential to the metabolism of carbohydrates, fats, and protein. Necessary for building and maintaining body tissues and for many other functions.
　Sources: Whole grains, milk, eggs, green vegetables, and liver.

B₃ (Niacin)

Functions: Energy production within the body. Necessary for healthy skin.
　Sources: Poultry, peanuts, meat, fish, mushrooms, and baked potatoes.

B₆ (Pyridoxine)

Functions: Necessary for the metabolism of protein. Needs increase when more protein is eaten. Also required for the functioning of the nervous system.
　Sources: Fish, pork, eggs, whole grains, fruits, nuts, and vegetables.

Biotin

Functions: Essential vitamin important to metabolism and as a carrier of carbon dioxide.
　Sources: Corn, egg yolks, liver, soy flour, and cereals.

C

Functions: Besides neutralizing free radicals as an antioxidant, vitamin C plays a major role in fighting infections. It also helps maintain bones, teeth, and blood vessels.
　Sources: Fruits, strawberries, tomatoes, potatoes, melons, broccoli, and peppers.

D

Functions: Helps the body absorb calcium.
　Sources: Exposure to strong sunlight; fish, eggs, and fortified milk.

E

Functions: One of the primary antioxidants, vitamin E helps sweep up free radicals. It also helps form cells, muscles, and other tissues.

Sources: Wheat bread, green leafy vegetables, whole-grain cereal, liver, peanuts, milk, seeds, and oatmeal.

Folate

Functions: Essential for the formation of DNA and for regeneration of cells in bone marrow and intestines. Known to be important during pregnancy for growth of the fetus.
Sources: Green leafy vegetables, legumes, oranges, and whole grains.

K

Functions: Helps process substances that are important in blood clotting.
Sources: Green leafy vegetables, cabbage, egg yolks, and soybean oil.

Pantothenic Acid

Functions: Important in metabolism of proteins, fats, and carbohydrates, in addition to the formation of various hormones.
Sources: Whole grains, legumes, egg yolks, and liver.

Minerals: Functions and Sources

Boron

Functions: Essential to calcium metabolism. Works with other minerals to prevent calcium loss.
Sources: Fruits and vegetables, especially apples, pears, broccoli, and carrots.

Calcium

Functions: Necessary to the maintenance of bones, teeth, the transmission of nerve impulses, and muscle contraction.
Sources: Milk, cheese, peas, salmon, sardines with bones, and dark, green leafy vegetables.

Chromium

Functions: Important in carbohydrate and lipid metabolism. Some research indicates it may accelerate fat metabolism but the jury is still out on whether it truly does.
Sources: Nuts, whole grains, cheese, meats, mushrooms, and asparagus.

Iodine

Functions: Necessary for normal cell metabolism and for the prevention of goiters.

Sources: Primarily iodized salt, but widely found in the food supply, especially in seafood and dairy products.

Iron

Functions: Essential to the development of hemoglobin. Part of energy and oxygen utilization in muscle.

Sources: Lean meats, fish, turkey, duck, Cornish hen, nuts, seeds, dried fruits, and green, leafy vegetables.

Magnesium

Functions: Necessary for many basic metabolic processes. Helps to hold calcium in tooth enamel and relaxes muscles after contraction. Helps in the conduction of nerve impulses and in the functions of several enzymes.

Sources: Green vegetables, nuts, seeds, legumes, chocolate, soybeans, and apricots.

Manganese

Functions: Activates some enzymes needed to utilize vitamin B_1 (thiamin) and vitamin C. Plays a role in bone development.

Sources: Whole grains, nuts, vegetables, fruit, instant coffee, tea, and cocoa powder.

Phosphorus

Functions: Required for energy production, it also helps form bones, teeth, cell membranes, and genetic material.

Sources: Poultry, fish, meat, milk, eggs, grains, and legumes.

Potassium

Functions: Needed for muscle contraction, nerve impulses, and the proper action of the heart and kidneys. Helps regulate blood pressure and the water balance in cells.

Sources: Most foods, particularly oranges and orange juice, bananas, potatoes with skin, whole grains, and most meat and dairy products.

Selenium

Functions: When working with vitamin E, selenium has powerful anti-oxidant capabilities that help regulate free radicals. It is also essential to the immune response and the functioning of the heart muscle.

Sources: Meats, seafood, eggs, whole grains, legumes, tomatoes, and Brazil nuts.

Sodium (Salt)

Functions: Regulation of the body's fluid balance, generation of nerve impulses and the metabolism of carbohydrates and protein.

Sources: Processed foods and table salt.

Zinc

Functions: Metabolism of protein, carbohydrates, fats, and alcohol. Necessary for many enzyme functions, the synthesis of proteins, tissue growth, and the healing of wounds.

Sources: Seafood, meat, liver, eggs, milk, beans, and whole-wheat bread.

Phytochemicals

Phytochemicals (*phyto* is the Greek word for "plant") are plants' natural protection against disease, sun damage, fungus, and bugs. Many of these chemicals also reduce disease risk and stimulate immunity in people. They are not considered essential substances, meaning you could live without them (not like vitamins and minerals), but they are also thought to be disease-fighting chemicals. So the more "fresh" plant foods you eat, the better off you'll be.

Phytochemicals are antioxidant in the way they work in the body. There are hundreds of these naturally occurring phytochemicals, but the primary ones are carotenoids (carrots, cantaloupes, red and yellow peppers, and sweet potatoes), flavonoids (fruits, vegetables, and wine), indoles (broccoli, cabbage, Brussels sprouts, and cauliflower), isoflavones (soy products), capsaicin (chili peppers and jalapeño peppers), lignans (flax seed), lycopene (tomatoes, watermelons, and pink grapefruit), catechins/tannins (berries and tea), garlic, and onions.

Some phytochemicals block the growth of blood vessels that feed tumors; others can inactivate enzyme systems that allow cancer cells to spread, while yet others have been seen to inhibit the production of hormones that promote cancer growth. Although these conclusions are still under investigation and are not totally conclusive, it is known that people who do not eat a lot of vegetables are more prone to colon cancer, while those who do eat a lot of vegetables have a reduced incidence of colon cancer.

Soy

This is one of the hottest areas of nutritional science being examined. Soy products are a tremendous protein source, especially for vegetarians. But not only is soy considered excellent in this regard, there is also much consideration given to its potential as an anticancer and anticoronary heart disease agent. Although many scientists feel the evidence is equivocal, there is research supporting the fact that women who consume diets rich in soy have fewer incidences of breast cancer. Additional scientific evidence has been reported that soy lowers blood total cholesterol and LDL cholesterol.

Other Supplements

Melatonin

Melatonin is one of the hottest supplements today. Melatonin's benefits are still debatable, but studies indicate many possible uses that may help avoid jet lag, help employees adjust to shift work, ease insomnia, boost the immune system, prevent cancer, protect cells from free-radical damage, and extend life. Still, I only recommend the use of melatonin for jet lag, and even then use caution; we really don't know a lot about hormone supplementation.

Jet lag is a recent phenomenon, and as any frequent flier will tell you, it can be a serious problem. Jet lag can be defined as the effects of traveling through two or more time zones (e.g., flying from Denver to Miami). Remember, due to time lost traveling east, it's easier to adjust when traveling west than traveling east.

Melatonin supposedly alleviates the common symptoms associated with jet lag by "resetting" the biological clock. Studies recommend taking 1 to 3 mg of melatonin prior to bedtime once you are in your new destination. It is important to take melatonin only *after* the trip, not before traveling. Other suggestions to avoid jet lag including drinking plenty of fluids and avoiding alcoholic and caffeine-containing beverages and foods.

It is recommended that melatonin be taken thirty minutes to two hours before bed for best results. One of the most common mistakes is taking melatonin too close to bedtime. It is not a prescription sleeping pill and does not work as quickly. The dosage is 1 to 3 mg to restore normal sleep patterns. The effect of melatonin will vary among individuals. Note that more is not better, and more can have a reduced effect.

DHEA (Adrenal Hormone Dehydroepiandrosterone)

DHEA is produced by the adrenal glands, where the body then converts it to testosterone, estrogen, and other steroids. Production is at a high at about age twenty-five and then declines steadily from there until, by age eighty, DHEA is 5 percent of what it was at age twenty-five. Functionally, it inhibits conversion of carbohydrates to fats and lowers blood pressure. Adverse side effects such as acne have been observed in people taking it as a supplement.

More than four thousand scientific studies have been conducted with DHEA, and still there is no complete and reliable protocol for its use. This is because most studies have been conducted with animals and not humans. DHEA is an "orphan drug," meaning that it has no parent company to guide its development through various stages of animal and human research. No pharmaceutical company will invest the money, with the drug being sold over-the-counter. I recommend caution with this hormone.

Bee Pollen

The claim behind bee pollen is that it increases energy levels and enhances physical fitness. The fact is that it has been studied extensively, investigating issues of strength, distance running, distance swimming, and other activities. The conclusion has been that bee pollen is *not* effective in increasing one's level of fitness. In addition, severe allergic reactions have been recorded in some cases.

Glucosamine Sulfate and Chondroitin

Both of these substances are naturally occurring in cartilage. It has been thought that the consumption of these supplements will reduce the symptoms of osteoarthritis. There is some scientific evidence that glucosamine can help, but scientists and physicians still advise caution until it is more completely investigated. Most published trials lasted only four to eight weeks when examining the role of glucosamine in treating osteoarthritis. Some physicians with whom I have spoken feel that the effect of glucosamine and/or chondroitin is more anti-inflammatory than it is anything else.

Lipoic Acid

This antioxidant influences glycolysis, or the process that converts blood sugar to energy. Since the body can make its own lipoic acid (in small amounts), it is not considered essential, as are vitamins and minerals. Body builders actually call it an "insulin mimicker" and use it to increase the muscular intake of sugar, possibly increasing glycogen (or starch) synthesis. Lipoic acid is also used in Europe as a treatment for diabetes and is considered to be a powerful antioxidant as well

Herbs

Since the FDA is just now beginning to regulate herbal supplements, there has been little reason for major pharmaceutical companies to study them. As a result, they have been produced in mass and distributed like crazy, and the sale of these products has become a gold mine.

Herbs are flooding the news and proliferate on the shelves of health food stores. If you venture into a healthfood store, you will be confronted by a great array of products. Since there have been volumes of books written about herbs and other supplements, I will provide only a brief overview about the science behind some of the more commonly questioned supplements.

There are a number of herbs that are either safe to use in moderation or that contain active ingredients that may produce useful physiological responses. Careful use of such products may (and I emphasize the word "may") provide useful relief.

Because herbs are plants, which is where medicines came from originally, that does not mean they are necessarily safe and effective. Your doctor needs to be aware if you are consuming any herbs, especially if you are on other forms of medication.

Herbs and their by-products have real value in medicine. If we could understand them better, standardize their production, and understand the dosages of what we need, we would be a lot better off.

Garlic

The supposed role of garlic to protect against cancer and cardiovascular disease and to lower cholesterol has gone way beyond the true scope of what has been studied. Recently, major studies in Germany and also at Yale have found that there were no differences in pretest and posttest cholesterol evaluation. Another study, however, examined forty-two thousand women aged fifty-five to sixty-nine, and observed that garlic consumption was inversely rated to the risk of cancer.

Echinacea

Is it truly possible that echinacea can boost your immune system to fight minor viral and bacterial infections, even the common cold? Recent studies indicate it can relieve the symptoms of a cold in some individuals. Almost everyone has heard of echinacea. As with all herbal products, there is a major concern with quality control. Since echinacea is totally unregulated, what you're buying may not contain much, if any, echinacea. Dosages are of great concern—no one knows what is correct. There have been very few adverse side effects reported, though it has been clearly stated that you should not take it for more than a few weeks. Not only does the herb lose its effectiveness, but there are other concerns as well. Scientists do say this about echinacea: There are types of people who should not try echinacea, such as those who know they are allergic to certain flowers, in addition to those people who have diseases such as lupus, rheumatoid arthritis, tuberculosis, and multiple sclerosis, and those who are HIV-positive. Be watchful of recommended dosages.

Ginseng

Very few herbs are more popular then ginseng. By some estimates, as many as six million people use ginseng regularly. The U.S. Food and Drug Administration classifies ginseng as a food, but several scientists suggest that it should be classified as a drug. In the most closely controlled scientific studies, ginseng has been found to not be significantly different than a placebo when evaluating performance, metabolic testing, and psychological tests. However, many studies on ginseng have found a positive effect on performance, stamina, and energy levels. This could be due to the way the studies were developed, the fact that there are several forms of ginseng, and the quality control among various products.

Saint-John's-Wort

This roadside weed with yellow flowers has been utilized externally and internally. It has been used as a popular herbal treatment for nervousness, sleep disorders, and depression. It is thought that it can reduce pain and anxiety. Some investigations have shown Saint-John's-wort to be as effective as some antidepressant medications. Although there seem to be few side effects, as with any supplement, however, before you begin taking it to reduce your anxiety levels, be sure to discuss this with your physician. It is not recommended for serious depression.

Ginkgo Biloba

There have been more clinical trials on ginkgo biloba than on any other herb. This herb is thought to improve circulation and to fight free radicals.

It has also been associated with the enhancement of memory. Ginkgo biloba has been prescribed in France and Germany for years against vascular disease and cerebral insufficiencies. In a study presented in an American Medical Association journal, three hundred patients, all diagnosed with mild to moderate dementia, improved their mental capacity, though about one-third got worse. Some experts believe it can slow down the progression of symptoms from Alzheimer's disease. There was some encouraging news from this study but, again, the major concern with ginkgo biloba is that commercially available products may not contain the same quality of preparation as herbs used in studies. Supplementation has caused upset stomach in numerous cases. To date, no one knows whether ginkgo biloba will help, or even how much ginkgo biloba is in what is out there in the market. Future research in this area may yield important results. Some scientists feel that you can boost your brain activity more effectively by mentally challenging yourself through doing jigsaw puzzles or crossword puzzles, reading a challenging book, or doing other brain and memory exercises.

Valerian Root

This has been shown in some studies to have a weak sedative and tranquilizer effect. It seems to act as a depressant of the central nervous system. Over a long history of use—more than a thousand years—there seem to be few side effects. Valerian root has a sleep-promoting action as well. Use is not recommended over long periods of time.

Kava Kava

This has been utilized for centuries in ways similar to valerian root. Kava kava has been shown to have a sedating effect on the central nervous system and to be a mild hallucinogen. Toxic effects may be possible. Discuss its use with your physician.

Saw Palmetto

Obtained from the red berries of a small palm tree, saw palmetto extracts have been utilized for treatment of benign enlargement of the prostate gland. It seems to inhibit conversion of testosterone into a chemical called DHT, which is thought to cause prostate enlargement. Benefits include easing urination and assisting in reducing frequent nighttime urination. In one study, 90 percent of the patients using saw palmetto considered its usage successful after three months. However, anyone experiencing pain or swelling of the prostate, or anyone having trouble urinating, should consult a physician.

Milk Thistle

This plant is found commonly throughout Europe. The seeds of milk thistle have been broken down into a compound called silymarin, which is considered by some experts to protect the liver. Some research supports its use as a liver protectant and as an antioxidant. Studies have demonstrated that silymarin may accelerate the regeneration of cells in an alcohol-damaged liver. However, because silymarin is not very water-soluble, it has trouble being digested in the gastrointestinal tract as a tea or in capsule form. To be effective, any milk thistle taken orally must be extremely concentrated.

Another Word of Caution

Again, before administering any of these supplements for yourself, be sure you consult your physician. Herbs and other supplements are not created equal. Until we have stringent scientific studies of herbal medicines and remedies, it is not smart to assume that they are automatically safe because they are "herbal." Do your own research.

Since the arena of supplements is so vast and somewhat ambiguous, I recommend that you consult with a registered dietitian (R.D.) in your area regarding general use of these products. If you do not know an R.D. in your area, simply call the American Dietetic Association at 1-800-366-1655.

Corporate Athlete Action Items

- Take a daily vitamin/mineral supplement as an insurance policy.
- Don't take hormonal or herbal supplements unless you are medically cleared and 100 percent sure of what you are taking and why you are taking them.
- Take a good look at the label of any supplement you are currently taking and compare its antioxidant ability with the recommended dosage.
- Write down your daily food intake for two consecutive days and evaluate the variety of food currently in your daily regimen. Note how it might improve so you get more of the appropriate vitamins and minerals.

Part III

THE JOY OF EXERCISE

11

The Benefits of Exercise

If you would see a person's soul, look at his body.
The body is a visible picture of what you think of your world.
—RALPH WALDO EMERSON

CORPORATE ATHLETE PRINCIPLE 11:

There's one type of stress that should always be a scheduled part of your day: exercise.

Welcome exercise into your life. Exercise is something you control. You determine when you will start; you constantly regulate the intensity; and you determine when it is time to stop.

It isn't the stressor that causes health-related problems but rather the feeling of helplessness and lack of recovery. Exercise is a means of exposing the body to stress and thereby training it. As working out on an exercise machine increases the endurance of muscle groups to withstand greater and greater resistance, so all exercise trains the body to not only deal with stress but also to increase its capacity for stress. As the body adapts to the stresses of exercise it moves to higher levels of efficiency and functional capacity.

Even Winners Take Time to Train

Race car driver Eddie Cheever Jr., forty-one, the winner of the 1998 Indianapolis 500, is not a person who reached a certain age, realized his health was failing, and decided to get back in shape.

"When you are competing at anything," Cheever says, "even in the boardroom, I think that if your body is in excellent condition, your mind will follow. If you are in physically poor condition, you are suffering, you have bad concentration, you can't get the job done that you want to do. And driving a race car, there is no room for being in bad shape."

Because we don't actually see race car drivers do their thing, most of us don't even think about their conditioning needs as athletes. After all, to a layperson, these drivers, although they must be alert while driving at high speeds, are sitting during the whole race.

"I know that the better shape I am in, I take myself out of being the weakest link," he says. "My job is to sit in the race car and concentrate. I *have* to concentrate, so the better shape I am in, the easier I can do that."

My partner Pat Etcheberry drastically changed Cheever's conditioning program to one that was designed specifically to his needs.

"I don't care how much I bench-press," Cheever says. "I don't care how much I can leg-press. That, to me, is totally irrelevant. I have to be able to sit in a race car and drive it as hard as I can for three and a half hours and not feel once in those three and a half hours that I am tired or that I should slow down or that I want to give up." So the mental aspect of the conditioning follows the physical aspect of it. "Pat changed my training pattern completely. The whole method of working out was totally different from what I did before," he adds. "I train harder now than I did before, but he has also made my job a lot easier in the car."

Exercise Will Make You Feel Better Every Day

Leonard Lauder, the chairman and chief executive of the Estee Lauder Companies, is a man who we might all agree is fairly busy. He carries around a gym bag everywhere he goes. He never uses the excuse "I don't have my gym clothes with me." In fact, he looked me in the eye and said, "If you want to exercise, you will do it."

And Lauder has aggressively spread his belief in corporate wellness to employees across his cosmetics empire, including companies such as Clinique and Origins Natural Resources.

If you exercise regularly, you will perform better in a wide range of stress tests than unfit subjects. If you exercise regularly, you'll have greater emotional stability. If you exercise regularly, you'll not only have a greater capacity for managing physical stress, you'll have a greater capacity for mental and emotional stress as well. People who exercise regularly experience fewer debilitating negative emotions, such as depression and anxiety. (Please don't misunderstand: People who exercise can certainly get depressed from time to time, but their experience with debilitating negative emotions is significantly less as a group than individuals who do not have exercise exposure.)

As a group, exercisers are more optimistic about life than nonexercisers, and have higher levels of self-confidence and self-esteem. Exercise also heightens feelings of self-control. The perception of control plays a pivotal role in managing stress, personal health, and life satisfaction.

Researchers have identified a number of consequences of the *lack of exercise* in adulthood:

- Increases in depression, moodiness, anxiety, fatigue, insomnia, and muscle weakness.
- Decreases in immunity, self-esteem, self-confidence, emotional stability, and frustration tolerance.

Exercise will also improve your self-image. You'll feel better about yourself and you'll look better. When you get up in the morning, you'll feel rejuvenated, leading to more energy than you've ever had at the office or at home.

Build Quality Time Through Fitness

Luke Rohrbaugh, fifty, is a senior vice president for investments with Prudential Securities. He lives and works in Harrisburg, Pennsylvania. This husband and father of two boys has spent the past twenty-eight years in the investment business. Joining the corporate world, Rohrbaugh adopted the work ethic of his native Hanover, Pennsylvania. "You got up early, went to work, and worked until you collapsed," he says. "If there wasn't sweat running down the crack of your ass by day's end, you weren't working hard enough."

That became his philosophy for a quarter century: *Go, go, go!*

In his school football playing days, Rohrbaugh tipped the scales at 270 pounds; today he hovers around 225. When the first of his boys was born nine years ago, keeping that weight became a challenge despite having exercise equipment—NordicTrack, Universal Gym, and free weights—in his basement.

"When the boys came along, I stopped working out at the gym," he says. "Too much going on, cramped lifestyle." You've heard the excuses; you've probably made them yourself. "I thought I'd work out at home four days a week. It never worked out that way. I'd come home from work and be a 225-pound lump of Jell-O. I couldn't give anything to my kids or my wife."

Rohrbaugh was wound pretty tight. His longtime routine was starting the day with up to three cups of hi-test—no decaf for him, thank you. Over the course of the day he'd consume as many as nine cups of coffee.

When Rohrbaugh was profiled and we looked at his routine, we made a number of suggestions. Now Rohrbaugh wakes up early, stretches, and, at a bare minimum, spends thirty minutes on his StairMaster and doing sixty push-ups. Then it's a trip to the sauna and a breakfast of two fresh, multigrain bagels, a ten-ounce glass of orange juice, *one* cup of coffee (decaffeinated), a multivitamin, and vitamins C and E, plus one baby aspirin. Before, he got no exercise and no breakfast. Today he's at his desk by 7:45 A.M., refreshed and ready to rock 'n' roll. "It's an hour later than I used to arrive," he says, "but I found I haven't missed anything *and* I got my workout in."

In the first year following this new regimen, Rohrbaugh missed only ten days of exercise—remarkable for someone who was not previously exercising. "I don't stay at hotels unless they have a gym now," he says. He has maintained his weight but has lost fat and gained muscle.

The coffee has been replaced by water—two liters per day.

"In the past, I'd be dead-ass tired when I got home, unable to do anything," he says. "Not anymore. Now the understanding my wife and I have is that my first fifteen minutes at home are mine. I get to turn back into Clark Kent. I get that time to get acclimated and decompress. After that, instead of me falling asleep at 8:00 P.M., I'm ready for my boys, who are more active than ever and are waiting eagerly for me to shoot hoops or work in the workshop. It has also helped in my relationship with my wife, Caryn. And instead of sleeping six hours a night, I sleep at least seven."

No More Excuses!

Here are some of the excuses that people use about not exercising or not being active. "I don't have time." "I'm always on the run." "Just can't fit it in." "I like watching TV, it's my recovery." "Exercise isn't recovery for me." "Exercise hurts." "I don't like to sweat."

But the real reason, the most important one, is that people don't have a strategy to make a commitment and then keep the commitment going. This is exactly why people go on diets and then go off diets, or why they stop smoking and then start again. They don't get a strategy into their behavior. That's why, in chapter 15, *The 21-Day Program,* we will create a lifestyle for you in which exercise becomes part of your daily regimen. Recovery from exercise will be important as well, but activity must be a scheduled part of every day.

Your Personal Business Plan

Most people have trouble maintaining an exercise program. All but the most devout have problems getting motivated and started on some days.

The good news is that you *can* train your body to be slim and energetic, and you can love doing it, too. But you must *want* it for yourself, for your own reasons, and you must have a sharp hunger for it. You may realize you *need* to do it, but you must train yourself to *want* to do it. Otherwise you'll fight it all the way, and nothing will change much. It can't be someone else's idea—someone else nagging you to do it. You must want to change for yourself first.

If you become more energetic, you'll enjoy your work more and you'll have enough stamina left at the end of the day to enjoy your family and your free time. If you have kids, no doubt you hope to see them grow up and be around as they get older. If you are competitive in your job, if you want an edge on your competition, if you want to be the best that you can be, being fit will allow you to work—*and play*—longer hours and harder than somebody who is not physically fit. As I work with people, I try to find out what they are looking for in their value system and then try to use that as the motivation.

My recommendation is that you take on energizing your mind and body as a business project and set it up like any other important project. Design your personal "business plan" and stick to it. It's difficult to imagine a more important personal project than increasing your physical and mental energy. Gaining more stamina will make all your other goals much easier to achieve.

Better Sweaty Than Dead

If Dave Nelson had not started taking better care of himself in 1997, he probably would be dead today.

Back then, Nelson was an out-of-shape, forty-four-year-old district sales manager for Merrill Lynch in nine states, from Tennessee to North Dakota. "I used to joke that between my wife and me, one of us was going to the gym five times a week. I went twice a year," he says. "I was always too busy. I'd leave for work at six in the morning. I was not one to get up at 4:00 A.M. and exercise. I'd get home at 6:00 or 7:00 P.M., tired, and I'd relax in front of the TV. [Exercise] was not a priority."

Nelson and several dozen million-dollar financial consultants came to LGE's campus in February 1997 for three days of full physicals, training, consultations, stretching, and fitness assessments. Six months later, the thirty-one people who stayed with the program returned to Orlando, and testing showed a marked improvement in all of them.

In January 1998, a month before the group's one-year anniversary, Nelson, a husband and father of two grown children, went through a life-changing event: quadruple bypass surgery. Unbeknownst to Nelson, heart disease was hereditary in his family. His eleven previous months of conditioning made it possible for him to qualify for a new, less-invasive surgical technique. "You had to meet a certain fitness standard—which I would not have had before starting the Mentally Tough program. Before, for example, my body fat was 31 percent; at the time of my surgery, it was 15 percent. I inadvertently positioned myself to at least be eligible for the less-invasive surgery."

As a result, he was up and around within twenty-four hours of the operation, and back to the office in three and a half weeks. And three months after the surgery, he was running three miles a day. "My heart could take it but my knees couldn't," he says, laughing, "so now I'm power-walking instead."

It's Never Too Late

Exercise will add *years to your life* and—through the added release of hormones such as endorphins—add *life to your years*. From two standpoints, job performance and longevity, it's vital to be moderately active. If you've been fighting it—making excuses, not finding time, or being resentful about its necessity—stop, and stop *now*, not tomorrow. Reconsider.

The body will adapt physically and mentally at any age. As long as you're still breathing, it's not too late to make significant progress at boosting your stamina and extending your life. This has been proven by studies conducted among people in their nineties. One group exercised with weights; the control group did nothing new. After a year, the exercisers had increased their mobility, strength, and mental alertness significantly compared to the control group—at ninety years old! So don't take the "It's too late for me" cop-out. At the same time, don't say "I'll start tomorrow." Get moving *today*, because you—your body, your mind, and your spirit—need it!

At the Tufts University Center for Aging, researchers identified a number of markers related to the aging process, and many of these same variables are influenced by exercise stress. Their general conclusion was that exercise, when done properly, slows the aging process. In just about all areas of stress exposure, the aging process is significantly slowed when the hormones and the forces exerted by stress are intermittently stimulated.

Some of the markers used to determine aging are things such as lean body mass, overall strength, basal metabolic rate, body fat, aerobic capacity, blood pressure, blood sugar tolerance, cholesterol levels, bone density, and body temperature regulation. Lean body mass and strength are considered to be the most important of the entire group, and it's noteworthy that all of these aging markers can be influenced in a significantly positive way by *regular* exercise.

The familiar notion that the older you are, the less you should do can have tragic consequences. More appropriate advice is that the older you get, the more important it is to *use it or lose it*. Clearly, exercise is one of the most powerful anti-aging agents we've ever discovered.

Cardiovascular and Metabolic Benefits of Exercise

People who exercise regularly experience the following improvements in their cardiovascular systems:

- **A decrease in resting heart rate.**   The heart responds to training by also increasing in strength and size. This means that with each heartbeat, the heart is able to eject more blood out to the body. This increased stroke volume means that a lower heart rate is possible to get the same amount of blood to the body.
- **An increase in maximal oxygen uptake.**   With exercise, the body is able to use more oxygen, as you are involved in physical activity. Therefore you can exercise for longer durations. Respiration is responsible for moving oxygen to the lungs and replenishing the blood, while circulation is important for transporting oxygen and nutrients to the cells. Metabolism then utilizes the oxygen in the cells to produce energy.
- **An increase in capillarization.**   These small vessels feed the cells of the body. With exercise it has been observed that there is an increase in the numbers of capillaries that will accelerate the rate at which waste products from exercise metabolism can be removed. This same process is also seen in the heart, which assists the lungs in oxygen delivery to the heart itself.
- **An increase in the ability of blood to carry oxygen.**   The more fit you become, the more oxygen you can transport because there is an increase in your red blood cell count. The red in the blood is actually iron in the form of hemoglobin. Hemoglobin transports oxygen throughout the blood.
- **Lower blood pressure.**   As you become fitter, your blood pressure will lower, decreasing your risk of cardiovascular disease.
- **A decrease in blood lipids.**   A regular aerobic exercise program will help control fats such as cholesterol and triglycerides in the blood. This reduces the risk of atherosclerosis, which can create mass obstructions in the arteries; it also reduces the risk of cardiovascular disease.

- **An increase in fat-burning enzymes.**   As you reach higher levels of fitness, the body's metabolism increases and necessitates an increase in enzymes that can burn more body fat and dietary fat.
- **An increase in the number and size of mitochondria, the energy building blocks of the body.**   These small structures are required for all cells in the body to function properly. As they get larger and increase in number, you are able to do more work.
- **A lower heart rate at given workloads.**   A higher level of fitness will allow you to work with greater efficiency. The cardiovascular system, due to stroke volume and the amount of blood sent out to the body per minute, causes the heart to beat at a much lower rate as a person becomes more trained.

Build Muscle to Burn Fat Faster

Pound for pound, muscle burns fat faster than fat burns fat. For every pound of muscle you gain (not much due to its density), you will burn an extra thirty to fifty calories per day. When you exercise, your muscles work while your body fat just goes along for the ride.

Some fat does get burned when you exercise, but only a tiny amount. Mainly you burn carbohydrates. Your next meal replaces those carbohydrates, and most likely, the fat you just burned, too.

Exercise is essential to weight loss, in a roundabout way and over the long haul. Muscle burns more fat twenty-four hours a day, and you burn most of your calories and fat when you're not exercising. The more muscle you have, the more fat you burn. You do *not* have to lift heavy weights, nor do you have to bulk up with your strengthening program.

The exercise machines and charts reporting how many calories are burned per hour with a particular exercise often grossly overestimate the amount of calories burned *during* the workout, but they also underestimate the effect of physical training. The higher rate of calorie-burning continues long *after* the exercise stops. Active bodies have a higher metabolic rate than sedentary bodies; they not only burn more fat by expending more energy, they also burn it faster, and keep on burning it faster, even during sleep.

Getting Stronger

When pro golfer Mike Hulbert came to us six years ago for conditioning help, my partner Pat Etcheberry told him that it is just as important to have a good general workout as to go out and pound balls on the range for three, four, or five hours. Not that the goal was to make him bigger to the naked eye; Pat's intention was to make him stronger and fitter in areas where he needed to be fit. And it paid off.

"I am in a lot better shape," Hulbert says, "and I am not getting any younger. I will be forty-two this spring, and it seems like each year, I feel better."

Hulbert has been a pro since 1981. When he first started on the pro tour, he was a runner who never did weight lifting. Now he has a conditioning system built around every tournament. He says, "Two hours before I play, I go into a fitness trailer on-site and warm up on a treadmill or bike, breaking a sweat before I play. I'll get stretched by one of the trainers. Then I grab something to eat. After a round, regardless of whether I had a good round or a really good round or a not so good round, instead of thinking about it and beating my brains in by hitting buckets of balls on a driving range, I will go back to the fitness trailer and work out for an hour."

His routine has made Hulbert stand out among his peers.

"Some guys think I am nuts," he admits. "Not so much because I warm up before a tournament, because lots of guys come in and get stretched. But I think where they go crazy is when they see me in there *after* the round, going crazy on the treadmill. *Then* they think I am nuts."

He believes that focusing on his conditioning and mental toughness will give him a longer career. "The competition is getting so strong, if you can get just a little bit of an edge, *just a little bit,* that could be a stroke here and there, and at the end of the week, that is a big, big difference. Or if we have to play more than eighteen holes, I will be fresher than the other guys. I'm not asking for much, but if I can just get an edge in one little area, then that is the difference in having a mediocre year to a good year, or a good year to a great year, and that is what I am shooting for."

Beginning Your Program

Exercise is like a 401k pension plan: The more you put in now, the more you'll have later. In the case of exercise, the more you do now, the more time and energy you'll have later to enjoy your pension plan.

Like shoes, however, one exercise routine doesn't fit all. You need to tailor your exercise routine to your condition, age, and life roles.

Seriously out-of-shape couch potatoes get overstressed merely by taking the long hike down the hall to the refrigerator; such individuals need exercise desperately, but they must approach it with great caution to avoid serious consequences. There is a training effect to being a couch potato, and these bodies have been trained for endurance sitting and have adapted to inactivity, so *any* movement is potentially stressful.

The group most in danger of overdoing exercise includes men under age fifty who, though athletic when younger, have not exercised much for ten years or more. These individuals often feel immune to the risks of suddenly becoming intensely active. They're not immune, however, as some grieving families discover. Get a medical checkup first, start slowly, and proceed with caution.

Researchers are now studying whether moderate exercise such as golfing with a hand-pulled cart, or leisurely thirty-minute strolls, offer any benefit. Many in the field say any exercise is certainly better than no exercise. This much is already clear: The average individual who goes out for at least moderately vigorous exercise will live much longer than someone who doesn't.

Today's research strongly suggests that you should exercise as frequently and as vigorously as you safely can if one of your goals is to prolong your highly functional years.

Study your lifestyle carefully before trying to raise your stamina. Allow for some backsliding. Anticipate having to fight off temptations to quit. Expect to readjust until you hit a workable schedule and formula. Count on it; you'll hit plateaus where progress seems to stall. Now you must tune in intently to your body's signals. Do a little more each week until your body tells you to ease up.

If you haven't been exercising or if you are older than thirty, get your doctor's approval first. Then start with three workouts a week, each session lasting thirty to forty-five minutes, the total time for all your work in aerobic conditioning, strength training, and flexibility. Don't fall into the trap of thinking one long workout a week is as good as three shorter ones spaced throughout the week. The difference is recovery. While one workout a week is better than none, it could injure you, creating problems ranging from aches and pains to heart attacks; three milder workouts a week put you on the road to greater energy, stamina, and longevity.

Periodization

Periodization training is the most widely accepted form of training among exercise physiologists, conditioning coaches, and sport psychologists for developing an athlete's physiological potential.

Seasonal sports such as track and field have utilized this form of training for years. By altering the activity as well as the volume, intensity, and frequency of training according to the time of year and its proximity to the sport's season, these athletes can peak physiologically for their respective sport. An Olympic athlete obviously wants to qualify and then perform at the highest level possible at the Olympic Games. However, a ranked tennis player does not have the luxury of the seasonal-sport athlete, since the tennis player competes throughout the year. This applies to the Corporate Athlete as well. You must compete all year long.

The periodization schedule for a ranked tennis player must be created around the athlete's tournament schedule and his or her fitness needs. In the case of Corporate Athletes, this would depend on when your most pressing business periods occur. Before you say, "Every day is a pressing day," please keep reading. Remember, a great tennis player doesn't know whether he or she will lose in the first round or advance all the way to the finals of a tournament. They must be ready all the time—just like you.

Periodization involves the peaking time of competition, the precompetition phase, the preparation phase, and the active rest phase. You are in recovery during the active rest phase. It is active recovery.

Within each periodization training scheme there are these four phases designed to systematically allow your mind and body to adapt appropriately, ensuring mental and physical peaking. Each phase may last from a few weeks to several months. It is psychologically and physiologically impossible to peak for every business event that occurs on an hourly basis, so the Corporate Athlete must identify which events to peak for, ranked by highest in importance.

A training schedule can be depicted and mapped out visually on a chart. The X-axis of the graph represents the calendar year divided into monthly time intervals. The Y-axis represents the Corporate Athlete's optimal level of intensity and business-specific training level. Each full cycle contains four phases:

- Phase I: The Preparation Phase
- Phase II: The Precompetitive Phase
- Phase III: The Competitive Peaking Phase
- Phase IV: The Active Rest Phase

Phase I: The Preparation Phase

During this phase, training is geared toward providing you with a firm base, a mental and physical fitness level in preparation for more intense business-specific training.

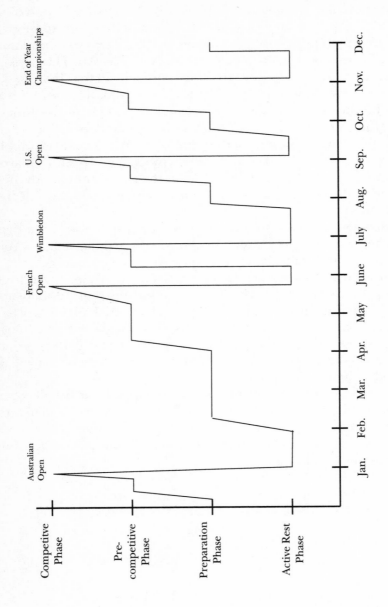

Figure 11.1. Periodization Schedule for the No. 1 Tennis Player in the World

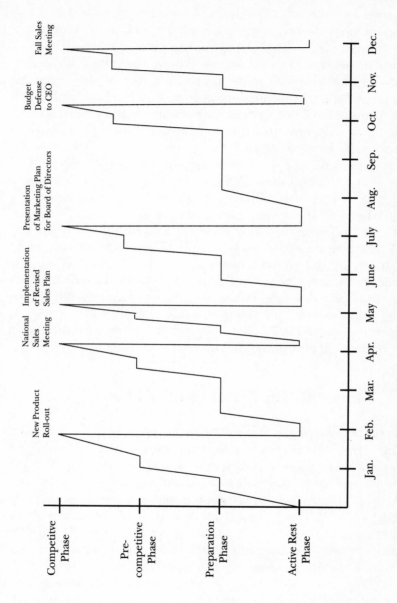

Figure 11.2. Periodization Schedule for the World's Best Marketing Executive

129

We develop the Corporate Athlete's base strength by first easing him or her into a program that emphasizes low-intensity high repetitions the first week (two to three sets of twelve to fifteen repetitions). Gradually we increase the intensity to a moderate level, at which you perform multiple sets (three to four) with eight to ten repetitions.

Your aerobic base should also be increased during this phase. Rhythmic/continuous-type exercise with some interval training of prolonged duration (twenty to forty minutes) is emphasized. Your level of training may vary from 55 percent to 85 percent of your maximum training heart rate, depending on your current fitness level. A strong aerobic base will allow you to recover efficiently throughout your day.

When you are in the preparation phase, you want to practice and review the mental and emotional habits that are fundamental to your success. Things such as positive thinking, mood control, nutrition, and the intensity of what you will be doing are essential to examine. For example, if you are preparing a major presentation, practice mental and emotional fundamentals of giving that speech in a low-intensity environment. If you are defending a budget or are involved in selling, use role-playing to rehearse how you will handle questions and/or conflicts and various pressures that might present themselves. You should also be performing visualization (and planning a daily schedule).

The level represented by Phase I indicates that further training must occur for you to be at an optimal physiological training level.

Phase II: The Precompetitive Phase

In the precompetitive phase, you will begin to taper your physical exercise program. You will also begin practicing with moderate to high intensity for your upcoming event. You want to begin practicing the mental and emotional habits that will be essential when you go into your arena, whether it is making a presentation, selling a service or an item, or managing conflict. Give yourself a frequent review of how such instances have gone in the past, of how they played out. Closely monitor your practice intensity and discipline. What is the motivation behind what you want to do? Have you connected it to your value system?

The last thing you want to feel, two or three weeks before you have to be on, is fatigued. This is the time when you must be getting ready to peak.

Visualization skills—creating images in your mind's eye of what lies ahead—should be practiced daily, and your emphasis should be on focus, concentration, and commitment to what you want to do, challenge and preparation for any adversity.

Phase III: The Competitive Peaking Phase

With your big day very near, you will definitely be decreasing the intensity of your physical training program. This should assure you adequate recovery before crunch time and give you incredible energy. You want to feel physically refueled and absolutely ready to go, no questions asked.

In the competitive peaking phase you are heading into the event. It might be the day before or a week before, but you are definitely heading into a peaking phase, when everything you've been working toward comes together. It is now showtime. All pistons are firing, all spark plugs are igniting. You are at maximum intensity. All your practice conditions should simulate as closely as possible to how it is really going to be.

Use daily visualization and closely monitor your performance. Again, monitor your levels of intensity, motivation, eagerness, discipline, emotional control, and moodiness. This is your dress rehearsal for the big event. Rituals are in place, time is in control, little can go wrong, you are energized and ready to go.

Phase IV: The Active Rest Phase

Once the event is over, you go into a phase of transition or active rest. For a short period of time you should be under no pressure and give yourself some (albeit very little in some corporate arenas) psychological rest. Your coworkers may raise an eyebrow, but plan to take a few days off after you peak. The recovery period is essential to avoid the negative results of overtraining such as chronic fatigue and motivation reduction.

You should be enduring very low intensity psychologically, and you can go though situations of self-reflection, self-evaluation, and future-goal-setting. Your goals should now be to have fun and celebrate the process you just completed. Relaxation exercises such as yoga and meditation, along with exercise and massage, can be extremely beneficial.

Jim Courier Visualizes the Process

For tennis player Jim Courier, winner of two Australian and two French Opens: "I need to rest, because I am always pretty active when I am training, and when I'm done for the day, it's important for me to sit down somewhere for two hours and let my body rest and recover."

This is exactly the opposite tack a Corporate Athlete must take.

"Periodization is something that a lot of people don't get and a lot of people don't do," he continues, "and I think a lot of people give up on what they are doing because they just get burned out on it. But periodizing an activity allows you to stay fresher and keep enjoying what you are doing a lot more. I know that has been an issue for most professional athletes in their careers."

Because he trains year-round, the days leading up to a major competition are filled with rest and relaxation. "That is fun time to me," he says. "Hopefully I have already done most of my heavy training in the months before. So I get as much rest as possible, and I am fresh when I go on the court." This is something not done in Corporate America. We often *go-go-go* right up to the moment of truth.

Even though few athletes want to win as badly as Jim Courier, he doesn't visualize the result. He visualizes the *process*. He will see himself serve the ball to a specific area of the service box and then see himself retrieving and returning the opponent's shot, going through how he intends to set himself up to hit a winning shot. He doesn't visualize a match days before it happens, for example. "I play out just a few points in the match in my head before I get on the court so it already feels familiar when I get out there."

And he gets nervous. "If I am *not* nervous, *that* is a bad sign. If I am not nervous, then I don't really care. If I am not excited about the match, then the outcome doesn't mean anything to me. So I like being nervous. That is one of the best things about the job. To most people, I guess 'nervous' has a negative connotation. For me, it has a positive connotation. It means I am excited, anxious to play, and I like that feeling of being on edge. I am never more alive than five minutes before the match. My heart starts pumping and the adrenaline is rushing."

Most tennis players are probably more nervous in the first round than they are when they get into the finals, because in the first round, they haven't yet gotten themselves "into" the tournament. Maybe you've experienced the same sensation making business presentations on the road.

"Each time I play," Courier says, "I have to get used to new surroundings. But by the time I reach a final, even if it is a major championship final, I have already played five or six matches there. And I must be playing very well, obviously, because I have won all my matches, so I am confident and comfortable. For that reason, there is much less anxiety at the end of the tournament for me than at the beginning. If I am in the final, I am in the groove. I am in my rhythm. I am probably more relaxed than ever."

Athletes apply periodization; people in business should, too. Jim Courier says, "I see a lot of people—in sports and in business—start with a really good plan and just get bored with it because they just keep doing the same thing over and over again. The human mind has a hard time staying eager when you just keep doing the same things. A lot of what we do as professional athletes is cycle on and cycle off, working hard for a month and then easing back for a little while, changing the routine enough to keep it fresh. I think that pattern is probably a good one for everybody, whether they are a pro athlete or not. It keeps you fresh, gives your body a chance to recharge and build, and probably plays well with your body's rhythms, too."

Interval Training

Here is the advice most people usually get: "Warm up for a few minutes, get your heart rate into your target range, keep it there, and after twenty to thirty minutes, cool down for a few minutes."

The problem with that is that it is steady-state training. But science has discovered that's *not* the best way to train. It's a good way to train. You will improve your health. But from a performance standpoint, the ideal way is interval training. This means you get your heart rate up and let your heart rate recover, then do it again and again.

An interval is defined as repeated bouts of high-intensity exercise with intermittent recovery (in our case, active rest) periods. This intermittent exercise allows a higher total volume of high-intensity work. Interval training is so important because your heart rate doesn't stay at one level for everything you do in life. If you are at home, and one of your kids gets hurt, your heart rate goes way up. Can you make wise decisions when your heart rate is at 150 or 160? Of course not.

Golfers work at keeping their heart rate as slow as possible before they execute a swing in a major tournament. If you work in an office and there is an emergency, you want to have a clear head. If you train at one level, keeping your heart rate at one level all the time, your body adapts to that, so when your heart rate accelerates because of an emotional stressor at work, it has a tendency to stay at that level. I want to teach you to recover very quickly, to get your heart rate lower.

If you go out and jog a mile, an easy, pleasant mile during which you relax and your mind moves very quickly, you will concentrate and think of many things, solving problems as you go. But if I make you run a mile for time and demand the fastest mile you ever ran, you won't have time to think. Your mind will be in survival mode, during which you cannot possibly think clearly.

If you are frequently under stress, you should do interval training because it increases the body's ability to tolerate stressful situations by exposing it to stress and then training recovery. It puts your mind and body under higher stress, gives you the opportunity to relax and lower the stress, then to repeat the stress/recovery cycle over and over again. The drawback to interval training is that if you don't know what you are doing, you can easily be hurt.

What about the issues of fat burning, aerobic training, and anaerobic training?

The lower the intensity of your heart rate (55% to 70%), the more you are freeing up fatty acids and burning them during the exercise program. When you are at 70 to 85 percent of your maximum heart rate, you will be in an aerobic state. Your body will utilize oxygen to create energy, and when you go above 85 percent, the utilization of oxygen can't keep up with your body's requirements for energy, so then it becomes somewhat *an*aerobic (without oxygen), and you will start burning the starch or glycogen that's in different parts of the body, such as muscles and the liver, for energy.

Your goal is to burn fat and increase your metabolism *after* exercise. The more you do interval training and the more you peak the peak and trough the trough, the higher your metabolism and the more fat you'll burn after exercise.

The key is that fat metabolism occurs following the exertion of the anaerobic (without oxygen) effort. Weight lifters, for example, will not burn fat as they actually lift the weight, but as the muscle recovers following a strenuous bout of lifting, there will be plenty of fat metabolism.

Once you have developed a good baseline for fitness, you will warm up for five minutes, get your heart rate into its target range, then oscillate inside that heart rate range for about 80 percent of your exercise time. About 20 percent of the time, though, I would like you to exercise above your target heart rate range a little bit and then also below your target heart rate range, so you really peak the peak and trough the trough. In that way you mimic the stress of life.

The greatest changes in aerobic capacity have been seen when high-intensity intervals are performed (e.g., at 85%) for two or three minutes, with a two-minute active rest interval. These high-intensity intervals improve central and peripheral circulation, capillarization in muscle, delay lactate production (production of waste), increase mitochondrial levels (which produces energy), improve enzyme concentration (improving system efficiency), and increase the number of lymphocytes (thus strengthening the immune system).

There is a minimum intensity below which a training effect will not occur, but there is a ceiling, too. As you increase your level of fitness, the ceiling you must attain will probably rise as well. Eighty-five percent of your maximal heart rate is considered the upper limit for obtaining aer-

THE BENEFITS OF EXERCISE

obic benefit, based on the premise that once you go beyond 85 percent of your maximum, you will begin utilizing starch in the muscle and from the liver for energy and will no longer utilize oxygen as efficiently.

Let's say that you're walking fast, attaining 85 percent of your maximum heart rate—the age-dependent rate of heartbeats per minute under maximal intensity. Now it's time to let it come down. Slow your pace, but use your arms to keep the blood flow working. In this recovery phase, practice the Ideal Performance State (IPS) walk, the walk of the confident fighter. Let your heart rate come down, and walk with your head up, shoulders level, arms loosely held at the side. If you can maintain that walk under fatigue, you can walk that way anywhere you go the rest of your life. When you do it often enough, it will just be *you*.

What you're doing by practicing the IPS walk is your rehearsal for how you will walk when you're going into a stressful meeting, when you're getting ready to make an important presentation, when you're defending the budget you've spent months developing. You will stride down the hallway toward that meeting with the IPS walk from the recovery phase of your interval training.

High-intensity intervals interspersed with low-intensity intervals provide a wide variety of stress to the system. The high-intensity interval challenges your body's systems to adapt. The low-intensity interval is a nice cooling-down period and prepares you for the next interval. For you as the Corporate Athlete, the correlation is between physical activity and preparing you for a mental activity or stress that you might encounter in the workplace. On the job, you will encounter high stress, low stress, high stress. It is not just a steady state all day long.

The good news about interval training is that anyone can perform intervals. You may not have to exercise as long, but be sure you are very warmed up before beginning the program. Do the speed work easily (you should never be totally out of breath) and train for recovery. Remember that the intensity of the hard bout of exercise is important, but so is the intensity of the recovery period.

Muscle Strength and Conditioning

If your training is aerobic, there will be little or no gain in strength. If your training involves light calisthenics and stretching, there will be little gain in strength. When you perform strength training properly, it is possible to expect 25 percent to 100 percent improvement in strength for each specific muscle group within three to six months. However, if you stop exercising, atrophy will occur. The basic requirement is three sessions per week per muscle group to improve strength of the specific muscle group, while two sessions per week will maintain the level of strength you have attained.

Muscular strength is defined as the ability of a muscle group to exert maximum force against a resistance in a single contraction. Muscular endurance is the ability of that muscle group to exert submaximal effort repeatedly over time. I believe that muscular strength and endurance are among the most overlooked fitness parameters. If the heart and the lungs don't work properly, disease can set in and overtake our bodies; without aerobic fitness, sickness can occur by compromising our total immune system. But mounting evidence over the past couple of decades has shown that muscular strength is absolutely essential to a person's overall health.

Any fitness program that is valuable considers the workout volume and intensity. Typically you should start out with lighter weights and more volume. Volume is the number of sets you perform times the repetitions times the intensity. As you get more trained, you can increase the volume. You also always want to work on balancing the muscles across joints. Work on the front of the joint and then the back of the joint to create balance across the joint—for example, the quadriceps on the front of the thigh and the hamstrings on the back of the thigh, since they both cross the hip and the knee.

If the Corporate Athlete has free weights available, we encourage that. But it is not so much a necessity as it is just a preference on our part. We feel that it gives your body more of an opportunity to develop completely on strength and on a coordination basis.

Yoga?

There are many paths to righteousness, as the old saying goes. Well, there are many paths to fitness as well. Steve Gray, LGE's director of corporate fitness and sports massage, welcomes the opportunity to introduce open-minded clients to yoga as an alternative to stretching and calisthenics to getting fit.

"I use yoga as a means of introducing people into a fun way to stretch," Gray says. "Yoga is one of the most popular growing classes in all of the health clubs and resorts, and I have found it to be very acceptable these days to get a wide range of people into stretching. It is a great way to incorporate stretching into movement."

The basis of yoga is being able to control the breath in a sequential series of movements, be that squatting up and down, bringing legs forward, arms over the head, or standing on one leg. There are hundreds of exercises in which you are required to maintain balance as well as control your breath and build strength, using the body almost as a weight. Gray teaches Corporate Athletes how to control their breathing and to use breathing to handle the stress of the movement of yoga.

Here is an interesting aside about yoga: Of all the classes we teach at LGE, exit surveys of our corporate clients indicate the yoga is one of their favorite parts of the program.

Maintain Your Flexibility

You should do stretching every day of your life. Stretching the muscles and tendons of your body will increase each joint's range of motion. When the range of motion of a joint becomes limited, daily functioning can become hampered. For example, with poor flexibility, you might easily pull a muscle running up stairs or wrench your hip and back as you lift your carry-on luggage on a plane.

There are days when you may say, "Okay, I've done my aerobics three days or five days this week, I've done my strength training three days, I need a day off." Well, even on those days off, take time to stretch. You can use it as another form of recovery. It will even help you get at peace with yourself on a busy day.

There are rules for stretching. No. 1, always warm up before you stretch. When you warm up to the point that you break a light sweat—jogging in place, skipping rope, or light calisthenics to break a sweat—then you know you've increased your internal body temperature. The tissues in your body will be much more pliable during the stretching you're going to take them through. Finally, stretch before *and* after an activity.

Doing slight stretching before you take a walk—stretching the Achilles tendon and maybe your hamstring and your lower back—helps prepare your body to do the work. As you get older, you start losing your range of motion. Many things you do in your day-to-day life, such as sitting behind the wheel of your car or behind a desk, are situations where your legs are bent for hours at a time, causing your hamstrings to get tight and your abdominals to get weak—and those are the main causes of back problems.

Put Your Heart (Rate) into It

Before starting cardiorespiratory conditioning, you must measure your heart rate. The most effective way of measuring heart rate is through the use of a heart rate monitor. If you don't have a heart rate monitor, however, here's the next best method, and it won't cost you a penny:

Hold your forearm in front of you with your palm up. Look down at your wrist and you'll see the midline of your wrist, the tendons in your wrist, and then between that midline and the thumb side you'll see a space—it's about an inch to an inch and a half, the space between the midline and the thumb side of your wrist. Take two fingers—do not use your thumb, because it has its own pulse—and press gently halfway between that space. You should feel your pulse. Some people might have a deeper pulse (you might have to move around a little bit), but your radial artery runs right through that area.

Count the number of heartbeats you feel for six seconds. Then multiply it times 10—or just add a zero—and you'll get a rough estimate of your heartbeat. It works best if you've been sitting still or even lying down for a few minutes before taking the measurement so you get a good evaluation of your resting heart rate.

A lot of people ask, "What's normal?" Normal could be 40 beats per minute to even 105, depending on the state you're in, when you've eaten, or how active you've been all day.

There is no normal resting heartbeat; there is a wide range of "normal." The average heart rate for men is 72 beats per minute, with women having an average heart rate of 78 beats per minute. Younger children have higher heart rates, and older adults have lower heart rates. Resting heart rates from 40 to 105 beats per minute are normal for certain individuals.

A proper exercise program of cardiovascular conditioning can reduce the resting heart rate by as much as 10 to 15 beats per minute. The heart rate also changes as your activities vary throughout the day. Most people's heart rate will fluctuate plus or minus a range of 40 beats per minute each day. Changes in postural position also affect the heart rate.

Another important factor: If your parents had a high heart rate, you're going to have a higher heart rate, too. You can bring that down with training, but if your parents had a genetically high heart rate, it's going to be almost impossible for you to have a very low heart rate. But you can bring down your resting heart rate with exercise.

Heart Rate Monitors

Taking your pulse manually can be very difficult while exercising, so many of our clients use a heart-rate monitor. If you are a beginner or a recreational exerciser, the heart rate monitor can scientifically provide you with the easiest intensity level at which you can work out and realize improvement. At this level there should be neither pain nor the sensation of being out of breath from exercise. The biggest advantage of the heart rate monitor is ensuring that the heart rate is in the optimum range for maximal benefits.

The heart rate monitor indicates the amount of exercise that burns the maximum amount of fat during the exercise program and the level of heart rate that will increase metabolism following exercise. This is a great aid and essential for training and weight loss.

If you are a seasoned exerciser and have attained a high level of fitness, you may begin your interval training by allowing your heart rate to oscillate between the upper range and the lower range of the target heart rate. For seasoned athletes, you may occasionally go above the target heart rate zone as you become fitter and as your sport demands, but be sure to allow for recovery in your training program. For this reason I recommend use of a heart rate monitor—to know exactly where your heart rate is during your workout.

Heart rate has been the exercise intensity indicator in scientific research for decades. At LGE we use monitors to determine the heart rate response to exercise intensity and the recovery mechanisms of heart rate to teach conditioning and overall recovery techniques. The heart rate monitor will provide a factor of safety and help motivate you to stay with the program. It is both a personal athletic trainer and a medical supervisor.

Corporate Athletes need a heart rate monitor with interval training, as it is difficult to know interval training results without a monitor. We also recommend you wear it to the office periodically to use as biofeedback during particularly stressful days.

Perceived Exertion

As you exercise, you can rate your perceived exertion on a numerical scale. The harder you exercise, the higher the perceived exertion will be.

After you have been exercising for three or four months you will begin to understand or perceive how you feel when your heart rate is at a certain level. It is this perceived exertion that will explain to you how hard you are exercising.

As you continue working out, cross-check your target heart rate zone against your perceived exertion. After a while it will be easy for you to predict your approximate heart rate based on how hard you are exercising and how you feel.

Getting a checkup is excellent advice—in fact, it's a must—for any sedentary person thinking about exercising. This is especially important for anyone who is at high risk because of obesity, smoking, diabetes, high blood cholesterol, hypertension, severe stress, or a family history of medical problems. So if you decide to improve your job performance and protect your health with exercise, by all means get all the medical help you can to prolong your life.

Corporate Athlete Action Items

- Get a yearly physical.
- Stretch every day.
- Think of your exercise program as a business plan. Write down your personal profits and losses by doing it or not doing it.
- Design a weekly schedule of your exercise time for interval training, strength training, and flexibility.
- Get access to a heart-rate monitor and identify your own perceived exertion levels. If you cannot find one, call us at LGE at 1-800-543-7764.
- Set up your own twelve-month periodization schedule by identifying the times of the year when you absolutely must be "on." No questions asked (e.g., defense of your budget, sales meeting with your company's largest distributor or client).
- Identify in your own life how you could use the concept of periodization (e.g., developing a new foundation for a specific skill, such as presenting new software, roll out practicing it, demonstrating it, then recovering from the stress of your performance).

Part IV

THE CORPORATE ATHLETE SPIRIT

12

Spiritual Fitness

The real voyage of discovery consists not in seeking
new landscapes but in having new eyes.

—MARCEL PROUST

CORPORATE ATHLETE PRINCIPLE 12:

Everybody has a spiritual side, whether you are Christian, Jewish, Buddhist, or agnostic— even if you are atheist.

As we travel throughout the world conducting Mentally Tough corporate training programs, we are constantly asked about the role of spirituality in business. Spirituality involves your core being—your soul, if you will. It delves into your personal mission and purpose, the truth about your life, and the issues of life that inspire you. Religion, on the other hand, often involves man-made classifications of how and when you should worship.

Spirituality is often associated with a Supreme Being. Religions have specific ways of believing and involve very specific ways of doing things. Many religions become ritualistic in the way they conduct worship.

I once heard a minister say, "If you don't believe you are spiritual, talk to anybody who went through World War II or the Vietnam conflict and found themselves pinned down in a foxhole. When bombs were going off all around them, they prayed. They may not have known who they were praying to, but they *were* praying."

How we access and apply our spiritual side determine how we deal with stress and tough times as they are presented throughout our life. This is the foundation for spiritual fitness.

Spirituality affects every aspect of our lives. It affects our business and our family, the sports we play, economics, politics, and romance. Spirituality involves moral, ethical, and religious attitudes, feelings, and values.

The human spirit is in many ways a very fragile entity. Whether something happens to you at work that is in some way shocking to your system, or it's a life-changing event, the human spirit is affected. Whether the crisis is physical, mental, or emotional, we often turn to our spirituality.

People often become content to obey their own personal religious laws outwardly without allowing spirituality to actually change their hearts or attitudes. But we must constantly try to improve the quality of our goodness. Some people follow religious beliefs only for physical or temporal benefits, not because they are spiritually hungry. You must constantly seek truth in your life.

It is not enough to be religious. Our actions and attitudes must be sincere. If not, we become hypocrites. Feeling that you are religious without living a life of substance is meaningless. If you only appear to have faith without putting it to work in your life, you are like a fruit tree that can bear no fruit. Religions sometimes focus too much on human effort. Following rules and rituals is not enough.

Our lives must back up our words. Do your actions agree with your words? The accumulation of knowledge alone in religion is empty. Knowledge should give us direction in our life, and then we must live it.

Why is it that we return to our spirituality only when significant events—such as the loss of a loved one, a divorce, relocating our entire family, or changing jobs—occur? I believe that *all time is sacred time* and that spirituality must be a habit for it to be really effective. Being spiritual only on Sunday is not enough for Christians, nor is being spiritual only on Friday nights or Saturday mornings enough for Jews. We have to resort to our spirituality daily.

With spirituality, whatever it means to you, if you don't practice it, it will never happen. Say to yourself every morning, "All time is sacred time." All we have to do is practice that phrase, and it almost becomes like a golden rule.

Someday, when you least expect it, the phrase "All time is sacred time" will mean something to you.

I recently conducted a corporate training program for a major pharmaceutical firm, and I asked about this phrase. One man said that he didn't believe it was true. Yet he went on to say that he had stopped smoking five years before on the day his first child was born. I asked him why he had stopped. He wanted to live to a ripe old age to see his child grow, and he knew that his smoking might prevent him from doing so, he said. I said, "Don't you believe at that moment you felt your time was sacred time, any time you could spend watching your child grow up into an adult was meaningful?" Tears welled in his eyes and suddenly he realized that he had lived that phrase. It was his emotional callus that prevented him from feeling the meaning behind the phrase.

Someday your health will be at the forefront of your life, you will have to deal with a serious family issue or will have to deal with your purpose in life. But the only time it will ever be meaningful to you is when you decide to do it for you. Why not now?

Look at the top causes of failure within corporations and you'll see a variety of interesting trends:

- People become isolated, and there is no accountability.
- People become independent rather than interdependent. Focus is lost.
- A loss of hope erodes morale among employees.
- People become too proud to get help.
- Values break down.

In an era when there is more pressure than ever to perform at high levels, we find that people more and more search for their own spirituality. We constantly need time for personal reflection and growth, and we increasingly realize the need for interdependence.

Spirituality Is the Cure

Your self-image is key. What do you think of yourself? Do you truly like yourself? What are your values? What are your needs as a human being? What is your body image? What are your feelings about yourself? How do you take care of yourself? What are your habits? How much self-confidence and self-love do you truly have? Once you internalize all those things, taking care of yourself, exercise, and eating well really become easy.

Why are you healthier when you exercise, when you eat better, when you pray, when you spend time with your family? How does the immune system improve with exercise? Let's talk about the miracle of the human machine, the grand design that is each of us. We have all this chaos, all these molecules and atoms put together.

Lower levels of stress and depression, as well as an increased ability to cope with stress, have been observed among people with high spiritual commitments. Basically, it comes down to this: If you are to be spiritually grounded, you must live your life consciously and not mechanically. By that I mean you must be present and mindful in all you do. Often we find ourselves mindlessly staring at a computer screen or daydreaming about being somewhere else other than where we are, and we actually become machines instead of conscious beings.

We go so far into this endeavor that we create a high, false drive that causes us to *go, go, go*. We confuse this with passion. If we don't succeed at whatever task we are attempting, we drop into a low, negative state of depression or a feeling of helplessness.

Spiritual people are very grounded. They stay in the middle and do not have so many ups and downs into the very negative states. To be competitive *and* to be spiritual is the struggle for most Corporate Athletes.

Spirituality is not a performance. You should not necessarily strive to perform for your family; you should attempt to make sure that you are *with* your family. Whatever your faith is, when you are in a state of being there and not performing, you are healthier and happier.

Are you a human being having a spiritual experience, or are you a spiritual being having a human experience? The issue becomes your personal faith. We know that this is true: If your real self is spiritually weak, it will be very difficult for you to handle all the trials *and* tribulations of corporate life. Only those people who have high self-esteem through their spiritual beliefs are the ones who can gravitate toward a positive response during tough times.

If you find inner peace, if you have inner tranquillity in your life due to your spiritual beliefs, you will be much better able to access the positive emotions necessary during a potentially negative situation.

What Is Important to You?

If you envision failure, you will fail, and if you envision success and believe in it, you will experience success. If you expect the worst, you will get the worst. And if you expect the best, you have a true shot at getting the best. Transcend what you do daily; that way you will be released from doubt and will hold nothing back. Give life itself your all. Faith in any idea and the belief in your ability to perform that idea will help you implement and perform whatever you need to do.

In addition to mental preparation for the day ahead, we need spiritual preparation. Whatever that is to you—whether you meditate, pray, or simply give yourself a few moments of silent contemplation—connect with it for a few minutes each day.

"I use the drive to work at 5:15 A.M. as prayer time," says Rodger Price of Johnson Controls. "When I haven't done that, I find later that I regret missing that time of reflection and meditation because it's important to me, it's something I ritualize to make sure it happens."

Turn the computer off at work, turn the radio off in your car, just take it easy. Turn off the environmental noise that you inadvertently surround yourself with every day. It's not easy, I know; I am a real victim of it myself. The sound track of my life has often been background noise, and I think I am in the majority. We feel a need for clutter around us, or else we don't feel like we are keeping busy, because we thrive on chaos.

The Values/Health Connection

I refer you to some recent research from the field of psychoneuroimmunology. Scientists have noted that every cell in the body is embedded with receptor sites that enable communication between cells. The chemical connection means that as you change your psychological and physiological state, each cell knows what is going on through this infinitely wise communication system. We know today, for example, that when you're happy there are biochemical events taking place throughout every cell in your body. Likewise, when you're angry or frustrated, a different biochemical event is occurring.

Scientists today theorize that for a person who is in a constantly negative state, the cell chemistry in the lining of the stomach, for example, changes so drastically that it becomes more receptive to the bacteria that cause ulcers. How many people do you know who always seem to be in a negative state? I would venture to say that at least one and possibly as many as five to six people immediately come to mind, people who surround you day after day. This creates a serious problem for us all because we are surrounded by this constant negativism.

A value is anything on which you place worth. It could be your belief in God, it could be the love you have for your child or for your spouse, it could be the love you have for a fiancée or for a parent or a sibling, it could be a love of nature. But whatever your value system is, you should emotionally connect to it. This is essential to surviving the tough times presented to us from day to day in business and in life.

One belief that I think is extremely important but is the most difficult to learn in business, in sports, or in life is this: *I love to compete more than I love to win.* But this is difficult because we are surrounded from day one with the fact that we should be winners.

In our society, we are afraid to make mistakes. Yet, there isn't a successful person I've met who has never made a mistake. In fact, I'd even go so far as to say that most of us got where we are today or we grew into the person we are today by the mistakes we made along the way. It was the tough times that molded and shaped us, not the easy times.

Say this to yourself: *When things get tough, I will stay in control of humor.* Show me someone who gets an emotional hit in the face or is presented with an incredible stressor, yet someone who can laugh or smile and access the feeling that this "problem" is going to be fun to solve, and I will show you a champion in his or her field or a champion in the making. But what usually happens is that we reprimand people who have fun or smile when things are supposed to be serious. We've heard it since our teenage years. "Wipe that smile off your face!" "What's so funny?" "Children should be seen and not heard." But humor is essential to being successful or achieving success.

Spirituality is in the center and in the surrounding circle of the performance triad. I say it is the heart and the soul of being a great performer.

Without spiritual energy we are nothing, because many of us are so weakened spiritually that we react to problems, we snap too quickly, we spend our days in a negative state of anger, frustration, defensiveness, or

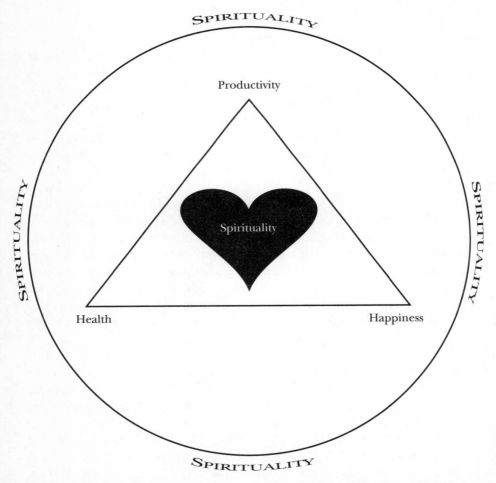

Figure 12.1. Spirituality Is the *Heart* and the *Soul* of the Performance Triad.

even in negative traumas such as depression, feelings of helplessness or hopelessness, or the feeling of being burned out. How do we find the spiritual energy I am referring to?

Actor Christopher Reeve may be the greatest optimist I know. The man who once soared high in the skies of Metropolis as Superman became a quadriplegic following a horseback riding accident several years ago. But despite his paralyzing injuries, he has sworn to maintain a normal life for himself and his family.

For starters, he demands regular electrical stimulation of the muscles of his immobile legs and arms because—even though he doesn't have the natural neurostimulation most people take for granted—he knows these muscles could otherwise move. Reeve believes that when researchers find a cure for his condition, his muscles must be ready. In the meantime, he will not let his muscles atrophy.

"When a cure is found," he says, "I will be ready to go."

I met Reeve when we were both part of the Peter Lowe International seminar tour. Onstage, Lowe asked Reeve, "Do you ever think, 'why me?'?"

And his answer was, "Well, why not me? There is a higher self, whether it is God or another higher being. But the world is full of good people. The key is what you do from here. You cannot live with 'That wasn't fair.' You can't say to yourself, 'That wasn't fair.' You have to say to yourself, 'Okay, given this, now what do I do?' At first you are overwhelmed. You say to yourself, 'I can't rebuild this house after the hurricane hit it. I just can't do it.' The only way you can do it is to get the hammer and lumber out and just do it. The same thing with me. I can't worry about, 'Oh, woe is me.'"

Lowe then asked Reeve to define success. "We are all one member of a five-billion-member family," Reeve said. "If I look out in this audience, and I look at you as a stranger, there is no connection. But when I look out at this audience, in this arena, I see people I have never met who are still friends and family. And if I take that approach, I rejoice in that, and then we connect to the entire human race."

Energy Levels and Spirituality

The word "enthusiasm" stems from the Greek "filled with God."

In business, we look at life as all or nothing. We become totally results-oriented. And if the results fail us, we lose confidence! We must determine why we have low self-esteem. If you have disempowering thoughts, you must believe that what you say about yourself and what you visualize about yourself are true.

We absolutely should not accept mediocrity in our lives. To generate a passion for what we do, we need a spiritual side. We also need morals, guilt, and ethics. The problem is that we often spend all of our time working on many minisolutions. We spend our lives dealing with symptoms of a problem, symptoms of what we think is going on when in fact we don't deal with the real cause of our problems. Often the *cause* of our problems is that we get caught up in the rat race so much that we cannot deal with our spiritual side.

Everyone says we need love, but we can't just talk about it, we must practice love. One way to do this is to forget the self and think of others. The Golden Rule applies no matter what your religious background: "Do unto others as you would have them do unto you." As you prepare for your day, create a mental picture of you *having* a good day.

Do not be awestruck by the accomplishments of other people. Seek out a confident mentor. Use positive affirmations and visualizations as you go through your day, and believe that you are a good person.

Embracing Growth, Not Results

If you saw the 1993 movie *Searching for Bobby Fischer,* you already know Josh Waitzkin. That film told the true story of this young chess prodigy, whose talent, as early as age seven, was favorably compared to that of Bobby Fischer. No one stays young forever, and the inspiration for *Searching* is now a twenty-one-year-old man, albeit one who is still highly regarded in the pressure-cooker world of professional chess.

Two years ago, with the help of David Striegel, Ph.D., myself, and others at LGE, Waitzkin returned to his original style with firmer grounding. Waitzkin was always introspective; we gave him psychological perspective on his performance, a sense for relating his performance state not only to chess but to everything.

"LGE taught me a language for how to approach the psychology of competition, which I really had no sense for. It was probably an unhealthy relationship that had to do with wrestling with demons and just crash-and-burn and a tormented, competitive life as opposed to a peaceful, competitive life. My spiritual movement toward Eastern thought, t'ai chi, Buddhism, and Taoism has helped me better relate."

There have been many times when Waitzkin needed a break from chess. Sometimes, when you are competing, a break is recovery. We taught him to take that recovery before he burns out.

"Burnout often relates to people who are looking at things in an entirely results-oriented way," Waitzkin says. "If, in a month or two, they are not moving toward their goal, they get frustrated as opposed to embracing growth. In my opinion, people who have a healthy relationship to their art and who are very good at it tend to be way less prone to burn out."

Waitzkin discovered what his Ideal Performance State was, then he identified the things that brought him back to it. That created a routine that regularly regenerates his performance. "If I discovered that doing a certain thing put me into the perfect frame of mind for chess, and I get in that routine every day, then I am slowly training my body to be in that state."

Face Your Own Truth

How can your personal spirituality help you thrive and go to the next level? Face the truth. Look into the mirror, look beyond your skin and into the very heart and soul of your being.

Claudine McIntee, vice president of training and development in Human Resources at Morgan Stanley Dean Witter, says getting in touch with her spirituality is a vitally important part of her day.

> I commute on the train every morning into Manhattan. I live in a suburb outside of New York City, and every morning that I travel in, I pray. It gets me focused and centered for the day. Every Wednesday, I also read to a fourth-grade student from an inner-city school for an hour and a half, trying to be a positive role model to her, showing that education is really important and that being a woman in a business or in industry, you can be very successful and independent. It is really very rewarding, because when I am crazy or I get worked up over something at work, I walk to see this kid and talk to her. My life is not that bad when you put it against this little kid who is just hoping that her mother and father are going to come home tonight. One day she told me that she was upset for her aunt because her cousin, who was eighteen months old, was accidentally shot by the father.
>
> Things like that are constant reminders of how fortunate and lucky I am, and I feel a sense of having been very fortunate in my life. I have had a lot of ups and downs and adversity in my personal life, and I feel that there were people in my life who have given to me. I feel a sense of responsibility to give back to others. So in being able to pass on that positive energy, it makes me feel good about myself. As a result, when I come back to work, I may be able to positively influence someone else who is having a bad day or getting worked up about something and somehow my positive energy is transmitted to that other person.

You never know when you are going to influence somebody, and you never know when you are going to touch someone. *American Health* magazine reported that research from the University of Michigan says that doing regular volunteer work, more than any other activity, dramatically increased life expectancy and probable vitality.

This is a contradictory issue for most people, because we have grown up in a society where you take care of no. 1. We grow up with the feeling that if you don't take care of yourself, no one else will. If you are to succeed, it is up to you. Personally, I agree with that last statement. If you're to be a success, it *is* 100 percent up to you. However, your definition of success is the most important thing. What is yours?

Rituals and Spirituality

Corporate Athletes must create rituals of success. Many rituals are crucial to your performance and to your life. Some of these include: the quantity and quality of sleep you get; the time you devote to exercise; how well you eat; routines you use before a major presentation or making a sale; habits you have as soon as you walk in the doorway at home; or routines you have for spending time alone. But one of the most important rituals and one of the areas where we as human beings truly break down is that of *spiritual* rituals.

Just as we scarf down or skip lunch; just as we fit in time to exercise; just as sometimes we sacrifice time with family or sacrifice sleep time, we often sacrifice our spiritual time as well. Like family time, we know that spiritual time heals our soul and brings us home to the deeper, more essential truths of life. Failure to make time for spiritual growth erodes the foundation of all other personal growth.

So what must you do to ritualize spirituality in your life? Certainly you can attend a service of the religion to which you belong. You could read inspirational materials written by priests, ministers, rabbis, or self-improvement specialists. Your could take a class dealing with life issues, or you could perform a community service. A close friend of mine goes to soup kitchens on the weekends to work with the homeless. You could meditate and access your inner self to make that personal connection with God or whatever force you rely on. And most importantly, you could pray.

The essence of prayer is not what is said or how or where, but how you communicate with your heart. Persistent prayer is necessary, but do not repeat prayers shallowly. We can never pray too much if our prayers are sincere and honest.

Finding time for prayer is not easy, but you must find the time, even if you must get up before sunrise. Make sure that all important life decisions are grounded in prayer and meditation. Admit your faults. And do this not only in prayer but to your fellow human beings as well. If you have caused problems for someone, ask for forgiveness from that person. Confessing what you have done and how you feel to family, friends, and even the public is crucial to praying effectively.

Prayer is one of the most important spiritual rituals you could possibly utilize. It revives the soul, strengthens the heart, improves your health, and enhances personal habits.

Spirituality as Recovery

Spirituality, and the practice of it, will assist you in obtaining emotional recovery. We often teach that time in *low positive*—that area where you have low energy but feel very good—is an extremely important part of being a performer in today's anxiety-ridden business world. Low positive energy stimulates healing and repair. The more stress you have in your life right now, the more important low positive energy becomes. Feelings of being at peace, relaxed, relieved, and reenergized are characteristic of being in a low positive energy state.

There are many ways in which you can access these feelings. You can pray or meditate. You can get outdoors by yourself and literally commune with nature. You can listen to music that enables you to access a state of relaxation. You can spend quality family time by emotionally connecting with various members of your family. Being able to relax—and relax often—is a key trait of someone who has a strong spiritual self.

You know how I made the transition from training athletes to training businesspeople. But maybe you're still skeptical: How can Jack Groppel, an athlete all his life, give me advice about spirituality?

Let me tell you a story.

I tore the cartilage of my right knee during the last dual meet of my collegiate tennis career and had postseason surgery in 1973. I hurt the left knee playing basketball the very next year, at twenty-two. As a result of these surgeries, I have nothing on the inside of my right knee and nothing on the outside of my left knee.

When I play a lot of tennis, I have soreness the next day and have trouble. When I reached my late thirties, the knees gave me some real problems. There were many sleepless nights from arthritic pain.

The biggest wake-up call of my life was related to these battered knees. It lasted eighteen months. During that time, I endured fear, pain, and debilitation. I had to stop exercising the way I loved, I had trouble in relationships—basically, I had a lot of trouble being me.

It all started in early August 1995, the morning that Hurricane Erin blasted central Florida. I took a ladder out and leaned it against the house to clean leaves from the rain gutters. When I came down the ladder, I felt a slight twist in my knee. The pain was minimal, definitely not anything excruciating, like I had suffered before. When I later went to the office, however, I felt serious pain in my left knee, and it had begun swelling. An orthopedic surgeon took 120 cc's of blood off my knee. The doctor said the problem was serious arthritis. After Hurricane Erin, I never jogged again. And I was used to jogging *every* day.

I was devastated when I realized I couldn't run anymore. I had to totally change my life. If you have bum knees like mine, you can swim. If you have no legs at all, you can use an upper-body ergometer. There is always, always, *always* something you can do. Develop muscle mass, and you can strength-train and do circuit training. To say that you can't do this because something hurts—well, something *always* hurts.

All went well until February 4, 1996. I was in Atlanta for three days attending the Super Show, the largest sporting goods show in the world. I was on my feet all day, each day.

When it was over, I flew to Miami. Changing planes, I went down an escalator behind an elderly woman. Apparently she should not have been walking by herself—she lost her balance and started to fall. I dropped my briefcase and jumped around her to the left, landing on my left leg to catch her. She was okay, but again I had slightly twisted my left knee. Saying a lot of prayers (as we all do when we get into scary situations), I prayed that I hadn't damaged the knee too significantly. But I had. By the time I got to the hotel I needed a wheelchair to get to my room. Not that I stayed long; the pain was so intense that I went to a hospital emergency room. I made my speech the next day on painkillers and with a huge cast around my knee.

Back home, my orthopedic surgeon decided that it would be necessary to operate. Two days after that operation, I was walking around with no crutches and feeling very little discomfort. Then I made a big mistake.

Five days later, my partner Jim Loehr and I were producing audiotape programs, and I needed to fly to Chicago. Landing at O'Hare International Airport on Wednesday, my knee started hemorrhaging. I couldn't get the bleeding to stop initially, but I finally did by tying a tight bandage around the area. During this trip, the knee became infected. I had three knee operations in one week to irrigate the knee with antibiotics, and a tube was placed into my heart to prevent bacteria from invading it. The staph infection was difficult to beat, and I was hospitalized for fifteen days. The pain was immeasurable. I was on crutches for a few weeks thereafter before switching to a cane.

A little over a month later, I was to speak at a Success Seminar in Atlanta's Georgia Dome before twenty-six thousand people. My goal was that I would walk on that stage with no crutches and with no cane and give the best presentation I possibly could. Not only did I need extensive therapy and rehabilitation for my knee, but I also had to have extensive practice and rehearsal for my presentation. I was slated to follow Christopher Reeve and precede Barbara Bush, so you could imagine the pressure I felt as a speaker, let alone getting my knee problems straightened out.

At that moment I made sure that God knew my goal also. I prayed that His will be done; I prayed that if it was His will that I accomplish this to *please* give me the strength to pull it off. When the day came, it was probably the most painful twenty-four hours of my life. But I did it! I walked onstage and made my presentation to twenty-six thousand people, as planned. I never felt such a feeling of accomplishment. It was another eight months before I could walk normally. I believe it was my faith that helped me and gave me the impetus to pull it off. Even when I felt I didn't have support from others, I always had my faith, and today my faith is stronger than it ever has been.

Wherever you are spiritually, regardless of your religious faith, keep growing. Make the following commitments to yourself: Keep searching for answers. Keep learning about spirituality. Keep developing your own spiritual growth and become emotionally connected to it. Never stop seeking your purpose in life and the truth about your life.

Corporate Athlete Action Items

- If someone asked you right now about your own spirituality, think through how you would explain it.
- Make a daily practice of accessing your own spiritual beliefs for the next twenty-one days. See what it does for you.
- Are you connected to your spiritual beliefs? If so, how?
- Would you consider yourself spiritually fit? Why or why not?
- Identify what you could do personally to improve your spiritual fitness.
- Identify what you currently do to live your life for others—for example, volunteering.
- Say to yourself daily, "All time is sacred time."

Part V

THE 21-DAY CORPORATE ATHLETE PROGRAM

13

Mark Your Starting Line: Determine Your Fitness and Nutrition Profile

No athlete is crowned but in the sweat of his brow.
—St. Jerome

CORPORATE ATHLETE PRINCIPLE 13:

Don't begin any physical, mental, or emotional conditioning program without determining your starting baseline.

In this section we'll combine everything you've learned so far about being a great Corporate Athlete and put it into action. Chapters 13 and 14 will help you determine your current fitness in terms of exercise, nutrition, values, and time management; chapter 15 will take that knowledge and guide you through a twenty-one-day program that will change and improve the rest of your life.

When new clients come to the LGE campus in Orlando, we don't just point them to the gym and tell them to get to work. That wouldn't be wise or safe. Instead, we take them through a battery of sophisticated mental, emotional, and physical profiling tests before starting them on any program. In the following pages you will take many of the same tests to determine your own baseline.

Great Ambitions Start with Smart Priorities

Mike Roscigno, thirty-six, is a person committed to personal and professional development who wanted to find "that balance so often

159

spoken of in today's business world without compromising my aspirations." Roscigno, the business development director for Andersen Consulting in the northeastern United States and Canada, was always running out of time during the day. "I was looking to be not only more efficient but best in class, too."

For Roscigno, realigning his priorities was a first step. He sat down with David Striegel, Ph.D., who coordinates individual training at LGE, and discussed his own core values. Immediately we recognized that Roscigno was not connecting his daily activities with his value system. His personal values didn't match up with the way he carried out his day. The two of them went through Roscigno's typical day and listed everything he did. There were two lists, actually—those things that matched up with his stated values and those that didn't. The idea is that your actions and behavior should reflect your deepest values.

"You want great health?" Striegel said, challenging Roscigno. "What do you do each day toward that goal besides driving yourself crazy? You want to be a great husband? I don't see any time for Tracy [Roscigno's wife] if you're at work from 8:30 A.M. till 8:30 P.M."

So typical of many Corporate Athletes with whom we work, Roscigno now starts his day at 5:45 A.M. with a twenty-five-minute run. "And when I leave the office now, I'm finished. Before, I'd go home and check my voice mail at the office to see if there was any work activity between the time I left the office and got home. But when you think about it, it's really pretty sick."

AEROBIC FITNESS

Target Heart Rate Test

Subtract your age from 220 and then compute first 70 percent, then 85 percent of that number. For example, if you're 40 years of age, subtract your age from 220, which gives you an estimated maximum heart rate of 180. Step two: 70 percent of 180 is 126, and 85 percent of 180 is 153. So if you're 40 years old, you've got a training heart rate that is between 126 and 153. Using the method of measuring heart rate for only 6 seconds, round those numbers down to 120 to 150. If you measure your heart rate for 6 seconds while you're being active, you'd like to be between 12 and 15 beats in 6 seconds.

Target Heart Rate Exercise Instruction

(*CAUTION: This is intended for experienced exercisers with no medical complications. A program for inexperienced exercisers is presented later.*) For the first month of exercise, here's what you might do. Warm up for five minutes. Get your heart rate into the target zone. How do you know when you're warmed up? You'll break a light sweat. But measure your heart rate. Practice measuring your heart rate all the time. When your heart rate is in the target zone, start walking very quickly—or maybe go up a hill, and you'll get your heart rate up to 85 percent of maximum. When you get to 85 percent, let it come down to 70 percent, then raise it again to 85 percent and let it come back down. If you have had a very sedentary lifestyle, fluctuations between 75 percent and 85 percent will not take much effort at first. You can do this by increasing the intensity of exercise—for example, by going up a hill, or by increasing the frequency of what you're doing. In other words, walking faster or sprinting if you're a runner. If you're not a runner, don't try sprinting until you're really warmed up. Remember to work your way into exercise slowly.

Once you've done this regularly for at least two months, you can really have some fun. You'll be able to go up even outside your target heart rate range. Maybe take your heart rate up to 90 percent. You may want to go to 95 percent. Then let your heart rate come down to even 65 percent or 60 percent. But the goal is that you peak the peak and trough the trough. By "peak the peak" I mean you will get your heart rate high and then "trough the trough" by bringing your heart rate way down. The goal is to spend about 80 percent of your exercise time oscillating in the target heart rate zone. Then you can spend 10 percent of the time above it and 10 percent of the time below it.

VO_2 Max

Every time you exercise, the heart, lungs, and skeletal muscles are challenged to grow stronger and improve their functional capacity. The oxygen use at which you hit your maximal effort is called the VO_2 Max. Exercise oxygen consumption is the best measure of metabolic rate during exercise and is determined by a VO_2 Max test.

A VO_2 Max test—available at hospitals, universities, and LGE—shows how fit you are aerobically, as well as your maximum ability to take in, transport, and use oxygen. It represents the maximal health and fitness of three major bodily systems: your lungs, which bring oxygen in; the heart, which pumps the oxygen out to the other muscles; and the muscles that use the oxygen for energy. Those three systems are challenged every time you exercise, and that is how you become more fit. They adapt to that stress every time you exercise by growing stronger during the recovery period.

The test produces a number we can compare with individuals of your same age, sex, and body weight to see where you are versus where you should be, and where you need to be going. It also can determine if you are healthy and if your heart and lungs look good. An exercise program can be prescribed based on the results of this test. At LGE, Brian Wallace, Ph.D., who holds accreditation from several agencies, oversees our physiological testing protocols and exercise prescription.

I recommend the VO_2 Max test both before you start an exercise program and then every six months to see what adaptations have taken place and how fit you have become. Once you reach the advanced level of aerobic fitness, we recommend being tested once a year.

Before conducting any of the tests that follow, please get medical clearance from your family physician.

Walking

For those who are sedentary or who never exercise very much, I recommend a one-mile-walk test developed by the Rockport Walking Institute to assess cardiorespiratory fitness.

Bear in mind that this is a weight-bearing test, so if you have a joint problem, it will be difficult to do. This test was designed for people aged twenty to sixty-nine and has been studied extensively.

The one-mile-walk test works on the same principle as many other distance-type run and/or jogging tests. People who have a higher level of cardiorespiratory fitness will walk one mile in a shorter time than those who are less conditioned. It is preferable to conduct this test on a quarter-mile track, perhaps at a high school or a college in your community.

Your goal is walking one mile as quickly as possible and measuring your heart rate immediately at the end of the test by counting your pulse for fifteen seconds. Refer to the section on heart rate and measuring heart rate to be sure you perform this task accurately. Be sure you warm up and stretch for the test so you will not get injured. (Please refer to table 13.1 to identify your cardiorespiratory fitness level. Identify the walking time and its corresponding postexercise heart rate on the appropriate chart for your age and gender.)

If you have been exercising for a while and are medically cleared for any form of exercise, another test you might try is the 1½-mile run. Again, the higher your level of fitness, the faster you will run a given distance. However, the intensity of a 1.5-mile run is not to be recommended for sedentary people, severely unconditioned people, people with joint problems, or people who are obese. The ideal site for a 1½-mile run is a ¼-mile track at your local high school or college. By utilizing a stopwatch and being able to measure your heart rate, you can get a reasonable evaluation of your cardiorespiratory fitness. Then you can look at your time and, according to your age, determine your level of cardiorespiratory fitness.

Table 13.1. Fitness Classification for One-Mile-Walk Test*

Fitness Category	Age 20–29	30–39	40+
Men			
Beginners	>18:00	>19:00	>21:30
	16:31–18:00	17:31–19:00	18:31–21:30
Intermed.	14:31–16:30	15:31–17:30	16:01–18:30
	13:01–14:30	13:31–15:30	14:00–16:00
Advanced	<13:00	<13:30	<14:00
Women			
Beginners	>18:31	>19:31	>20:01
	17:01–18:30	18:01–19:30	19:01–20:00
Intermed.	15:01–17:00	16:01–18:00	18:00–19:00
	13:31–15:00	14:01–16:00	14:31–17:59
Advanced	<13:30	<14:00	<14:30

*Times are given in minutes and seconds (> = greater than; < = less than). Because the one-mile-walk test is designed primarily for older or less-conditioned individuals, the fitness categories listed here do not include a "superior" category.

Table 13.2. Fitness Categories for Cooper's 1.5-Mile-Run Test to Determine Cardiorespiratory Fitness*

Fitness Category	Age 20–29	30–39	40–49	50–59	60+
Men					
Beginners	>16:00	>16:30	>17:30	>19:00	>20:00
	14:01–16:00	14:46–16:30	15:36–17:30	17:01–19:00	19:01–20:00
Intermed.	12:01–14:00	12:31–14:45	13:01–15:35	14:31–17:00	16:16-19:00
	10:46–12:00	11:01–12:30	11:31–13:00	12:31–14:30	14:00–16:15
Advanced	9:45–10:45	10:00–11:00	10:30–11:30	11:00–12:30	11:15–13:59
	<9:45	<10:00	<10:30	<11:00	<11:15
Women					
Beginners	>19:00	>19:30	>20:00	>20:30	21:00
	18:31–19:00	19:01–19:30	19:31–20:00	20:01–20:30	20:31–21:00
Intermed.	15:55–18:30	16:31–19:00	17:31–19:30	19:01–20:00	19:31–20:30
	13:31–15:54	14:31–16:30	15:56–17:30	16:31–19:00	17:31–19:30
Advanced	12:30–13:30	13:00–14:30	13:45–15:55	14:30–16:30	16:30–17:30
	<12:30	<13:00	<13:45	<14:30	16:30

*Times are given in minutes and seconds (> = greater than; < = less than).

FLEXIBILITY

The primary test utilized to evaluate your general flexibility is called the standard sit-and-reach test. The American College of Sports Medicine recommends using this test to examine low back and hip flexibility. It evaluates the range of motion of the trunk as you stretch the lower back muscles and the muscles in the back of your thighs.

You will need a yardstick or a tape measure of equivalent length to measure the distance you are able to reach. With the yardstick lying flat on the floor, place a piece of tape across the yardstick at right angles to the fifteen-inch mark.

Since there is the chance of injury due to stretching, be sure you warm up properly. This is an essential component prior to testing because if you try to stretch forcefully and your body is too cold, you could strain the muscles. Also, before performing this test, please bear in mind that to prevent injury you should not bounce or use ballistic stretching of any type.

Flexibility Testing Instruction

Sit down with the yardstick between your legs. Remove your shoes and be sure the heels of your feet touch near the edge of the taped line and that your feet are about ten to twelve inches apart. Slowly reach forward with both hands as far as possible on the yardstick. Once you have reached as far as comfortably possible, hold that position momentarily. Keep your hands parallel and make sure your fingertips are in contact with the yardstick. Your score is simply measured, beginning with zero being able to touch your toes. If you can reach past your toes, measure the number of inches in positive numbers (e.g., 2 inches past your toes is +2). If you are 2 inches short of reaching your toes, this would be −2. Make sure you keep your knees straight and that they are held down during the testing movement. It also helps if you exhale and drop your head as you are reaching. Refer to table 13.3 to examine your level of flexibility.

Now you can use stretching techniques to improve your flexibility, but be sure you follow proper techniques. I don't want you to force stretching. Only stretch the body part until you feel a slight pull, slight tightness, very slight discomfort, not pain. If you feel pain, you've gone too

Table 13.3. Scoring and Ranks for the Sit-and-Reach Test*

Sit-and-Reach Score (Measurements are in inches)	Fitness Classification
≤ −1	Beginner or needs work
0 to +1	Intermediate but still needs a little work
≥ +2	Excellent

*Note that these norms are for both men and women (aged 18 to 50 years). Units for the sit-and-reach score are inches and indicate the distance of your fingertips from your toes. Negative numbers indicate that you cannot reach your toes, whereas positive numbers indicate the number of inches that you can reach past your toes.

far. I emphasize the words *slight tightness.* That's when you stop, and you hold it for twenty to thirty seconds. Do not bounce. This is called ballistic stretching. A lot of people think that if they bounce they will improve their range of motion around a joint. No; you'll only hurt yourself if you do a bouncing type of stretching.

STRENGTH

To get a rough estimate of your starting strength level, we recommend two tests. It is extremely important, however, that you recognize whether you have any limitations that would prevent you from performing these tests. For example, any joint pain, muscle soreness in the areas being tested, or other debilitations that could be problematic will prevent you from doing this. For example, a bad back should prevent you from performing the abdominal curl test.

The Upper-Body-Strength Test

Recommended by the American College of Sports Medicine, this test calls for men to assume a standard push-up position: head up, hands placed shoulder width apart, and back straight. One complete repetition of a push-up is counted only if your chest comes to within three to four inches of the floor.

For women, assume a modified push-up position with the knees flexed to ninety degrees and the ankles crossed in a kneeling position. Score the maximum number of push-ups you can perform without rest, then refer to table 13.4 for your age and gender norms.

Table 13.4. Age and Gender Norms on Push-up Test*

| Fitness Category | *Age* | | | | |
	20–29	*30–39*	*40–49*	*50–59*	*60+*
Men					
Advanced	≥48	≥40	≥31	≥26	≥24
	38–47	31–39	25–30	20–25	19–23
Intermed.	30–37	25–30	19–24	14–19	11–18
	23–29	18–24	12–18	10–13	7–10
Beginners	≤22	≤17	≤11	≤9	≤6
Women					
Advanced	≥37	≥32	≥25	≥21	≥15
	31–36	25–31	19–24	18–20	13–14
Intermed.	24–30	20–24	14–18	13–17	6–12
	18–23	12–19	7–13	7–12	3–5
Beginners	≤17	≤11	≤6	≤6	≤2

*≥ = greater than or equal to; ≤ = less than or equal to.

The Abdominal Muscular Endurance Test

This test involves a bent-leg curl-up. Lie down on a solid surface with your face up, bending the knees at approximately one hundred degrees. Feet should be flat on the floor and kept in place throughout the exam. Cross your arms over your chest, with each hand on the opposite shoulder. Keeping your head, neck, and shoulders in alignment, raise your head and shoulders up off the floor. The back of the head may not come in contact with the floor, and the hands cannot be moved from the shoulders. The upper body must come to a nearly upright position (i.e., touching your elbows to your thighs). The repetition should be performed in a two-step cadence ("up one-two, down one-two").

You should count as many repetitions as you are able to perform within this cadence. The test is completed if you cannot maintain the appropriate cadence or if you accomplished one hundred repetitions. Please don't cheat on this test, as you would only be cheating yourself! Now review table 13.5 for your gender to see your level of fitness.

Table 13.5. Muscular Strength and Endurance Scoring Table

	Abdominal Crunches	
	Men	*Women*
Advanced	100	100
	100	100
	100	
Intermediate	66	69
	45	49
	38	37
Beginner	33	34
	29	31
	26	27
	22	24
	18	21
	16	15

NUTRITION

The Where-Are-You-Starting-From Nutrition Questionnaire

Answer True or False for each question.
1. "Broiled," "steamed," and "baked" are low-fat terms.   _____
2. The most important nutrient you can consume is water.   _____
3. Fat is the major source of energy for the body.   _____

4. There is no ideal body weight or fat-to-muscle ratio for a particular individual. ____

5. You should eat a small meal at least two hours before facing a major performance test (a crucial meeting or negotiation, making an important presentation, giving a speech). ____

6. The words "lite" and "lean" on a label mean the food is healthier. ____

7. Most red meat is high in fat. ____

8. You should get most of your energy from carbohydrates. ____

9. The skin on a chicken breast is mostly fat and contains more than one hundred calories. ____

10. Raw vegetables are better for you than cooked vegetables. ____

11. Sugar can make you hyperactive or out of control. ____

12. You can become addicted to sugar. ____

13. Honey has the same effect on you as sugar. ____

14. You should wait until you're thirsty to take a drink of water. ____

15. A vitamin and mineral supplement is probably appropriate for active people of any age, regardless of their diet. ____

16. Active people need to consume fat. ____

17. The fried fish at most fast-food restaurants is higher in calories than hamburger. ____

18. The sugar found in fruit is nutritionally good for you, and you can have as much as you want. ____

19. Dietary cholesterol is found only in meats, dairy products, and other animal food products. ____

20. Protein and fat cause food to stay in the stomach longer. ____

21. Vitamins and minerals are major sources of energy. ____

Answers:

1. True	7. True	13. True	19. True
2. True	8. True	14. False	20. True
3. False	9. True	15. True	21. False
4. True	10. True	16. True	
5. True	11. False	17. True	
6. False	12. False	18. False	

Evaluating Your Score

18 or more correct—You possess excellent nutritional knowledge, but are you committed to using this knowledge in your daily life?

15 to 17 correct—You're doing okay, but make sure you keep your commitment up.

14 or fewer correct—You need to improve your nutritional knowledge. Improving your diet is difficult if you're not more aware of your nutritional needs.

TIME MANAGEMENT

Corporate Athletes often tell us they simply don't have time to apply the Corporate Athlete program to their particular life. They say they're swamped, too busy and inundated, but all they need is a simple plan for constructing how they will live their day (and other days for the rest of their lives). The following time management worksheet has helped many people such as yourself identify how to better spend the day and accomplish what they must in the time available to them.

Most people don't realize what brings them passion. But if you take a look at what you do on a daily—and hourly—basis and then compare that with what you say are your values and beliefs, a ray of reality will shine in. In working with clients, we set up a dichotomy between what you tell us your values are, and what your behavior tells us they really are. If they're not the same, either you don't know what your values and beliefs are and you are just kind of going off in a random direction, or you do, and you are just not living by them. Which one is it? We don't make a judgment as to good or bad.

If one of your deepest values involves your family, specifically a child, we will ask you to describe special moments with that child. "I remember the first time she called my name, the first time she pedaled a bike, her first day of school. . . ." Emotion just drips off of those examples. So whatever changes we help you make in your schedule will tie back to those things. What are you doing to generate the next wave of special moments?

Use your answers to this to determine where you are successful or not successful at reaching your values. The chart could be used for travel days. It could also be used for normal days—whatever that means for you. Your goal is to identify what specifically must be done to connect you *and* your life to what is important to you.

Step 1. Values: What's important to you?

Many Corporate Athletes thrive on fear in a very chaotic workplace. If fear is your modus operandi, failure is not far behind. And losing yourself and your values are far worse than losing the bid, the deal, or the job. Values are critical to your success, both in this program and in life.

Faith, children, spouse, parents, success, money, friends, power, exercise, humor, rest . . . the list goes on. There are no right or wrong answers and whatever you write down should be *your* truth. Also, you may have only three or four items that come to mind, or you could have fifty, but make the list natural, don't force it, and let it reflect you.

1. _____

2. _____

3. _____

4. _____

5. _____

6. _____

7. _____

8. _____

9. _____

10. _____

Step 2. Write down the exact time constraints on you.

For example, list when you *must* be at work, when you *can* leave work, when the kids *must* get up to get ready for school, when you *must* go to sleep, when you *must* get up, etc.

4:00 A.M. _____

4:30 A.M. _____

5:00 A.M. _____

5:30 A.M. _____

6:00 A.M. _____

6:30 A.M. _____

7:00 A.M. _____

7:30 A.M. _____

8:00 A.M. _____

8:30 A.M. _____

9:00 A.M. _____

9:30 A.M. _____

10:00 A.M. _____

10:30 A.M. _____

11:00 A.M. _____

11:30 A.M. _____

12:00 noon _____

12:30 P.M. _____

1:00 P.M. _____

1:30 P.M. _____

2:00 P.M. _____

2:30 P.M. _____

3:00 P.M. _____

3:30 P.M. _____

4:00 P.M. _____

4:30 P.M. _____

5:00 P.M. _____

5:30 P.M. _____

6:00 P.M. _____

6:30 P.M. _____

7:00 P.M. _____

7:30 P.M. _____

8:00 P.M. _____

8:30 P.M. _____

9:00 P.M. _____

9:30 P.M. _____

10:00 P.M. _____

10:30 P.M. _____

11:00 P.M. _____

11:30 P.M. _____

12:00 midnight _____

12:30 A.M. _____

1:00 A.M. _____

1:30 A.M. _____

2:00 A.M. _____

2:30 A.M. _____

3:00 A.M. _____

3:30 A.M. _____

Step 3. Are you getting any values met during your day now?

If so, write that down. Is there *any* flexibility in your schedule? If so, write that down. For example, perhaps you read to your children each night at 8:30 P.M. to connect with them.

Step 4. Review your value list and place a check by any value that is already met during your day.

For example, you always connect with your spouse at 7:30 P.M., right after dinner. If the time when that value is met is not down, place it in the schedule. Maybe you always get time alone right after dinner to read a chapter in a great book, or you awake at 5:30 A.M. before anyone else in the house so you can squeeze in your exercise time.

Step 5. Is there anywhere you can expand your day?

For example, can you go to bed later and get up a half hour earlier to have quiet time to put your faith into action, to meditate, or to exercise? If so, consider this in your schedule.

Step 6. Update.

Your life and the demands upon it are fluid. Constantly revisit your value system and your schedule. If you are having a child, your value system will likely change. If you are changing priorities at your job, your time constraints will change.

Corporate Athlete Sample Goals

Before you start your 21-day program in chapter 15, identify your mental, emotional, physical, and spiritual goals. Here are a few examples to get you started:

- I want to be a better team player.
- I want more energy than I've ever had before.
- I want as much energy at the end of the day as when I started my day.
- I want to be able to *connect* with my clients and develop better relationships with them.
- I want to learn to be more resilient in how I handle stressors at the office.
- I want to find time in my day to satisfy my spiritual needs.
- I want to improve the way I speak in public, both formally and informally.
- I want to become a better user of my computer and the Internet.
- I want to improve my cold-calling skills.
- I want to be a better member of my family.
- I want to be a great friend.
- I want to get on an exercise regimen and stick to it.
- I want to lose ten pounds of fat but gain four pounds of muscle (lean body mass) so my percent of body fat will change markedly but my weight may not change much.
- I want to learn to eat strategically. At least three meals per day plus two strategic snacks will be how I live my life.
- I want to cut my coffee intake to two cups per day.
- I want to drink at least eight glasses of water per day.
- I want to cut my alcohol intake down to no more than one drink per day.

Your Corporate Athlete Goals

1. _____

2. _____

3. _____

4. _____

5. _____

6. _____

7. _____

8. _____

9. _____

10. _____

14

Before You Go into Training . . .

Training is everything. The peach was once a bitter almond;
cauliflower is nothing but cabbage with a college education.
—MARK TWAIN

CORPORATE ATHLETE PRINCIPLE 14:

What separates a *great* Corporate Athlete from a good
Corporate Athlete? Often it is patience, persistence,
and perfect practice—the four P's.

Practice and hard work are crucial in sports and in your business life, but
practice alone will not make you perfect. Practice will only make it permanent. For example, if you "practice" skipping breakfast or scarfing
your lunch or fitting in time for exercise or fitting in time for family, those
practices will make those situations permanent. If you want to reach your
dreams for your life, productivity, health, and happiness, you must *think,*
act, and *train* like a corporate Olympian. You must become *emotionally*
connected to what you want.

Training Made the Difference

When veteran NFL quarterback Jim Harbaugh came to our company in
1994, many people thought he was washed up in professional football.
    After seven years with the Chicago Bears, he was literally booed out
of town by the team's fans. "Imagine anything you have heard and then
quadruple it," he acknowledges, "and that's what I heard every time my
name was called over the loud speaker and for every incomplete pass. It
was pretty brutal. My confidence was kind of shot." The Indianapolis Colts
picked Harbaugh up as a free agent for the '94 season, during which he
started ten games, was benched for four, and then returned for the final
two. His performance left a great deal to be desired.
    Harbaugh wasn't looking for a personal trainer at the time, but he

174

wasn't ready to leave the game yet, either. He had heard about my partner Pat Etcheberry's work as a fitness trainer for world-class athletes and figured he had nothing to lose. During the entire off-season between 1994 and '95, Harbaugh, then thirty-one years old, devoted himself to Pat's tutelage. The results were astounding.

"The next season, I had an amazing year, my best year," Harbaugh says. In 1995 he was the offensive player of the year, led the NFL in quarterback ratings, went to the Pro Bowl, was the Comeback Player of the Year, and led his team to the NFC championship game. He also jumped from making $800,000 a year to a four-year, $15 million deal.

What changed? Well, Harbaugh was always known as a guy who worked hard, exercised hard, and was a brutally tough competitor. But despite his best efforts, he had never trained in a job-specific manner before. During the football season he did the same conditioning routines as the fifty other guys on the team—whether they were running backs, kickers, or defensive ends. In the off-season he regularly played racquetball and basketball and lifted weights.

Pat threw it all out and started Harbaugh down a different, highly individualized path. A quarterback performs markedly different tasks physically than an offensive lineman, just as a senior vice president of merchandising mentally does different tasks than a vice president of human resources. What Harbaugh did need was a focus on four sport-specific skills: speed, explosion, quickness, and agility.

Harbaugh is one of a generation of mature quarterbacks who have stayed in the game for twelve years, long after the average player has hung up his cleats. In the 1998 season, for example, the star quarterbacks were not rookie phenoms but grown men in their mid- to late-thirties with names such as Elway, Testaverde, Flutie, Chandler, and even fortysomething Steve DeBerg.

"When you get older, you need that one-on-one of a personal trainer because you don't always have the energy you had as a twenty-one-year-old," Harbaugh says. And isn't it true of Corporate Athletes as well? "Meanwhile, you are playing against twenty-one-, twenty-two- and twenty-three-year-old guys, because the average pro career is like three and a half years. I have to get to bed before 11:00 P.M., I have to eat right, I have to get sleep. You can't be going out partying and expect to wake up and be working in the sand pits in the morning."

Getting Started

The body is made of muscle, bone, and tendons, and it is made to move. The body is not designed to be a gel. We *must* move. How much movement is a minimum amount for you? First of all, don't get caught up in the scenario that if you are on your feet all day (e.g., a counter manager or a lawyer) you are getting exercise. All you are getting are sore joints. You must devote three hours and fifteen minutes a week to your exercise program. For you to get basic health benefits, that's a minimum time commitment. That would take care of your abdominal work, your aerobic and interval time, your strengthening and flexibility.

Do small things that may help you make the process work for you. For instance, take a phrase from the world of computers and try multitasking:

- When you come home, if you hate doing sit-ups, if you hate stretching, do them while you watch the news or a sitcom rerun.
- Include your family in walks. Don't just go out by yourself, because in families who tend to get interested in fitness together, each of the individual members tends to carry on with it. Combine time-saving methods with methods of reconnecting with your family.
- Incorporate your exercise periods into the day as a means of having ritualized time to yourself, where this is *your sacred time* that no one can violate.

At the same time, don't expect too much too soon. People have the tendency to say, "Hey, it took me twenty-five years to get out of shape, but I am going to get back in shape in two months (or even sooner)." Isn't it obvious what is wrong with that equation? Give yourself time.

We see many businesswomen at LGE who never exercised because there weren't sports available to them in high school when they were growing up. The difference in attitudes toward exercise and the difference in self-assurance between them and younger women is striking. We get a tremendous sense of satisfaction in people who are taking the first step in their journey and seeing how they develop and blossom.

If a beginner exercises three times a week, at proper intensity and duration, that person will see about a 25 percent increase in his or her functional capacity, strength, or aerobic fitness over a three-month period, and maybe another 15 to 20 percent over the next three months.

Many people begin their exercise program by doing too much, too fast, too soon. They say, "Back in college, I used to get out and run, I used to play basketball," or "I used to lift this much weight," and then they go out and try to do too much. They get so sore the next day that they can't get out of bed, or they get hurt. You have to start slowly and move through the program.

Therefore, regardless of where you are in your fitness level, it may be smart to initiate your new program with a beginner phase. This will introduce you to the frequency of training, the duration and intensity of each training session.

My clients often feel a little soreness after beginning an exercise program. A little soreness is healthy; excruciating pain is not. I explain the healthy soreness this way: It's your body thanking you for getting started!

I will introduce you to three different 21-day programs, the first being for an absolutely sedentary beginner who has not exercised much at all; the second for an intermediate exerciser, someone whose level of fitness is in the medium or average range; and finally a level of training that is designed for those in excellent fitness condition.

Adaptations in aerobic fitness should occur fairly rapidly, and significant improvements will be seen within several weeks. Studies show vast improvements in aerobic capacity following ten weeks of regular aerobic training. Remember: *More is not necessarily better.* So don't drive yourself into the ground. Be smart about your training.

As you exercise, consider the intensity of how hard you work out. For this reason we refer to the target training zone. A beginner should always start with a low target heart rate zone after obtaining medical approval to exercise.

Strengthen Your Abdominals

A football player who had a history of back problems went down with a leg injury during a Green Bay Packers/San Francisco 49ers game. "And when the back goes, it all goes," said TV announcer John Madden. "The legs, the arms, everything, because everything is so integrally connected to the back."

That is true not only for a football player, but for the Corporate Athlete as well. If your back is killing you and you are in a very important meeting, it is very hard to stay focused on what you are trying to think about. That, in turn, leads to mental errors. The no. 1 cause of low back pain is weak abdominal muscles. And if your back is hurting you, you may stay home a couple of days in a year that you otherwise would be at work. A high predominance of absenteeism occurs due to low back pain.

We see an awful lot of people with back pain. It makes many of them physically dysfunctional. So if we get people in that kind of shape, certainly we want to start them on something gentle. Stretching hamstrings and strengthening abdominals are the best means of ensuring that they will be structurally symmetrical enough to withstand the rigors of taking it to the next step, which is doing treadmill walking or bike riding or whatever it may be. Abdominal strength is critical to maintaining postural integrity.

Many Corporate Athletes have never done abdominal work, so let's start with the basics. (If possible, have someone read the following instructions aloud while you get in position to exercise.)

First, find a firm surface. You can have a small, thin pad underneath you, but you should really have tremendous support for the back. Don't do this in bed, for example. A bed collapses too much, and it's kind of funny to try to do abdominal curls in bed anyway.

Exercise Instructions

Get on a firm surface, lying flat on your back. Keep your feet flat on the floor, and bend your knees so that they're at about a one-hundred-degree angle. Now cross your arms over your chest with your hands on your shoulders. Your right hand should be on your left shoulder, your left hand on your right shoulder. Identify something on the ceiling, maybe the intersection of how the ceiling tiles fit, or a spot on the ceiling—something straight above your head. Keep your eyes on that spot.

Control your neck movements and keep your eyes fixed on the spot you choose. Keep your head, neck, and trunk in a straight alignment. Now curl your shoulders toward your pelvis. Don't lift your trunk off the floor. You're going to curl your rib cage and shoulders toward your pelvis. You only need to come off the floor so that your shoulder blades are no longer touching the floor. That's about the middle of your trunk. You don't need to go any farther than that because if you do, you will kick in the hip flexors and they will facilitate your movement upward. If you only move as much as I'm explaining right now—in other words, curling up so your shoulder blades are off the floor—you'll isolate the abdominal muscles.

If you want to work on the muscles on the side of the abdomen—the oblique muscles—rotate a little to the right, which will bring the left shoulder blade just a hair higher off the floor. Then straighten up and go back down. On the next curl, rotate to the left.

How fast should you do this? Count "one thousand one, one thousand two," and your shoulder blades should be off the floor. And then down—"one thousand one, one thousand two," and your shoulders should be back on the floor. You're not trying to set a world land speed record, *boom-boom, one-two-three-four-five*. It's "one thousand one, one thousand two, I'm up; one thousand one, one thousand two, I'm down." Once you get the timing, you won't need to count the thousand. It'll be "up one-two, down one-two; up one-two, down one-two."

If you've already been doing abdominal work, or once you've done the beginner abdominal position for a month or two, here's the way to set up: Again, you'll want to be on a firm surface, a thin mat or the floor. Put your hands behind your head. Your hands will not pull your head forward. Your hands will only support your head, elbows out to the side.

Locate a spot on the ceiling again, keeping your eyes fixed on it. Don't bend your head or flex at the neck. Do not curl your neck forward. Your head, neck, and trunk should be aligned. Now repeat the instructions for beginners. Curl your shoulders and rib cage toward your pelvis until your shoulder blades are off the ground.

What makes this the advanced form? Because what you've done by raising your arms up around your head, elbows out to the side, is increase the leverage, and that forces your abdomen and your abdominal muscles to work harder. You can work on the oblique muscles or the muscles on the sides by rotating a little on the way up. But make sure you straighten out and keep your eyes on the spot on the ceiling so you don't pull or strain your neck. The role of the hands is supporting the head. You should not feel stress in the neck if you do these exercises properly.

Your eventual goal is one hundred per day. Because the abdominal muscles consist of four groups of muscles, the long muscles of the abdomen, the transverse muscles, and the obliques only need about twelve hours of recovery before you can stress them again. It's probably the only group of muscles in the body that doesn't require at least forty-eight to seventy-two hours of rest. So you can do abdominal work every day. Now, if you haven't done any abdominal work, don't do a hundred tonight. You will be very sore tomorrow.

Using the technique that is most appropriate for you, whether you're a beginner or advanced, do one set of twenty-five abdominal curls per day for seven days. The second week, do *two* sets of twenty-five. You do not need to do these together. You could do one set in the morning and one in the afternoon or evening. By the third week, do three sets of twenty-five. You'll gradually increase your capability to expose yourself to more stress. By the fourth week you can do either four sets of twenty-five at different times throughout the day or you can do two sets of fifty, but you're able to do one hundred abdominal curls per day after just three weeks of exercise. If you do it as described above, you should reach one hundred abdominals per day without too much force or pain. Remember, while pain is a signal to stop, discomfort is very healthy.

You may be interested in why we put abdominal conditioning ahead of the heart and the lungs, even though cardiovascular disease is the no. 1 killer in the United States. In all the years that we have been training Corporate Athletes, we have found that if we send you out doing aerobic conditioning right off the bat you'll do it, you'll be religious about it. But within four weeks, a majority of people will stop because they will experience lower back pain. And what's the no. 1 cause of lower back pain? Weak abdominal muscles. So our approach is that the abdomen is the core of the body. Strengthen the abdominal muscles before you do anything else. Strong abdominal muscles support the back and minimize the onset of lower back pain. Abdominal conditioning is crucial to your being a great Corporate Athlete and performing at your best.

Go for Cardiorespiratory Fitness

Alternating your heart rate response during exercise is what interval training is all about: The heart rate goes up during the intense phase and then is taught to recover during the active recovery phase. Recovery during the interval training for your aerobic program does not involve total rest but a form of active rest.

Most newer computerized exercise machines have interval training programs that will increase speeds and/or resistance to increase the intensity and then give you a trough of active rest that teaches the heart a recovery mechanism.

Interval Exercise Program and Instruction for *Beginners*

Warm up for at least five minutes. Begin the interval program by walking at a moderate speed for a hundred yards, followed by a slow walk of a hundred yards, followed by a brisk walk of a hundred yards, followed by a slow walk of a hundred yards, again followed by a moderate walk of a hundred yards, and continue this: slow, brisk, slow, brisk, and so on. Be cautious and listen to your body as you exercise. After about fifteen minutes (twenty minutes total), cool down with a slow walk for five minutes.

Interval Exercise Program and Instruction for *Intermediate* Exercisers

Following a five-minute warm-up where you have broken a sweat, you can begin by doing a fast jog of a hundred yards, followed by a brisk walk of a hundred yards, again followed by a fast jog of a hundred yards, again followed by a brisk walk of a hundred yards, then a sprint of a hundred yards, followed by a slow jog at a hundred yards, followed by a sprint of a hundred yards, followed by a brisk a walk of a hundred yards, followed by a sprint of a hundred yards, followed by a jog of a hundred yards. After fifteen minutes (twenty minutes total), cool down for five minutes with a moderately paced walk down to a slow walk by the end.

Interval Exercise Program and Instruction for *Advanced* Exercisers

After your warm-up, you can vary the intervals as much as you like. There is no set rule for how you do them. You could do intervals as described previously, or you could even train using intervals on a high-school track, where you run a 440-yard dash (one loop around the track) as fast as you can, then jog the second, and alternate accordingly. The intervals are basically up to you; just don't do intervals all the time. And be sure that when you're finished with the intervals, you cool down for at least five minutes.

Regardless of your skill level, if you're looking for a sport that provides all the benefits of interval training, tennis is one of the best. When you are stressed as you play a point in tennis, your heart rate goes up. You then have twenty to thirty seconds between points when your heart rate will come down. The U.S. Tennis Association has programs in your community. Check them out at www.usatennis.com to get information about your community tennis association.

The Warm-up

Your body's tissues are not soft and pliable; they're tight and rigid. Heating your body softens and makes the tissues more flexible. Adequate warm-up is vital for everyone before exercise, but especially so for the poorly conditioned or for those who are older. By getting your body ready for the more strenuous exercise to come, the warm-up greatly reduces the chances of injury.

What you are trying to do is very gradually and progressively get your heart to beat a little faster, your lungs to bring in more air and more oxygen. Warming up your bloodflow and muscles improves the contraction process. You are trying to very gradually alleviate the stress on your cardiovascular system rather than just getting right into exercise.

Warm-up Instruction. Break a sweat by walking briskly, cycling, or running in place. Once you've started sweating, you should do mild stretching, going through your complete stretch routine so your body will be as flexible as possible for your heavy exercise session.

A warm-up period could be five to ten minutes long and involve many different forms of activity. Since it takes more force to injure a warm muscle than a cold muscle, the activities you choose are important during your warm-up. Include low-intensity exercises such as light calisthenics (jumping jacks, jogging, or jumping rope), bicycling, or using a step machine. The main goal is to break a sweat. Sweating indicates that your body is warmed and ready for at least the initial parts of your exercise program.

The Cool-down

The last segment of an aerobic training session is the cool-down.

Once exercise is completed, your goal is to reduce the strain on the heart and reduce the risk of muscle and tendon injury. Abruptly stopping your exercise program causes blood to pool in the areas of the body where effort occurred, minimizing the return of blood to the heart. Don't just go from an immediate interval *boom-boom-boom-boom* exercise program to an abrupt halt. This could bring about dizziness or faintness. The heart won't keep up with the body's need, and it could create a new problem.

You must cool down slowly. The cool-down involves low-intensity activity as previously described, gradually bringing your bodily processes (heart rate, internal body temperature, etc.) toward the normal range for you. *Cool-down Instruction.* Take three to five minutes to cool down, letting your heart rate come down naturally, giving your body recovery. Cool down by walking slowly, jogging if you've been running fast, bringing your heart rate down gradually.

Increase Your Muscle Strength and Conditioning

How do you strength-train? Technique is of the utmost importance. If you're going to join a club and use machines and free weights, I definitely recommend that you see a personal trainer. Get on your own personal program, but remember that the technique you learn in lifting weights and moving resistance is key to the benefits and the success you will have in your strength-training program.

At LGE, we emphasize technique. For example, everybody understands the bicep muscle of the arm. When your palms are facing forward, your elbows and upper arms held at the side, and you bring your palm up toward your head (flexing at the elbow), you are stressing the bicep muscle. When you use an exercise band, you will stress the muscle slowly and then allow the muscle to slowly return to its original length by extending the arm. Do this gradually as well. Again, you're not trying to set a world record for speed. Slow the contraction and then slow as you lengthen it as well. These two types of contraction, one shortening the muscle, one lengthening the muscle, are important to getting the full benefits of strength training.

Any resistance program needs to be closely monitored at its outset. Otherwise it is easy to overtrain and become quite sore. Perform a total body-strength training program. Work on all the muscle groups that go across joints (e.g., the quadriceps and hamstring muscles that are on the front and back sides of the thigh, respectively, and across the knee and hip). A good strength training session usually involves about a thirty- to forty-five-minute workout three days during the week on alternating days. Most muscles require forty-eight hours of recovery to receive the full benefit of resistance training.

Exercise Instruction

Most individuals will want to work out at about 75 to 80 percent of their maximum ability for each muscle group. This means that if you can bench-press one hundred pounds, your training level would be at seventy-five to eighty pounds. The goal would be to perform three sets of eight to ten repetitions with approximately thirty seconds to one minute between sets. With practice you will comfortably be able to increase to ten to twelve repetitions at this prescribed intensity level, and you can increase the weight slightly.

Within three months—it does take ninety days to change a behavior, after all—most people will be gaining strength at a pretty good pace, exercising three times a week, doing three sets of each exercise.

Always Remember Flexibility

Flexibility training reduces the risk of injuries in your muscles, in your joints, especially when you are getting involved in an exercise program such as this one. You will be stressing muscles and joints in a way that you may not be used to, and if you hurt them or injure them, then you will be out again.

Always stretch both sides of your body. If you play a unilateral sport like tennis, for example, and you're a right-handed player, you still want to stretch the left side of your body. Whether you're playing soccer or basketball during your lunch hour, or going out for a round of golf this afternoon, always stretch both sides of the body. But remember this. Flexibility may be the most important area for you to be an active person throughout the rest of your life. The reason why people get injured is more related to a lack of flexibility and a lack of conditioning than to poor muscle strength or poor aerobic capacity. So flexibility training is absolutely essential to you living an active, fulfilling life as a true Corporate Athlete.

After warming up, and at the end of your exercise program, you should perform a total body flexibility routine. Stretch each major body part about its primary joint (e.g., the upper arm about the shoulder, the thigh about the hip, the calf about the ankle and knee, the back, and the abdominals). Remember: *No pain, no gain* has no place in a Corporate Athlete's exercise routine. Hold each stretch for twenty to thirty seconds, rest, and repeat.

Should I Hire a Personal Trainer?

A personal trainer is often necessary for motivation, leadership, and guidance. You could use the services of a trainer if you realize that you just don't have the body of knowledge to train yourself or you don't understand the reference books that lead some people through an exercise program.

You want someone who can take you through the exact techniques, someone who consistently researches and upgrades and experiments with new techniques in making exercise fresh, fun, and effective. But make sure it's a person who is certified, trained professionally to do these techniques the right way. Finally, find someone who is used to working with Corporate Athletes and not someone who expects you to become a Mr. or Ms. America type or an NFL middle linebacker.

We believe that American College of Sports Medicine, National Strength and Conditioning Association, and American Council on Exercise credentials probably are the best. This is not to discredit other certifying agencies, but these three reflect a high degree of understanding of the body. People who are well rounded in various strength-building techniques and certification, such as yoga instructors, are certainly valid in their specific fields as standard personal trainers. Look for someone who gives you the information you need to make exercise worthwhile, safe, and fun.

Being held accountable is a big part of staying with the Corporate Athlete program. Having an obligation to show up and, certainly, making a financial commitment are pretty important factors in making people stay on track. That's why personal trainers can be so beneficial.

Instead of hiring a personal trainer, some people arrange to exercise with a friend or a coworker. A good partner is good because it keeps you going, but a bad one can really hurt you because you have to keep yourself motivated, and then you have to motivate the other person, so it has to be somebody with whom you click.

15

The 21-Day Program

It's supposed to be hard! If it wasn't hard,
everybody would do it!
—JIMMY DUGAN, MANAGER, ROCKFORD PEACHES

CORPORATE ATHLETE PRINCIPLE 15:

Don't exercise to get healthier. Exercise to perform at higher levels at work and with your family.

You'll get healthier, but exercise because it will make you the best Corporate Athlete you could possibly become. The mind and the body truly are one.

The following program includes twenty-one-day instructions for beginner, intermediate, and advanced exercisers as you evaluated yourself in chapter 13 (or as a personal trainer evaluated you).

Make sure that you warm up before beginning any exercise program, and be sure to cool down after each workout.

This training log arms you with ammunition against the temptation to quit the program or revert to old methods. It shows how to reward yourself during your self-evaluation and how to break down bad habits within twenty-one days.

Instructions for Completing
the Corporate Athlete Training Log

Give yourself a "+" on your daily log for each of the following you completed:

____ I used very little (less than 1 teaspoon) or no butter/margarine today.

185

_____ I added only minimal amounts or no salt to my food today.

_____ I had either no alcohol today or I had only one drink. (One drink = one 12-oz. beer or one 4-oz. glass of wine.)

_____ I ate strategically today to enable myself to perform at high levels.

_____ I grazed all day long by eating at least five small meals.

_____ I had the proper amount of total fat intake.

_____ The fat I did consume was mostly monounsaturated (e.g., olive oil)

_____ Any animal protein I consumed was low in fat (chicken with no skin, etc.)

_____ I consumed an adequate amount of fiber. (A well-balanced diet containing fruits, vegetables and grains usually provides adequate fiber.)

_____ My total cholesterol consumption was no more than moderate or less. (Moderate cholesterol is 290 mg. One egg contains 270 mg of cholesterol.)

_____ I drank at least eight glasses (8 oz. each) of water. (One glass of fresh juice may be substituted for one glass of water.)

_____ I followed the recommended plan of 55 percent carbohydrates, 25 percent protein, and 20 percent fat.

_____ I minimized my intake of simple sugars (candy, chocolate, cakes).

_____ I took a multivitamin, multimineral supplement.

_____ I said "no" to the desire for desserts.

_____ I ate nothing that was fried or deep-fat fried.

_____ I ate no or very little (less than one teaspoon) mayonnaise or salad dressing—even if it was low-fat or fat-free.

_____ I consumed no doughnuts, Danish pastry, or croissants.

_____ I limited my intake of caffeine to not more than two small cups of coffee; three small cups of tea; or one can of soda.

_____ I minimized my intake of soft drinks today (no more than 12 oz).

_____ I ate no or no more than 4 oz. of red meat.

_____ I ate at least three servings of green, leafy vegetables.

_____ I never felt thirsty.

_____ I read at least one nutrition label in detail

_____ I ate a healthy breakfast.

_____ I skipped no meals.

_____ I experienced true enjoyment when eating.

_____ I feel that I ate in a healthy manner.

_____ I perceived that I was eating intelligently throughout the day.

_____ I took the time to eat and I took my time when eating.

_____ I did not feel food-deprived.

_____ I felt good about myself and my relationship with food.

_____ I never felt I was on a diet.

_____ I consumed at least two servings of fruit.

_____ My eating habits did not affect my quality of sleep.
_____ I performed my exercise routines today.
_____ I continued my search for spiritual improvement today.
_____ I felt energized today.

Your daily goal is 30 points.
Add your daily scores and log your weekly total for reference in following weeks.
Weekly goal: 210 points.
Twenty-one-day goal: 630 points.

DAY 1

Exercise

	Abdominal	Aerobic Training		Strength		Flexibility
	Level	Time	Type	% Max.	Time	Time
Beginner	25	10 min.	Steady	60	20 min.	5 min.
Intermediate	2×25	20 min.	Steady	70	20 min.	10 min.
Advanced	4×25	30 min.	Steady	80	30 min.	10 min.

Nutrition

Breakfast

Protein source _____

Carbohydrate source _____

Fat source _____

Fluid _____

Breakfast idea: Egg Beaters omelette with low-fat cheese, or another suggestion from pages 258–59.

Strategic Morning Snack

Protein source _____

Carbohydrate source _____

Fat source _____

Fluid _____

Nut breads with low-fat cream cheese, or another suggestion from pages 262–63.

Lunch

Protein source _____

Carbohydrate source _____

Fat source _____

Fluid _____

Lunch idea: Skim or low-fat milk, fruit juice, or fresh fruit can be included with any of these selections, or another suggestion from pages 259–60.

Strategic Afternoon Snack

Protein source _____

Carbohydrate source _____

Fat source _____

Fluid _____

Treasure logs: roll thin meat slice with low-fat cheese or low-fat cheese spread, or another suggestion from pages 262–63.

Dinner

Protein source _____

Carbohydrate source _____

Fat source _____

Fluid _____

Dinner idea: Whole wheat spaghetti with low-fat tomato sauce, or another suggestion from pages 260–62.

Evening Snack

Carbohydrate source _____

Fat source _____

Fluid _____

Fruits, vegetables, or yogurt; minimal protein.
(Minimize protein in your evening snack to avoid poor sleep patterns.)

Nutrition/Exercise/Sleep

Nutrition

Five or more meals   Yes____ No____

Small meals   Yes____ No____

Healthy meals   Yes____ No____

Exercise

No. of abdominals _____

Cardiovascular training _____ Time _____

No. of recovery waves _____ Max. HR _____

Interval _____ Steady state _____

Strength time _____ Stretching time _____

Total exercise time today _____

Sleep

Time to bed _____ Time up _____

Nap: Yes _____ No _____

Total sleep time including nap _____

Train recovery:

    Recovery every 90 minutes: Yes _____ No _____

Emotional response to crisis du jour:

    High   Medium   Low

Achieved stress/recovery balance today:

    High   Medium   Low

Level of productivity today:

    High   Medium   Low

Level of overall energy rating today:

    High   Medium   Low

Things accomplished: Performance

_____

_____

_____

_____

Things accomplished: Health

_____

_____

_____

_____

Things accomplished: Happiness

_____

_____

_____

_____

DAY 2

Exercise

	Abdominal	Aerobic Training		Strength		Flexibility
	Level	Time	Type	% Max.	Time	Time
Beginner	25	10 min.	Steady	Rest	Rest	5 min.
Intermediate	2×25	20 min.	Steady	Rest	Rest	10 min.
Advanced	4×25	20 min.	Steady	Rest	Rest	10 min.

Nutrition

Breakfast

Protein source _____

Carbohydrate source _____

Fat source _____

Fluid _____

Breakfast idea: Egg white omelette with tomato and mushrooms, or another suggestion from pages 258–59.

Strategic Morning Snack

Protein source _____

Carbohydrate source _____

Fat source _____

Fluid _____

Peanut butter crackers with 1 percent or skim milk, or another suggestion from pages 262–63.

Lunch

Protein source _____

Carbohydrate source _____

Fat source _____

Fluid _____

Lunch idea: Grilled low-fat cheese and tomato on whole wheat, or another suggestion from pages 259–60.

Strategic Afternoon Snack

Protein source _____

Carbohydrate source _____

Fat source _____

Fluid _____

Low-fat granola or crunchy mix: unsugared cereal (Cheerios, Chex, etc.) mixed with raisins, peanuts, sunflower seeds, etc., or another suggestion from pages 262–63.

Dinner

Protein source _____

Carbohydrate source _____

Fat source _____

Fluid _____

Dinner idea: Beef vegetable stew and low-fat biscuits, or another suggestion from pages 260–62.

Evening Snack

Carbohydrate source _____

Fat source _____

Fluid _____

Fruits, vegetables, or yogurt; minimal protein.

Nutrition/Exercise/Sleep

Nutrition

Five or more meals   Yes_____ No_____

Small meals   Yes_____ No_____

Healthy meals   Yes_____ No_____

Exercise

No. of abdominals _____

Cardiovascular training _____ Time _____

No. of recovery waves _____ Max. HR _____

Interval _____ Steady state _____

Strength time _____ Stretching time _____

Total exercise time today _____

Sleep

Time to bed _____ Time up _____

Nap: Yes _____ No _____

Total sleep time including nap _____

Train recovery:

    Recovery every 90 minutes: Yes _____ No _____

Emotional response to crisis du jour:

      High   Medium   Low

Achieved stress/recovery balance today:

      High   Medium   Low

Level of productivity today:

      High   Medium   Low

Level of overall energy rating today:

      High   Medium   Low

Things accomplished: Performance

_____

_____

_____

_____

Things accomplished: Health

_____

_____

_____

_____

Things accomplished: Happiness

_____

_____

_____

_____

DAY 3

Exercise

	Abdominal	Aerobic Training		Strength		Flexibility
	Level	Time	Type	% Max.	Time	Time
Beginner	25	10 min.	Steady	60	20 min.	5 min.
Intermediate	2×25	20 min.	Steady	70	20 min.	10 min.
Advanced	4×25	35 min.	Interval	70–85	30 min.	10 min.

Nutrition

Breakfast

Protein source _____

Carbohydrate source _____

Fat source _____

Fluid _____

Breakfast idea: Cold, healthy cereal (e.g., Total, Wheat Chex, Cheerios, etc.) with low-fat milk, or another suggestion from pages 258–59.

Strategic Morning Snack

Protein source _____

Carbohydrate source _____

Fat source _____

Fluid _____

Cornbread and tomato juice, or another suggestion from pages 262–63.

Lunch

Protein source _____

Carbohydrate source _____

Fat source _____

Fluid _____

Lunch idea: Chef's salad: lettuce with hard-boiled egg whites, sliced deli cuts (e.g., cheese, turkey, and tomatoes) with low-fat dressing on the side, or another suggestion from pages 259–60.

Strategic Afternoon Snack

Protein source _____

Carbohydrate source _____

Fat source _____

Fluid _____

Tuna fish: on crackers, in sandwiches, or another suggestion from pages 262–63.

Dinner

Protein source _____

Carbohydrate source _____

Fat source _____

Fluid _____

Dinner idea: Low-fat chicken enchiladas with low-fat refried beans and salad, or another suggestion from pages 260–62.

Evening Snack

Carbohydrate source _____

Fat source _____

Fluid _____

Fruits, vegetables, or yogurt; minimal protein.

Nutrition/Exercise/Sleep

Nutrition

Five or more meals   Yes_____ No_____

Small meals   Yes_____ No_____

Healthy meals   Yes_____ No_____

Exercise

No. of abdominals _____

Cardiovascular training _____ Time _____

No. of recovery waves _____ Max. HR _____

Interval _____ Steady state _____

Strength time _____ Stretching time _____

Total exercise time today _____

Sleep

Time to bed _____ Time up _____

Nap: Yes _____ No _____

Total sleep time including nap _____

Train recovery:

       Recovery every 90 minutes: Yes _____ No _____

Emotional response to crisis du jour:

       High   Medium   Low

Achieved stress/recovery balance today:

       High   Medium   Low

Level of productivity today:

       High   Medium   Low

Level of overall energy rating today:

       High   Medium   Low

Things accomplished: Performance

_____

_____

_____

_____

Things accomplished: Health

_____

_____

_____

_____

Things accomplished: Happiness

_____

_____

_____

_____

DAY 4

Exercise

	Abdominal	Aerobic Training		Strength		Flexibility
	Level	Time	Type	% Max.	Time	Time
Beginner	25	10 min.	Steady	Rest	Rest	5 min.
Intermediate	2×25	20 min.	Steady	Rest	Rest	10 min.
Advanced	4×25	20 min.	Steady	Rest	Rest	10 min.

Nutrition

Breakfast

Protein source _____

Carbohydrate source _____

Fat source _____

Fluid _____

Breakfast idea: Bran cereal with berries with low-fat milk, or another suggestion from pages 258–59.

Strategic Morning Snack

Protein source _____

Carbohydrate source _____

Fat source _____

Fluid _____

Celery sticks or cucumber boats stuffed with cottage cheese, cheese spread, tuna salad, or egg salad (all low-fat), or another suggestion from pages 262–63.

Lunch

Protein source _____

Carbohydrate source _____

Fat source _____

Fluid _____

Lunch idea: Tuna fish salad (tuna canned in spring water with low-fat mayonnaise) sandwich on whole wheat bread, or another suggestion from pages 259–60.

Strategic Afternoon Snack

Protein source _____

Carbohydrate source _____

Fat source _____

Fluid _____

Ants on logs: celery filled with peanut butter and dotted with raisins, or another suggestion from pages 262–63.

Dinner

Protein source _____

Carbohydrate source _____

Fat source _____

Fluid _____

Dinner idea: Microwavable dinners from Lean Cuisine, Budget Gourmet, or Healthy Choice; look for no more than 2 grams of fat per 100 calories, or another suggestion from pages 260–62.

Evening Snack

Carbohydrate source _____

Fat source _____

Fluid _____

Fruits, vegetables, or yogurt; minimal protein.

Nutrition/Exercise/Sleep

Nutrition

Five or more meals	Yes____	No____
Small meals	Yes____	No____
Healthy meals	Yes____	No____

Exercise

No. of abdominals _____

Cardiovascular training _____ Time _____

No. of recovery waves _____ Max. HR _____

Interval _____ Steady state _____

Strength time _____ Stretching time _____

Total exercise time today _____

Sleep

Time to bed _____ Time up _____

Nap: Yes _____ No _____

Total sleep time including nap _____

Train recovery:

　　　Recovery every 90 minutes: Yes _____ No _____

Emotional response to crisis du jour:

　　　High　　　Medium　　　Low

Achieved stress/recovery balance today:

　　　High　　　Medium　　　Low

Level of productivity today:

　　　High　　　Medium　　　Low

Level of overall energy rating today:

　　　　　High　　　　　Medium　　　　　Low

Things accomplished: Performance

_____

_____

_____

_____

Things accomplished: Health

_____

_____

_____

_____

Things accomplished: Happiness

_____

_____

_____

_____

DAY 5

Exercise

	Abdominal	Aerobic Training		Strength		Flexibility
	Level	Time	Type	% Max.	Time	Time
Beginner	25	10 min.	Steady	60	20 min.	5 min.
Intermediate	2×25	20 min.	Steady	70	20 min.	10 min.
Advanced	4×25	35 min.	Interval	70–85	30–40 min.	10 min.

Nutrition

Breakfast

Protein source _____

Carbohydrate source _____

Fat source _____

Fluid _____

Breakfast idea: Low-fat yogurt with fresh fruit, or another suggestion from pages 258–59.

Strategic Morning Snack

Protein source _____

Carbohydrate source _____

Fat source _____

Fluid _____

Fruit and low-fat cheese kabobs: alternate fruit and cheese cubes, or another suggestion from pages 262–63.

Lunch

Protein source _____

Carbohydrate source _____

Fat source _____

Fluid _____

Lunch idea: Peanut butter and jelly sandwich on whole wheat bread, or another suggestion from pages 259–60.

Strategic Afternoon Snack

Protein source _____

Carbohydrate source _____

Fat source _____

Fluid _____

Canned fruit chunks or slices: pineapple, pear, mandarin orange, etc., and cottage cheese, or another suggestion from pages 262–63.

Dinner

Protein source _____

Carbohydrate source _____

Fat source _____

Fluid _____

Dinner idea: Creamed chicken or tuna (made with reduced-sodium canned mushroom soup and low-fat milk) over rice or noodles with garden fresh peas, or another suggestion from pages 260–62.

Evening Snack

Carbohydrate source _____

Fat source _____

Fluid _____

Fruits, vegetables, or yogurt; minimal protein.

Nutrition/Exercise/Sleep

Nutrition

Five or more meals   Yes____ No____

Small meals   Yes____ No____

Healthy meals   Yes____ No____

Exercise

No. of abdominals _____

Cardiovascular training _____ Time _____

No. of recovery waves _____ Max. HR _____

Interval _____ Steady state _____

Strength time _____ Stretching time _____

Total exercise time today _____

Sleep

Time to bed _____ Time up _____

Nap: Yes _____ No _____

Total sleep time including nap _____

Train recovery:

      Recovery every 90 minutes: Yes _____ No _____

Emotional response to crisis du jour:

      High   Medium   Low

Achieved stress/recovery balance today:

      High   Medium   Low

Level of productivity today:

      High   Medium   Low

Level of overall energy rating today:

      High   Medium   Low

Things accomplished: Performance

_____

_____

_____

_____

Things accomplished: Health

_____

_____

_____

_____

Things accomplished: Happiness

_____

_____

_____

_____

DAY 6

Exercise

	Abdominal	Aerobic Training		Strength		Flexibility
	Level	Time	Type	% Max.	Time	Time
Beginner	Rest	Rest	Rest	Rest	Rest	10 min.
Intermediate	Rest	Rest	Rest	Rest	Rest	20 min.
Advanced	4×25	20 min.	Steady	Rest	Rest	10 min.

Nutrition

Breakfast

Protein source _____

Carbohydrate source _____

Fat source _____

Fluid _____

Breakfast idea: Toasted cinnamon-raisin bagel with low-fat cream cheese, or another suggestion from pages 258–59.

Strategic Morning Snack

Protein source _____

Carbohydrate source _____

Fat source _____

Fluid _____

Fruit smoothie and pretzels or other bread group, or another suggestion from pages 262–63.

Lunch

Protein source _____

Carbohydrate source _____

Fat source _____

Fluid _____

Lunch idea: Tossed salad (various lettuces with cut-up vegetables) with nuts, or another suggestion from pages 259–60.

Strategic Afternoon Snack

Protein source _____

Carbohydrate source _____

Fat source _____

Fluid _____

Low-fat cheese slices or spreads on low-fat crackers or rice cakes, or another suggestion from pages 262–63.

Dinner

Protein source _____

Carbohydrate source _____

Fat source _____

Fluid _____

Dinner idea: Fettuccine with low-fat cream sauce, or another suggestion from pages 260–62.

Evening Snack

Carbohydrate source _____

Fat source _____

Fluid _____

Fruits, vegetables, or yogurt; minimal protein.

Nutrition/Exercise/Sleep

<u>Nutrition</u>

Five or more meals	Yes____	No____
Small meals	Yes____	No____
Healthy meals	Yes____	No____

<u>Exercise</u>

No. of abdominals _____

Cardiovascular training _____ Time _____

No. of recovery waves _____ Max. HR _____

Interval _____ Steady state _____

Strength time _____ Stretching time _____

Total exercise time today _____

Sleep

Time to bed _____ Time up _____

Nap: Yes _____ No _____

Total sleep time including nap _____

Train recovery:

      Recovery every 90 minutes: Yes _____ No _____

Emotional response to crisis du jour:

      High   Medium   Low

Achieved stress/recovery balance today:

      High   Medium   Low

Level of productivity today:

      High   Medium   Low

Level of overall energy rating today:

      High   Medium   Low

Things accomplished: Performance

_____

_____

_____

_____

Things accomplished: Health

_____

_____

_____

_____

Things accomplished: Happiness

_____

_____

_____

_____

DAY 7

Exercise

	Abdominal	Aerobic Training		Strength		Flexibility
	Level	Time	Type	% Max.	Time	Time
Beginner	2×25	15 min.	Steady	60	20 min.	10 min.
Intermediate	2×25	20 min.	Steady	75	20 min.	10 min.
Advanced	Rest	Rest	Rest	80	30–40 min.	20 min.

Nutrition

Breakfast

Protein source _____

Carbohydrate source _____

Fat source _____

Fluid _____

Breakfast idea: Plain bagel with jelly, or another suggestion from pages 258–59.

Strategic Morning Snack

Nutrition

Breakfast

Protein source _____

Carbohydrate source _____

Fat source _____

Fluid _____

Apple and peanut butter, or another suggestion from pages 262–63.

Lunch

Protein source _____

Carbohydrate source _____

Fat source _____

Fluid _____

Lunch idea: Low-fat quiche and sliced tomatoes, or another suggestion from pages 259–60.

Strategic Afternoon Snack

Protein source _____

Carbohydrate source _____

Fat source _____

Fluid _____

Dried apricots and raw almonds, or another suggestion from pages 262–63.

Dinner

Protein source _____

Carbohydrate source _____

Fat source _____

Fluid _____

Dinner idea: Macaroni and red clam sauce, or another suggestion from pages 260–62.

Evening Snack

Carbohydrate source _____

Fat source _____

Fluid _____

Fruits, vegetables, or yogurt; minimal protein.

Nutrition/Exercise/Sleep

Nutrition

Five or more meals   Yes_____ No_____

Small meals   Yes_____ No_____

Healthy meals   Yes_____ No_____

Exercise

No. of abdominals _____

Cardiovascular training _____ Time _____

No. of recovery waves _____ Max. HR _____

Interval _____ Steady state _____

Strength time _____ Stretching time _____

Total exercise time today _____

Sleep

Time to bed _____ Time up _____

Nap: Yes _____ No _____

Total sleep time including nap _____

Train recovery:

      Recovery every 90 minutes: Yes _____ No _____

Emotional response to crisis du jour:

      High   Medium   Low

Achieved stress/recovery balance today:

      High   Medium   Low

Level of productivity today:

      High   Medium   Low

Level of overall energy rating today:

      High   Medium   Low

Things accomplished: Performance

_____

_____

_____

_____

Things accomplished: Health

_____

_____

_____

_____

Things accomplished: Happiness

_____

_____

_____

_____

WEEKLY SUMMARY

Emotional performance for the week—avg. _____

Five or more meals: number of days _____

Small meals: number of days _____

Ate healthy: number of days _____

Abdominals: total number _____

Interval: time _____

Steady state: time _____

Strength training: total time _____

Stretching: total time _____

Exercise: total time _____

Sleep: total time for the week (incl. naps) _____

Recovery: average for the week _____

Energy: average for the week_____

DAY 8

Exercise

	Abdominal	Aerobic Training		Strength		Flexibility
	Level	Time	Type	% Max.	Time	Time
Beginner	2×25	15 min.	Steady	Rest	Rest	10 min.
Intermediate	3×25	25 min.	Interval	Rest	Rest	10 min.
Advanced	5×25	20 min.	Interval	Rest	Rest	10 min.

Nutrition

Breakfast

Protein source _____

Carbohydrate source _____

Fat source _____

Fluid _____

Breakfast idea: Bran banana bars or other healthy, fruit-filled breakfast bars, or another suggestion from pages 258–59.

Strategic Morning Snack

Protein source _____

Carbohydrate source _____

Fat source _____

Fluid _____

Granola bar (low-fat), or another suggestion from pages 262–63.

Lunch

Protein source _____

Carbohydrate source _____

Fat source _____

Fluid _____

Lunch idea: Chicken salad (white meat with low-fat mayonnaise) sand-wich on pumpernickel bread, or another suggestion from pages 259–60.

Strategic Afternoon Snack

Protein source _____

Carbohydrate source _____

Fat source _____

Fluid _____

Ginger snaps and skim milk, or another suggestion from pages 262–63.

Dinner

Protein source _____

Carbohydrate source _____

Fat source _____

Fluid _____

Dinner idea: Pita pockets stuffed with three-bean salad, or another sug-gestion from page 260–62.

Evening Snack

Carbohydrate source _____

Fat source _____

Fluid _____

Fruits, vegetables, or yogurt; minimal protein.

Nutrition/Exercise/Sleep

Nutrition

Five or more meals	Yes____	No____
Small meals	Yes____	No____
Healthy meals	Yes____	No____

Exercise

No. of abdominals _____

Cardiovascular training _____ Time _____

No. of recovery waves _____ Max. HR _____

Interval _____ Steady state _____

Strength time _____ Stretching time _____

Total exercise time today _____

Sleep

Time to bed _____ Time up _____

Nap: Yes _____ No _____

Total sleep time including nap _____

Train recovery:

            Recovery every 90 minutes: Yes _____ No _____

Emotional response to crisis du jour:

       High   Medium   Low

Achieved stress/recovery balance today:

       High   Medium   Low

Level of productivity today:

       High   Medium   Low

Level of overall energy rating today:

       High   Medium   Low

Things accomplished: Performance

_____

_____

_____

_____

Things accomplished: Health

_____

_____

_____

_____

Things accomplished: Happiness

_____

_____

_____

_____

DAY 9

Exercise

	Abdominal	Aerobic Training		Strength		Flexibility
	Level	Time	Type	% Max.	Time	Time
Beginner	2×25	15 min.	Steady	65	20 min.	10 min.
Intermediate	3×25	20 min.	Steady	70%	20 min.	10 min.
Advanced	5×25	35 min.	Interval	70–90	30–40 min.	10 min.

Nutrition

Breakfast

Protein source _____

Carbohydrate source _____

Fat source _____

Fluid _____

Breakfast idea: Oatmeal with skim milk, or another suggestion from pages 258–59.

Strategic Morning Snack

Protein source _____

Carbohydrate source _____

Fat source _____

Fluid _____

Dry cereal and raw vegetables, or another suggestion from pages 262–63.

Lunch

Protein source _____

Carbohydrate source _____

Fat source _____

Fluid _____

Lunch idea: Breast of turkey on rye bread, or another suggestion from pages 259–60.

Strategic Afternoon Snack

Protein source _____

Carbohydrate source _____

Fat source _____

Fluid _____

Bloody Mary mix with celery, or another suggestion from pages 262–63.

Dinner

Protein source _____

Carbohydrate source _____

Fat source _____

Fluid _____

Dinner idea: Ravioli with low-fat cheese and lean ground chuck, or another suggestion from pages 260–62.

Evening Snack

Carbohydrate source _____

Fat source _____

Fluid _____

Fruits, vegetables, or yogurt; minimal protein.

Nutrition/Exercise/Sleep

Nutrition

Five or more meals	Yes____ No____
Small meals	Yes____ No____
Healthy meals	Yes____ No____

Exercise

No. of abdominals _____

Cardiovascular training _____ Time _____

No. of recovery waves _____ Max. HR _____

Interval _____ Steady state _____

Strength time _____ Stretching time _____

Total exercise time today _____

Sleep

Time to bed _____ Time up _____

Nap: Yes _____ No _____

Total sleep time including nap _____

Train recovery:

Recovery every 90 minutes: Yes _____ No _____

Emotional response to crisis du jour:

High   Medium   Low

Achieved stress/recovery balance today:

High   Medium   Low

Level of productivity today:

High   Medium   Low

Level of overall energy rating today:

High   Medium   Low

Things accomplished: Performance

_____

_____

_____

_____

Things accomplished: Health

_____

_____

_____

_____

Things accomplished: Happiness

_____

_____

_____

_____

DAY 10

Exercise

	Abdominal	Aerobic Training		Strength		Flexibility
	Level	Time	Type	% Max.	Time	Time
Beginner	2×25	15 min.	Steady	Rest	Rest	10 min.
Intermediate	3×25	25 min.	Interval	Rest	Rest	10 min.
Advanced	5×25	20 min.	Steady	Rest	Rest	10 min.

Nutrition

Breakfast

Protein source _____

Carbohydrate source _____

Fat source _____

Fluid _____

Breakfast idea: English muffins with jelly spread, or another suggestion from pages 258–59.

Strategic Morning Snack

Protein source _____

Carbohydrate source _____

Fat source _____

Fluid _____

Grapes and nuts, or another suggestion from pages 262–63.

Lunch

Protein source _____

Carbohydrate source _____

Fat source _____

Fluid _____

Lunch idea: Cashew butter and banana sandwich on whole wheat, or another suggestion from pages 259–60.

Strategic Afternoon Snack

Protein source _____

Carbohydrate source _____

Fat source _____

Fluid _____

Raw vegetables, or another suggestion from pages 262–63.

Dinner

Protein source _____

Carbohydrate source _____

Fat source _____

Fluid _____

Dinner idea: Rice and bean burrito, or another suggestion from pages 260–62.

Evening Snack

Carbohydrate source _____

Fat source _____

Fluid _____

Fruits, vegetables, or yogurt; minimal protein.

Nutrition/Exercise/Sleep

Nutrition

Five or more meals   Yes_____ No_____

Small meals   Yes_____ No_____

Healthy meals   Yes_____ No_____

Exercise

No. of abdominals _____

Cardiovascular training _____ Time _____

No. of recovery waves _____ Max. HR _____

Interval _____ Steady state _____

Strength time _____ Stretching time _____

Total exercise time today _____

Sleep

Time to bed _____ Time up _____

Nap: Yes _____ No _____

Total sleep time including nap _____

Train recovery:

Recovery every 90 minutes: Yes _____ No _____

Emotional response to crisis du jour:

    High   Medium   Low

Achieved stress/recovery balance today:

    High   Medium   Low

Level of productivity today:

    High   Medium   Low

Level of overall energy rating today:

    High   Medium   Low

Things accomplished: Performance

_____

_____

_____

_____

Things accomplished: Health

_____

_____

_____

_____

Things accomplished: Happiness

_____

_____

_____

_____

DAY 11

Exercise

	Abdominal	Aerobic Training		Strength		Flexibility
	Level	Time	Type	% Max.	Time	Time
Beginner	2×25	15 min.	Steady	65	20 min.	10 min.
Intermediate	3×25	20 min.	Steady	70–85	20 min.	10 min.
Advanced	5×25	40 min.	Interval	65–85	30–40 min.	10 min.

Nutrition

Breakfast

Protein source _____

Carbohydrate source _____

Fat source _____

Fluid _____

Breakfast idea: Cream of Wheat with soy milk and cantaloupe slices, or another suggestion from pages 258–59.

Strategic Morning Snack

Protein source _____

Carbohydrate source _____

Fat source _____

Fluid _____

Toasted oatmeal squares and low-fat milk, or another suggestion from pages 262–63.

Lunch

Protein source _____

Carbohydrate source _____

Fat source _____

Fluid _____

Lunch idea: Cold pasta salad: stuffed tortellini with cut-up fresh vegetables, or another suggestion from pages 259–60.

Strategic Afternoon Snack

Protein source _____

Carbohydrate source _____

Fat source _____

Fluid _____

Protein drink, or another suggestion from pages 262–63.

Dinner

Protein source _____

Carbohydrate source _____

Fat source _____

Fluid _____

Dinner idea: Vegetarian lasagna, or another suggestion from pages 260–62.

Evening Snack

Carbohydrate source _____

Fat source _____

Fluid _____

Fruits, vegetables, or yogurt; minimal protein.

Nutrition/Exercise/Sleep

Nutrition

Five or more meals	Yes____ No____
Small meals	Yes____ No____
Healthy meals	Yes____ No____

Exercise

No. of abdominals _____

Cardiovascular training _____ Time _____

No. of recovery waves _____ Max. HR _____

Interval _____ Steady state _____

Strength time _____ Stretching time _____

Total exercise time today _____

Sleep

Time to bed _____ Time up _____

Nap: Yes _____ No _____

Total sleep time including nap _____

Train recovery:

      Recovery every 90 minutes: Yes _____ No _____

Emotional response to crisis du jour:

      High   Medium   Low

Achieved stress/recovery balance today:

      High   Medium   Low

Level of productivity today:

      High   Medium   Low

Level of overall energy rating today:

      High   Medium   Low

Things accomplished: Performance

_____

_____

_____

_____

Things accomplished: Health

_____

_____

_____

_____

Things accomplished: Happiness

_____

_____

_____

_____

DAY 12

Exercise

	Abdominal	Aerobic Training		Strength		Flexibility
	Level	Time	Type	% Max.	Time	Time
Beginner:	2×25	15 min.	Interval	Rest	Rest	10 min.
Intermediate	Rest	Rest	Rest	Rest	Rest	20 min.
Advanced	5×25	20 min.	Steady	Rest	Rest	10 min.

Nutrition

Breakfast

Protein source _____

Carbohydrate source _____

Fat source _____

Fluid _____

Breakfast idea: Fruit smoothie (apple, strawberries, bananas, dates, and apple juice).

Strategic Morning Snack

Protein source _____

Carbohydrate source _____

Fat source _____

Fluid _____

Spring-water-packed tuna with crackers, or another suggestion from pages 262–63.

Lunch

Protein source _____

Carbohydrate source _____

Fat source _____

Fluid _____

Lunch idea: Corkscrew pasta with peas, roast chicken, and peppers, or another suggestion from pages 259–60.

Strategic Afternoon Snack

Protein source _____

Carbohydrate source _____

Fat source _____

Fluid _____

Bagel with low-fat cream cheese, or another suggestion from pages 262–63.

Dinner

Protein source _____

Carbohydrate source _____

Fat source _____

Fluid _____

Dinner idea: Stir-fry vegetables, or another suggestion from pages 260–62.

Evening Snack

Carbohydrate source _____

Fat source _____

Fluid _____

Fruits, vegetables, or yogurt; minimal protein.

Nutrition/Exercise/Sleep

Nutrition

Five or more meals	Yes____ No____
Small meals	Yes____ No____
Healthy meals	Yes____ No____

Exercise

No. of abdominals _____

Cardiovascular training _____ Time _____

No. of recovery waves _____ Max. HR _____

Interval _____ Steady state _____

Strength time _____ Stretching time _____

Total exercise time today _____

Sleep

Time to bed _____ Time up _____

Nap: Yes _____ No _____

Total sleep time including nap _____

Train recovery:

      Recovery every 90 minutes: Yes _____ No _____

Emotional response to crisis du jour:

      High   Medium   Low

Achieved stress/recovery balance today:

      High   Medium   Low

Level of productivity today:

      High   Medium   Low

Level of overall energy rating today:

      High   Medium   Low

Things accomplished: Performance

_____

_____

_____

_____

Things accomplished: Health

_____

_____

_____

_____

Things accomplished: Happiness

_____

_____

_____

_____

DAY 13

Exercise

| | Abdominal | Aerobic Training | | Strength | | Flexibility |
	Level	Time	Type	% Max.	Time	Time
Beginner	Rest	Rest	Rest	60	20 min.	20 min.
Intermediate	4×25	20 min.	Steady	75	20 min.	10 min.
Advanced	Rest	Rest	Rest	80	30–40 min.	20 min.

Nutrition

Breakfast

Protein source _____

Carbohydrate source _____

Fat source _____

Fluid _____

Breakfast idea: Apple-bran muffin (low-fat) with unsweetened apple-sauce, or another suggestion from pages 259–60.

Strategic Morning Snack

Protein source _____

Carbohydrate source _____

Fat source _____

Fluid _____

Skim milk and an apple, or another suggestion from pages 263–63.

Lunch

Protein source _____

Carbohydrate source _____

Fat source _____

Fluid _____

Lunch idea: Low-fat yogurt with wheat bread with peanut butter, or another suggestion from pages 259–60.

Strategic Afternoon Snack

Protein source _____

Carbohydrate source _____

Fat source _____

Fluid _____

A regular-size energy bar, or another suggestion from pages 262–63.

Dinner

Protein source _____

Carbohydrate source _____

Fat source _____

Fluid _____

Dinner idea: Vegetable stew, or another suggestion from pages 260–62.

Evening Snack

Carbohydrate source _____

Fat source _____

Fluid _____

Fruits, vegetables, or yogurt; minimal protein.

Nutrition/Exercise/Sleep

Nutrition

Five or more meals   Yes____ No____

Small meals   Yes____ No____

Healthy meals   Yes____ No____

Exercise

No. of abdominals _____

Cardiovascular training _____ Time _____

No. of recovery waves _____ Max. HR _____

Interval _____ Steady state _____

Strength time _____ Stretching time _____

Total exercise time today _____

Sleep

Time to bed _____ Time up _____

Nap: Yes _____ No _____

Total sleep time including nap _____

Train recovery:

       Recovery every 90 minutes: Yes _____ No _____

Emotional response to crisis du jour:

      High   Medium   Low

Achieved stress/recovery balance today:

      High   Medium   Low

Level of productivity today:

　　　　High　　　　Medium　　　　Low

Level of overall energy rating today:

　　　　High　　　　Medium　　　　Low

Things accomplished: Performance

_____

_____

_____

_____

Things accomplished: Health

_____

_____

_____

_____

Things accomplished: Happiness

_____

_____

_____

_____

DAY 14

Exercise

	Abdominal	Aerobic Training		Strength		Flexibility
	Level	Time	Type	% Max.	Time	Time
Beginner	3×25	15 min.	Steady	Rest	Rest	10 min.
Intermediate	4×25	30 min.	Interval	Rest	Rest	10 min.
Advanced	6×25	20 min.	Steady	Rest	Rest	10 min.

Nutrition

Breakfast

Protein source _____

Carbohydrate source _____

Fat source _____

Fluid _____

Breakfast idea: Toaster waffle with strawberries, or another suggestion from pages 258–59.

Strategic Morning Snack

Protein source _____

Carbohydrate source _____

Fat source _____

Fluid _____

Frozen yogurt with nuts, or another suggestion from pages 262–63.

Lunch

Protein source _____

Carbohydrate source _____

Fat source _____

Fluid _____

Lunch idea: Egg salad with low-fat mayonnaise (limit egg consumption to one per week), or another suggestion from pages 259–60.

Strategic Afternoon Snack

Protein source _____

Carbohydrate source _____

Fat source _____

Fluid _____

Rice cakes with low-fat milk, or another suggestion from pages 262–63.

Dinner

Protein source _____

Carbohydrate source _____

Fat source _____

Fluid _____

Dinner idea: Vegetable, cheese, and chicken calzone, or another suggestion from pages 260–62.

Evening Snack

Carbohydrate source _____

Fat source _____

Fluid _____

Fruits, vegetables, or yogurt; minimal protein.

Nutrition/Exercise/Sleep

Nutrition

Five or more meals   Yes____ No____

Small meals   Yes____ No____

Healthy meals   Yes____ No____

Exercise

No. of abdominals _____

Cardiovascular training _____ Time _____

No. of recovery waves _____ Max. HR _____

Interval _____ Steady state _____

Strength time _____ Stretching time _____

Total exercise time today _____

Sleep

Time to bed _____ Time up _____

Nap: Yes _____ No _____

Total sleep time including nap _____

Train recovery:

        Recovery every 90 minutes: Yes _____ No _____

Emotional response to crisis du jour:

        High   Medium   Low

Achieved stress/recovery balance today:

        High   Medium   Low

Level of productivity today:

        High   Medium   Low

Level of overall energy rating today:

        High   Medium   Low

Things accomplished: Performance

_____

_____

_____

_____

Things accomplished: Health

_____

_____

_____

_____

Things accomplished: Happiness

_____

_____

_____

_____

WEEKLY SUMMARY

Emotional performance for the week—avg. _____

Five or more meals: number of days _____

Small meals: number of days _____

Ate healthy: number of days _____

Abdominals: total number _____

Interval: time _____

Steady state: time _____

Strength training: total time _____

Stretching: total time _____

Exercise: total time _____

Sleep: total time for the week (incl. naps) _____

Recovery: average for the week _____

Energy: average for the week_____

DAY 15

Exercise

	Abdominal	Aerobic Training		Strength		Flexibility
	Level	Time	Type	% Max.	Time	Time
Beginner	3×25	20 min.	Interval	60–70	20 min.	10 min.
Intermediate	4×25	20 min.	Steady	80	20 min.	10 min.
Advanced	6×25	45 min.	Interval	70–90	30–40 min.	10 min.

Nutrition

Breakfast

Protein source _____

Carbohydrate source _____

Fat source _____

Fluid _____

Breakfast idea: Oat bran waffle (homemade) with fruit, or another suggestion from pages 258–59.

Strategic Morning Snack

Protein source _____

Carbohydrate source _____

Fat source _____

Fluid _____

Bran muffin with apple cider, or another suggestion from pages 262–63.

Lunch

Protein source _____

Carbohydrate source _____

Fat source _____

Fluid _____

Lunch idea: Sardines on pumpernickel bread, or another suggestion from pages 259–60.

Strategic Afternoon Snack

Protein source _____

Carbohydrate source _____

Fat source _____

Fluid _____

Graham crackers with low-fat milk, or another suggestion from pages 262–63.

Dinner

Protein source _____

Carbohydrate source _____

Fat source _____

Fluid _____

Dinner idea: Chicken fajitas with low-fat refried beans, or another suggestion from pages 260–62.

Evening Snack

Carbohydrate source _____

Fat source _____

Fluid _____

Fruits, vegetables, or yogurt; minimal protein.

Nutrition/Exercise/Sleep

Nutrition
_____

Five or more meals   Yes_____ No_____

Small meals   Yes_____ No_____

Healthy meals   Yes_____ No_____

Exercise
_____

No. of abdominals _____

Cardiovascular training _____ Time _____

No. of recovery waves _____ Max. HR _____

Interval _____ Steady state _____

Strength time _____ Stretching time _____

Total exercise time today _____

Sleep
_____

Time to bed _____ Time up _____

Nap: Yes _____ No _____

Total sleep time including nap _____

Train recovery:

          Recovery every 90 minutes: Yes _____ No _____

Emotional response to crisis du jour:

          High   Medium   Low

Achieved stress/recovery balance today:

> High   Medium   Low

Level of productivity today:

> High   Medium   Low

Level of overall energy rating today:

> High   Medium   Low

Things accomplished: Performance

_____

_____

_____

_____

Things accomplished: Health

_____

_____

_____

_____

Things accomplished: Happiness

_____

_____

_____

_____

DAY 16

Exercise

	Abdominal	Aerobic Training		Strength		Flexibility
	Level	Time	Type	% Max.	Time	Time
Beginner	3×25	15 min.	Steady	Rest	Rest	10 min.
Intermediate	4×25	30 min.	Interval	Rest	Rest	10 min.
Advanced	6×25	20 min.	Steady	Rest	Rest	10 min.

Nutrition

Breakfast

Protein source _____

Carbohydrate source _____

Fat source _____

Fluid _____

Breakfast idea: Whole-wheat pancakes with blueberries, or another suggestion from pages 258–59.

Strategic Morning Snack

Protein source _____

Carbohydrate source _____

Fat source _____

Fluid _____

Apricot halves and Fig Newtons, or another suggestion from pages 262–63.

Lunch

Protein source _____

Carbohydrate source _____

Fat source _____

Fluid _____

Lunch idea: Vegetarian mix (lettuce, beans, peppers, broccoli, cauliflower) in a pita pocket, or another suggestion from pages 259–60.

Strategic Afternoon Snack

Protein source _____

Carbohydrate source _____

Fat source _____

Fluid _____

Low-fat yogurt with blueberries, or another suggestion from pages 262–63.

Dinner

Protein source _____

Carbohydrate source _____

Fat source _____

Fluid _____

Dinner idea: Vegetarian pizza, or another suggestion from pages 260–62.

Evening Snack

Carbohydrate source _____

Fat source _____

Fluid _____

Fruits, vegetables, or yogurt; minimal protein.

Nutrition/Exercise/Sleep

Nutrition

Five or more meals	Yes____	No____
Small meals	Yes____	No____
Healthy meals	Yes____	No____

Exercise

No. of abdominals _____

Cardiovascular training _____ Time _____

No. of recovery waves _____ Max. HR _____

Interval _____ Steady state _____

Strength time _____ Stretching time _____

Total exercise time today _____

Sleep

Time to bed _____ Time up _____

Nap: Yes _____ No _____

Total sleep time including nap _____

Train recovery:

　　　Recovery every 90 minutes: Yes _____ No _____

Emotional response to crisis du jour:

　　　High　　　Medium　　　Low

Achieved stress/recovery balance today:

　　　High　　　Medium　　　Low

Level of productivity today:

　　　High　　　Medium　　　Low

Level of overall energy rating today:

　　　High　　　Medium　　　Low

Things accomplished: Performance

_____

_____

_____

_____

Things accomplished: Health

_____

_____

_____

_____

Things accomplished: Happiness

_____

_____

_____

_____

DAY 17

Exercise

	Abdominal	Aerobic Training		Strength		Flexibility
	Level	Time	Type	% Max.	Time	Time
Beginner	3×25	25 min.	Interval	55–70	20 min.	10 min.
Intermediate	3×25	25 min.	Interval	55–70	30 min.	10 min.
Advanced	6×25	45 min.	Interval	70–90	30–40 min.	10 min.

Nutrition

Breakfast

Protein source _____

Carbohydrate source _____

Fat source _____

Fluid _____

Breakfast idea: Pita stuffed with fresh fruit salad, or another suggestion from pages 258–59.

Strategic Morning Snack

Protein source _____

Carbohydrate source _____

Fat source _____

Fluid _____

Air-popped popcorn, or another suggestion from pages 262–63.

Lunch

Protein source _____

Carbohydrate source _____

Fat source _____

Fluid _____

Lunch idea: Flounder (baked, without breading), or another suggestion from pages 259–60.

Strategic Afternoon Snack

Protein source _____

Carbohydrate source _____

Fat source _____

Fluid _____

Raisins and nuts, or another suggestion from pages 262–63.

Dinner

Protein source _____

Carbohydrate source _____

Fat source _____

Fluid _____

Dinner idea: Low-fat chicken stir-fry, or another suggestion from pages 260–62.

Evening Snack

Carbohydrate source _____

Fat source _____

Fluid _____

Fruits, vegetables, or yogurt; minimal protein.

Nutrition/Exercise/Sleep

Nutrition

Five or more meals	Yes____ No____
Small meals	Yes____ No____
Healthy meals	Yes____ No____

Exercise

No. of abdominals _____

Cardiovascular training _____ Time _____

No. of recovery waves _____ Max. HR _____

Interval _____ Steady state _____

Strength time _____ Stretching time _____

Total exercise time today _____

Sleep

Time to bed _____ Time up _____

Nap: Yes _____ No _____

Total sleep time including nap _____

Train recovery:

      Recovery every 90 minutes: Yes _____ No _____

Emotional response to crisis du jour:

      High   Medium   Low

Achieved stress/recovery balance today:

      High   Medium   Low

Level of productivity today:

      High   Medium   Low

Level of overall energy rating today:

      High   Medium   Low

Things accomplished: Performance

_____

_____

_____

_____

Things accomplished: Health

_____

_____

_____

_____

Things accomplished: Happiness

_____

_____

_____

_____

DAY 18

Exercise

	Abdominal	Aerobic Training		Strength		Flexibility
	Level	Time	Type	% Max.	Time	Time
Beginner	3×25	20 min.	Interval	Rest	Rest	10 min.
Intermediate	Rest	Rest	Rest	Rest	Rest	20 min.
Advanced	6×25	20 min.	Interval	Rest	Rest	10 min.

Nutrition

Breakfast

Protein source _____

Carbohydrate source _____

Fat source _____

Fluid _____

Breakfast idea: French toast with fresh mixed fruit, or another suggestion from pages 259–60.

Strategic Morning Snack

Protein source _____

Carbohydrate source _____

Fat source _____

Fluid _____

Pretzels and cheese cubes, or another suggestion from pages 262–63.

Lunch

Protein source _____

Carbohydrate source _____

Fat source _____

Fluid _____

Lunch idea: Low-fat cottage cheese with fruit and melba toast, or another suggestion from pages 259–60.

Strategic Afternoon Snack

Protein source _____

Carbohydrate source _____

Fat source _____

Fluid _____

Frozen fruit juice bar, or another suggestion from pages 262–63.

Dinner

Protein source _____

Carbohydrate source _____

Fat source _____

Fluid _____

Dinner idea: Filet of sole (baked, without breading), or another suggestion from pages 260–62.

Evening Snack

Carbohydrate source _____

Fat source _____

Fluid _____

Fruits, vegetables, or yogurt; minimal protein.

Nutrition/Exercise/Sleep

Nutrition

Five or more meals	Yes_____ No_____
Small meals	Yes_____ No_____
Healthy meals	Yes_____ No_____

Exercise

No. of abdominals _____

Cardiovascular training _____ Time _____

No. of recovery waves _____ Max. HR _____

Interval _____ Steady state _____

Strength time _____ Stretching time _____

Total exercise time today _____

Sleep

Time to bed _____ Time up _____

Nap: Yes _____ No _____

Total sleep time including nap _____

Train recovery:

    Recovery every 90 minutes: Yes _____ No _____

Emotional response to crisis du jour:

    High   Medium   Low

Achieved stress/recovery balance today:

    High   Medium   Low

Level of productivity today:

    High   Medium   Low

Level of overall energy rating today:

    High   Medium   Low

Things accomplished: Performance

_____

_____

_____

_____

Things accomplished: Health

_____

_____

_____

_____

Things accomplished: Happiness

_____

_____

_____

_____

DAY 19

Exercise

	Abdominal	Aerobic Training		Strength		Flexibility
	Level	Time	Type	% Max.	Time	Time
Beginner	Rest	Rest	Rest	70	20 min.	20 min.
Intermediate	4×25	20 min.	Interval	70–85	20 min.	10 min.
Advanced	Rest	Rest	Rest	85	30–40 min.	20 min.

Nutrition

Breakfast

Protein source _____

Carbohydrate source _____

Fat source _____

Fluid _____

Breakfast idea: Orange breakfast milkshake with orange juice, low-fat milk, and bananas, or another suggestion from pages 258–59.

Strategic Morning Snack

Protein source _____

Carbohydrate source _____

Fat source _____

Fluid _____

Cereal based, fruit-filled bar, or another suggestion from pages 262–63.

Lunch

Protein source _____

Carbohydrate source _____

Fat source _____

Fluid _____

Lunch idea: Skinless chicken breast and skim mozzarella sandwich on a hard roll, or another suggestion from pages 259–60.

Strategic Afternoon Snack

Protein source _____

Carbohydrate source _____

Fat source _____

Fluid _____

Peanuts and fruit, or another suggestion from pages 262–63.

Dinner

Protein source _____

Carbohydrate source _____

Fat source _____

Fluid _____

Dinner idea: Cornish hen (skinless baked, without stuffing), or another suggestion from pages 260–62.

Evening Snack

Carbohydrate source _____

Fat source _____

Fluid _____

Fruits, vegetables, or yogurt; minimal protein.

Nutrition/Exercise/Sleep

Nutrition

Five or more meals   Yes____ No____

Small meals   Yes____ No____

Healthy meals   Yes____ No____

Exercise

No. of abdominals _____

Cardiovascular training _____ Time _____

No. of recovery waves _____ Max. HR _____

Interval _____ Steady state _____

Strength time _____ Stretching time _____

Total exercise time today _____

Sleep

Time to bed _____ Time up _____

Nap: Yes _____ No _____

Total sleep time including nap _____

Train recovery:

          Recovery every 90 minutes: Yes _____ No _____

Emotional response to crisis du jour:

      High   Medium   Low

Achieved stress/recovery balance today:

      High   Medium   Low

Level of productivity today:

      High   Medium   Low

Level of overall energy rating today:

      High   Medium   Low

Things accomplished: Performance

_____

_____

_____

_____

Things accomplished: Health

_____

_____

_____

_____

Things accomplished: Happiness

_____

_____

_____

_____

DAY 20

Exercise

	Abdominal	Aerobic Training		Strength		Flexibility
	Level	Time	Type	% Max.	Time	Time
Beginner	4×25	20 min.	Interval	Rest	Rest	10 min.
Intermediate	4×25	30 min.	Steady	Rest	Rest	10 min.
Advanced	6×25	20 min.	Steady	Rest	Rest	10 min.

Nutrition

Breakfast

Protein source _____

Carbohydrate source _____

Fat source _____

Fluid _____

Breakfast idea: Scrambled egg substitute with English muffin, or another suggestion from pages 258–59.

Strategic Morning Snack

Protein source _____

Carbohydrate source _____

Fat source _____

Fluid _____

Fresh fruit and yogurt, cheese, or lean deli cuts, or another suggestion from pages 262–263.

Lunch

Protein source _____

Carbohydrate source _____

Fat source _____

Fluid _____

Lunch idea: Bean and bulgur salad, or another suggestion from pages 259–60.

Strategic Afternoon Snack

Protein source _____

Carbohydrate source _____

Fat source _____

Fluid _____

Low-fat cheese cubes with pretzels or low-fat crackers, or another suggestion from pages 262–63.

Dinner

Protein source _____

Carbohydrate source _____

Fat source _____

Fluid _____

Dinner idea: Tuna steak (grilled), or another suggestion from pages 260–62.

Evening Snack

Carbohydrate source _____

Fat source _____

Fluid _____

Fruits, vegetables, or yogurt; minimal protein.

Nutrition/Exercise/Sleep

Nutrition

Five or more meals	Yes____ No____
Small meals	Yes____ No____
Healthy meals	Yes____ No____

Exercise

No. of abdominals _____

Cardiovascular training _____ Time _____

No. of recovery waves _____ Max. HR _____

Interval _____ Steady state _____

Strength time _____ Stretching time _____

Total exercise time today _____

Sleep

Time to bed _____ Time up _____

Nap: Yes _____ No _____

Total sleep time including nap _____

Train recovery:

      Recovery every 90 minutes: Yes _____ No _____

Emotional response to crisis du jour:

      High   Medium   Low

Achieved stress/recovery balance today:

      High   Medium   Low

Level of productivity today:

      High   Medium   Low

Level of overall energy rating today:

      High   Medium   Low

Things accomplished: Performance

_____

_____

_____

_____

Things accomplished: Health

_____

_____

_____

_____

Things accomplished: Happiness

_____

_____

_____

_____

DAY 21

Exercise

	Abdominal	Aerobic Training		Strength		Flexibility
	Level	Time	Type	% Max.	Time	Time
Beginner	4×25	25 min.	Interval	60–70	25 min.	10 min.
Intermediate	4×25	25 min.	Interval	65–85	30 min.	10 min.
Advanced	6×25	45 min.	Interval	75–90	30–40 min.	10 min.

Nutrition

Breakfast

Protein source _____

Carbohydrate source _____

Fat source _____

Fluid _____

Breakfast idea: Low-fat granola with fresh fruit cup, or another suggestion from pages 258–59.

Strategic Morning Snack

Protein source _____

Carbohydrate source _____

Fat source _____

Fluid _____

Applesauce and low-fat muffin or whole grain bread, or another suggestion from pages 262–63.

Lunch

Protein source _____

Carbohydrate source _____

Fat source _____

Fluid _____

Lunch idea: Lean roast beef sandwich on rye bread, or another suggestion from pages 259–60.

Strategic Afternoon Snack

Protein source _____

Carbohydrate source _____

Fat source _____

Fluid _____

Hard-boiled eggs (limit egg consumption to one per week) and tomato juice, or another suggestion from pages 262–63.

Dinner

Protein source _____

Carbohydrate source _____

Fat source _____

Fluid _____

Dinner idea: Salmon almondine (baked, without butter), or another suggestion from pages 260–62.

Evening Snack

Carbohydrate source _____

Fat source _____

Fluid _____

Fruits, vegetables, or yogurt; minimal protein.

Nutrition/Exercise/Sleep

Nutrition

Five or more meals	Yes_____ No_____
Small meals	Yes_____ No_____
Healthy meals	Yes_____ No_____

Exercise

No. of abdominals _____

Cardiovascular training _____ Time _____

No. of recovery waves _____ Max. HR _____

Interval _____ Steady state _____

Strength time _____ Stretching time _____

Total exercise time today _____

Sleep

Time to bed _____ Time up _____

Nap: Yes _____ No _____

Total sleep time including nap _____

Train recovery:

　　　Recovery every 90 minutes: Yes _____ No _____

Emotional response to crisis du jour:

　　　High　　　Medium　　　Low

Achieved stress/recovery balance today:

　　　High　　　Medium　　　Low

Level of productivity today:

　　　High　　　Medium　　　Low

Level of overall energy rating today:

High   Medium   Low

Things accomplished: Performance

_____

_____

_____

_____

Things accomplished: Health

_____

_____

_____

_____

Things accomplished: Happiness

_____

_____

_____

_____

WEEKLY SUMMARY

Emotional performance for the week—avg. _____

Five or more meals: number of days _____

Small meals: number of days _____

Ate healthy: number of days _____

Abdominals: total number _____

Interval: time _____

Steady state: time _____

Strength training: total time _____

Stretching: total time _____

Exercise: total time _____

Sleep: total time for the week (incl. naps) _____

Recovery: average for the week _____

Energy: average for the week_____

Breakfast Ideas (twenty-six selections)

Fresh fruit, low-fat, or skim milk and/or fruit juice can be served with any or all of the following selections:

Apple-bran muffin (low-fat) with unsweetened applesauce

Banana bran muffin (low-fat) with skim milk

Bran banana bars or other healthy fruit-filled breakfast bars

Bran cereal with berries with low-fat milk

Cold healthy cereal (e.g., Total, Wheat Chex, Cheerios) with low-fat milk

Cream of Wheat with soy milk and cantaloupe slices

Egg Beaters omelette with low-fat cheese

Egg white omelette with tomato and mushrooms

English muffins with jelly spread

French toast with fresh mixed fruit

Fruit smoothie (apple, strawberries, bananas, dates, and apple juice)

Fruit smoothie (bananas, dates, coconut milk, orange, and papaya juice)

Fruit smoothie (cashews, bananas, dates, and coconut milk)

Low-fat granola with fresh fruit cup

Low-fat yogurt with fresh fruit

Muesli with rice milk and mixed dried fruits

Oat bran waffle (homemade) with fruit

Oatmeal with skim milk

Orange breakfast milkshake with orange juice, low-fat milk, and bananas

Pita stuffed with fresh fruit salad

Plain bagel with jelly

Poached eggs and rye toast (two eggs, no more than once per week)

Scrambled egg substitute with English muffin

Toasted cinnamon-raisin bagel with low-fat cream cheese

Toaster waffle with strawberries

Whole-wheat pancakes with blueberries

Lunch (thirty-five selections)

Skim or low-fat milk, fruit juice, or fresh fruit can be included with any of these selections:

Entrées

Avocado and cheese sandwich on whole-wheat bread with alfalfa sprouts

Bean and bulgur salad

Breast of turkey on rye bread

Canned tuna in spring water on pita bread

Cashew butter and banana sandwich on whole wheat

Chef's salad: lettuce with hard-boiled egg whites, sliced deli cuts (e.g., cheese, turkey, and tomatoes) with low-fat dressing on the side

Chicken salad (white meat with low-fat mayonnaise) sandwich on pumpernickel bread

Cold pasta salad: stuffed tortellini with cut-up fresh vegetables

Corkscrew pasta with peas, roast chicken, and peppers

Egg salad (limit egg consumption to two per week) with low-fat mayonnaise

Grilled low-fat cheese and tomato on whole wheat

Hummus sandwich on pita bread

Lean roast beef sandwich on rye bread

Low-fat cottage cheese with fruit and melba toast

Low-fat quiche and sliced tomatoes

Low-fat yogurt with whole-wheat bread with peanut butter

Nicoise salad: romaine lettuce, tuna, hard-boiled egg whites, green beans, tomatoes, cooked new potatoes, and a few olives

Peanut butter and jelly sandwich on whole-wheat bread

Protein salad with seeds, cashews, egg whites, tomatoes, and lettuce

Red beans and rice

Sardines on pumpernickel bread

Skinless chicken breast and skim mozzarella sandwich on a hard roll

Soy hot dog sandwich

Tossed salad (various lettuces with cut-up vegetables) with nuts

Tuna fish salad (tuna canned in spring water with low-fat mayonnaise) sandwich on whole-wheat bread

Vegetarian burger

Vegetarian mix (lettuce, beans, peppers, broccoli, cauliflower) in a pita pocket

Waldorf salad (with low-fat mayonnaise) with brown rice

Soups

Look for lower sodium varieties (e.g., 500 mg or less per serving). With soups such as the following, you can add a salad with low-fat dressing and/or healthy breads:

Beef barley soup

Black bean soup

Chicken and noodle soup

Chicken and rice soup

Cream of broccoli soup

Lentil soup

Tomato bisque soup

Dinner Ideas (fifty-seven selections)

Add a tossed salad with low-fat dressing, fresh fruit, and/or steamed vegetables with any or all of these:

Angel hair pasta with tomato and basil

Baked shrimp (without breading)

Baked whiting (without stuffing)

Beef vegetable stew and low-fat biscuits

Broiled scallops (without breading)

Brown rice and steamed vegetables

Cajun grilled chicken (or turkey, skinless)

Calamari (grilled)

Chicken fajitas with low-fat refried beans

Clam and pasta salad

Cornish hen (skinless baked, without stuffing)

Creamed chicken or tuna (made with reduced-sodium canned mushroom soup and low-fat milk) over rice or noodles with garden fresh peas

Curried baked chicken (skinless, without cream)

Fettuccine with low-fat cream sauce

Filet of sole (baked, without breading)

Flounder (baked, without breading)

Grilled mahimahi (dolphin)

Grilled swordfish

Ground lean chuck (broiled)

Herb grilled vegetables

Herbed roasted chicken (skinless)

Kidney beans and rice

Lemon chicken with steamed squash

Low-fat chicken enchiladas with low-fat refried beans and salad

Low-fat chicken stir fry

Low-fat crab quiche

Low-fat linguini primavera

Low-fat macaroni and cheese

Low-fat mushroom risotto

Low-fat turkey tacos

Low-fat vegetable casserole

Macaroni and red clam sauce

Manicotti with vegetables

Microwavable dinners from Lean Cuisine, Budget Gourmet, or Healthy Choice

Orange roughy (grilled)

Perch with pine nuts

Pita pockets stuffed with three-bean salad

Pork tenderloin

Potato stuffed peppers (without cheese)

Ravioli with low-fat cheese and lean ground chuck

Rice and bean burrito

Salmon almondine (baked, without butter)

Snapper (broiled)

Steamed garden vegetables

Stir fry vegetables

Teriyaki chicken with pineapple wedges and rice pilaf

Tilefish (steamed)

Tofu with broccoli and mushrooms

Top sirloin (broiled) (no more than twice per week)

Tuna steak (grilled)

Veal chop with boiled barley

Vegetable, cheese, and chicken calzone

Vegetable stew

Vegetarian lasagna

Vegetarian pizza

Venison steak with wild rice

Whole-wheat spaghetti with low-fat tomato sauce

Snacks (forty-five selections)

Air-popped popcorn

Ants on logs: celery filled with peanut butter and dotted with raisins

Apple and peanut butter

Applesauce and low-fat muffin or whole-grain bread

Apricot halves and Fig Newtons

Bagel with low-fat cream cheese

Bloody Mary mix with celery

Bran muffin with apple cider

Canned fruit chunks or slices: pineapple, pear, mandarin orange, etc., and cottage cheese

Cantaloupe and multigrain fruit bar

Cereal-based fruit-filled bar

Celery sticks or cucumber boats stuffed with cottage cheese, cheese spread, tuna salad, or egg salad (all low-fat)

Cornbread and tomato juice

Dried apricots and raw almonds

Dry cereal and raw vegetables

Fresh fruit and yogurt, cheese, or lean deli cuts

Frozen fruit juice bar

Frozen yogurt with nuts

Fruit and low-fat cheese kabobs; alternate fruit and cheese cubes

Fruit smoothie and pretzels or other bread group

Ginger snaps and skim milk

Graham crackers with low-fat milk

Granola bar (low-fat)

Grapes and nuts

Hard-boiled eggs (limit egg consumption to two per week) and
   tomato juice

Low-fat cheese cubes with pretzels or low-fat crackers

Low-fat cheese slices or spreads on low-fat crackers or rice cakes

Low-fat granola or crunchy mix: unsugared cereal (Cheerios, Chex,
   etc.) mixed with raisins, peanuts, sunflower seeds, etc.

Low-fat yogurt with blueberries

Nut breads with low-fat cream cheese

Peanut butter crackers with 1 percent or skim milk

Peanuts and fruit

Pretzels and cheese cubes

Protein drink

Raisins and nuts

Raw vegetables

Regular-size energy bar

Rice cakes with low-fat milk

Skim milk and an apple

Spring-water-packed tuna with crackers

Toasted oatmeal squares and low-fat milk

Trail mix

Treasure logs: roll thin meat slice with low-fat cheese or low-fat
   cheese spread

Tuna fish on crackers or in sandwiches

Zucchini, carrot, pumpkin breads with apple butter or peanut butter or low-fat cream cheese

Part VI

MANAGERIAL
FITNESS

16

Spreading the Corporate Athlete Message

> Everybody talks about wanting to change things and help and
> fix, but ultimately all you can do is fix yourself. And that's a
> lot. Because if you can fix yourself, it has a ripple effect.
>
> —Film director Rob Reiner

Corporate Athlete Principle 16:

Containing the cost of employee absenteeism, burnout, turnover, and health care through fitness, nutrition, and wellness programs is necessary for increasing performance in Corporate America.

A man stopped to talk to two workers he saw breaking granite.

"What are you doing?" he asked the first worker.

"I'm trying to break this granite," the first worker said.

Then he turned to the second worker. "What are you doing?" he asked.

"I'm on a team building a cathedral," the second worker answered.

Some people in business see one tree at a time. Some see the whole forest before them.

Corporate America is caught in a vicious cycle. In an era of reengineering and restructuring, the ever-increasing demand for employees to accomplish more with fewer resources has pushed them as never before. Employees overwork their mental and emotional capacities and severely undertrain for the physical demands of their work. The result is an imbalanced pattern of stress and recovery that compromises performance and, over time, slowly erodes employee health and happiness.

Do you share the belief that if you're not sick, you're healthy enough to perform at high levels at the office and with your family? Unfortunately, few people think in terms of setting health goals beyond hoping

267

to avoid infectious diseases, accidents, and migraines. This attitude precludes putting much effort into reaching the peak of vigorous vitality.

The economic impact on Corporate America has been dramatic. Health care costs are spiraling out of control—from $12 billion in 1950 to more than $1 trillion in 1998 and still growing. The average health care cost in America, currently at $2,500 per person per year, is almost two times higher than any other industrialized nation's. More than half of that expense is being absorbed by business and industry, virtually eliminating after-tax profits in many instances.

Current estimates indicate that more than one million deaths each year may be attributed to unhealthy lifestyles. Premature deaths cost Corporate America more than $50 million annually as well as almost 200 million workdays of lost production. Many of these deaths are middle-aged men and women at the peak of their working years. Ironically, as many as 80 percent of these deaths could be prevented by adopting a healthy lifestyle.

Look at the first half of the twentieth century. What did medicine overtake? The plague, polio, tuberculosis, typhoid, typhus—all of them major, debilitating diseases.

Now look at health care in the second half of the century. We're under attack by cardiovascular disease, cancer, and AIDS. We have had to deal with environmentally induced diseases. We know that many cancers are related to nutrition and lack of activity. Sure, there are cancers and cardiovascular diseases that are caused genetically, but I believe we cop out by blaming too much on genetics.

One of the big concerns in Corporate America today is the value of human capital. Are our human resources as good as they should be? Are we taking good care of our human capital?

Despite this, employee maintenance has been afforded a lower priority than rapid growth and shareholders' equity concerns. Replacement costs for broken or worn-out employees are only beginning to be fully understood by corporations. In fact, the American Heart Association estimates that the cost of recruiting replacements drains another $1 billion each year from Corporate America. Equally devastating are the hidden costs. Out-of-shape employees tend to get sick more often and recover more slowly; efficiency and productivity suffer; and chronic fatigue and lethargy increase the risk of on-the-job accidents.

Contain the Cost of Health Care through Wellness Programs

As a result of the staggering rise in medical costs, many organizations are beginning to realize that keeping employees healthy costs less than treating them once they are sick. With an eye on the future, forward-thinking companies in Corporate America are shifting their focus, finding that an investment in employee health translates into substantial dividends over the long run.

Dramatic breakthroughs in fitness technology, nutrition, and sports medicine, coupled with strong scientific evidence, now links participation in fitness and wellness programs to higher job productivity, lower medical costs, and happier employees. Most of this research is being conducted and reported by organizations that have already implemented fitness/wellness programs and includes a wide diversity of *Fortune* 1,000 companies.

The impact of exercise and nutrition on virtually every aspect of an employee's life is well documented. Avoiding crash-and-burn diets; using clean-burning, high-energy foods; and following a high-performance lifestyle provide the underpinnings for the mental toughness needed to perform at optimal levels.

On a day-to-day basis, physical stress exposure can provide the ultimate recovery mechanism from high-level corporate stress. Muscles, tendons, and ligaments are stretched, pumped, and challenged through a full range of motion, stimulating a dormant physiology—alleviating muscle tension, dissipating stress hormones, and diverting the mental strain to the working muscles. Blood vessels and capillaries open up, driving more blood, oxygen, and nutrients to underworked areas and moving toxic buildup of stress by-products away from overworked areas and out of the body. Mental acuity, alertness, creativity, and alpha waves (associated with calmness and relaxation) are stimulated. Decision-making, efficiency, time management, concentration, and morale all improve for Mentally Tough Corporate Athletes while mental errors are reduced. These Corporate Athletes also enjoy intermittent relief from feelings of fatigue, anxiety, depression, frustration, and anger generated in today's intensely competitive workplace.

On a long-term basis, the effects of proper exercise, diet, and attitude are no less dramatic. Most notably, the strength, resilience, and efficiency of the cardiovascular, respiratory, and muscular systems improve dramatically, making employees less susceptible to the debilitating effects of corporate stress, such as endless time pressure, longer workdays, and constant change, and resulting in fewer errors and faster solutions. Daily work activities that were once chores become much easier and more enjoyable. An enhanced capacity for work and stress tolerance heightens an employee's creativity and rejuvenates his or her attitude.

For the corporation, these benefits translate into decreased absenteeism, employee turnover, disability, and sick days; lower incidence of disease and death; shorter duration of illness and fewer relapses, as well as greater physical work capacity, productivity, and creativity. Further, it has been reported that those employees with the highest job performance ratings also rated high in fitness and exercise participation. When combined with attitudinal training, the benefits are even greater.

All these benefits, in turn, demonstrate a significant impact on the bottom line. And the bottom line in Corporate America is cost effectiveness. All research clearly projects positive trends in the benefit-to-cost return from corporate fitness programs. In fact, some health care insurers and companies are already creating premiums based on fitness levels.

Today's evidence clearly demonstrates that properly run corporate fitness and wellness programs can be justified on a dollars-and-cents basis. Depending on the extent of the wellness/fitness program, employers save $1.24 to $8.33 per $1.00 spent on the program. The more comprehensive the program and the greater the support from upper management, the greater the savings.

Managing Your Time Is Managing Your Life

Charlie Hughes, fifty-four, president and CEO of Land Rover/North America, needs a pretty high tolerance for stress.

Wearing him down is the same hamster treadmill dance we all experience, except his was of the transatlantic variety. "Working for a company based in the United Kingdom, there's a huge amount of travel," Hughes says. "I travel probably 50 percent of the time."

Hughes's job has more to do with leadership than with day-to-day operations. "Over time, that—and the travel requirements—take a toll if you don't have the preparation or understanding you get in the Mentally Tough course, if you don't follow a regular schedule, if you don't take breaks, if you give up exercise for long periods of time. And I *do* view myself in this job as an athlete."

On the exercise front, Hughes has been a runner for the past twenty years. "I'd run when it was *convenient*," he says, "and I could never understand why I wasn't in good shape. Now I run every day. Plus a hundred stomach crunches every day. I recently had a physical at Johns Hopkins. After my doctor got all the results back, he said, 'Charlie, you are five years younger than when I met you three years ago. Whatever you're doing, keep doing it. You're as healthy as I've ever seen you.'"

Before leaving home every day, Hughes uses the checklist in chapter 15. "I do it in the morning right before I do my mental preparation. If it looks like I'm going to rush out the door and skip it, my wife says, 'Don't.' I spend seven or so minutes on it; taking that time to get ready for the day is far more powerful than it sounds. 'Mentally Tough' is the right expression."

The Seven-Phase Campaign to
Boost Employee Productivity and Loyalty

Here's a practical program to boost employee productivity and loyalty. When it's fully implemented, it can make an enormous difference in the job performance of your entire workforce:

1. **Top-level commitment must be strong enough to provide meaningful encouragement and incentives.**   No substantial or permanent improvement in corporate culture, performance, and profitability will occur without such top-level support.

2. **Management must communicate what changes it hopes employees will make in their personal lifestyles.**   This has to be done in a manner that will get them enthusiastic about improving their health. Trainers and coaches can assist.

3. **Recognize and reward healthy lifestyles.**   Since lifestyle quality controls performance, let it be known that it will be an important consideration in making promotions. Identify employees who already have healthy lifestyles and those who make significant progress in improving their way of life, and recognize them in the newsletter and with perks.

4. **Put your vending machines on a diet.**   In one company I worked with recently, of twenty-two items in a vending machine, twenty of them were more than 50 percent fat, and the other two items were 100 percent sugar. That is an accident waiting for a place to happen.

Require the vendors who supply the food and drinks for vending machines to include healthy, low-fat foods instead of candy, potato chips, and other high-fat snacks that tend to push some of your people toward poor cognitive performance and even early heart attacks.

Employee dissatisfaction with these changes can be minimized by first convincing everyone of its personal importance to them, and also by making the change over time. I recommend the following healthful snacks for vending machines:

- Fat-free pretzels
- Fig Newtons
- Apples, bananas, and other fruits, along with vegetables and salads if your machines are serviced daily or if your facility has an employee cafeteria where fresh fruit can be offered
- Canned fruit juices (but not sugar-added fruit drinks)
- Turkey sandwiches with lettuce and tomato on rye bread
- Packaged raisins
- Trail mix
- Peanuts (though high in fat, peanuts are high in nutrients)

- Cinnamon raisin bagels (the flavor deters the perceived need for cream cheese)
- Tuna sandwiches on whole-wheat bread
- Grilled chicken breast sandwiches on multigrain bread

5. Eliminate the term "coffee break" from the human resources vocabulary. Use "recovery break" instead. Gradually reduce the accessibility and convenience of coffee in step with the progress of your educational program. Offer a variety of pure fruit juices and caffeine-free brands of soft drinks instead.

6. Provide in-plant exercise facilities and make them available during work hours. Encourage their use to provide recovery waves that will permit employees in mentally and emotionally stressful positions (boring, repetitive work is emotionally stressful) to maintain their performance at peak levels throughout the workday.

7. Encourage work groups to begin their shifts with a routine of stretches and calisthenics. This is done in other countries and has been shown to improve alertness and teamwork on the job. Some corporations are beginning this approach and have been amazed at the results in improved productivity.

Corporate Athlete Action Items

- Identify what could be done to environmentalize your work area or department.
- Initiate the process today and get the ball rolling to improve your work spaces (e.g., cafeterias, vending machines, break-out areas, and conference rooms).
- Discuss this concept with coworkers and with supervisors to get it into the corporate culture.

Want What You Need

The future has several names. For the weak, it is "Impossible."
For the fainthearted, it is the "Unknown."
For the thoughtful and valiant, it is "Ideal."

—VICTOR HUGO

You've heard that life is a journey—a long distance race, not a sprint. By now you realize that it is actually a marathon of sprints that must be followed by recovery throughout the entire trek. And that journey is to be enjoyed day by day, hour by hour, and minute by minute.

It is too easy to make an excuse not to do the important things in life. We learn from a very early age to make excuses. We call it "Cover your assets." CYA, for short. We learn how to make excuses for why we can't take that test today, why we don't have last night's homework, why the project is late and over budget. Why we don't have time to be with our family tonight.

No more excuses!

There are three types of people in Corporate America:

- those who make things happen
- those who watch things happen
- those who wonder what happened

Let's not make excuses any longer. Let's decide what is important. What is your value system? What is important to you? Let's work from there. If your health is important, *make* it important. If your spirituality is important, *make* that important. If your family is no. 1, *make* it no. 1.

Only you can say, "These are the most important things to me," and only you can prove it by making it so. But for goodness' sake, we cannot deal with excuses any longer.

In most jobs, business is the crisis du jour. There's always something coming around the corner. You've got to keep yourself together while you're doing six other things and see your way through. People will come to you all day, and they all want five minutes of your time. Those "five" turn into an hour, and you can't turn them away. Then it becomes an excuse for not doing the things you want to and should be doing.

273

You picked up this book for a reason. That reason might be to be more productive in your work life or more productive in your home life, with your family, to be better for them. Maybe you picked it up to be healthier. Maybe you picked it up to be happier. We can talk about motivation, but motivation must come from within.

For example, in life-changing events, such as when someone stops smoking and never starts again, or if someone loses an incredible amount of weight and never puts it back on, usually the stimulus was a major, provocative life event.

When people lose a substantial amount of weight or when they stop smoking, very often they say something like "I saw my child being born, and I wanted to see her grow up," or "I am getting married, and I want to be really good for my spouse." It could be something simple, but still life-changing to you; that is the issue. Whatever makes a connection with you will be something that is very important to you, and that is the issue.

Instead of looking for excuses, look for what makes a task such as good exercise, better nutrition, or spending time with family worthwhile.

You already know that eating better is meaningful and that exercising is meaningful. But you must look inside: Are you exercising just to lose weight? Why not really find out why? Because if you want to lose weight, then you are dealing with self-image. If you want to get more connected to someone, then it is love or self-esteem. Identify the need you are trying to meet by changing your lifestyle. Once you identify your needs and then start getting your needs organized—and once you behave based on your needs—suddenly you won't be needing to make excuses any longer. Once you become emotionally connected to whatever you desire, then prioritization is easy. You will have your values lined up, you will know what your needs are, you will listen very closely to your needs and say "No" to many of your wants. A need is: you *need* nourishment for lunch. A want is: you *want* that Dairy Queen hot fudge sundae. Separate your needs and your wants. Then the goal becomes that your wants actually become your needs.

You need sleep, nutrition, exercise, time with family, friends, a sense of belonging, self-esteem. You need to love and you need to be loved. When these needs become your wants, you will be headed toward self-fulfillment. When you *want* to sleep well, you will live your life to meet that goal. When you *want* to exercise, you will live your life to meet that goal.

Once you do all these things, self-esteem and a sense of belonging will be easily found.

Many Corporate Athletes have told me that nothing will happen in their companies until upper management decides that the culture should change. That always amazes me. You cannot wait for the CEO to say "As of today, our culture will change." You must make a change in your life and then let other people see you and let you lead by example. Imagine the Founding Fathers of the United States in 1776 saying, "Let's wait and see what happens"!

You must be the master of your own life. You have your own free will; exercise it! People are extremely powerful in their own lives, but unfortunately, most of us don't realize the power we possess. Cultures only change when *you*, as an individual, stimulate change. Don't wait for someone else to change your life. You have the power. Use it!

Making and Keeping Commitments to Change

As with everything worthwhile in life, making and keeping a commitment to the Mentally Tough program takes effort and planning. Few skills are more valuable. Learning how to do this opens up unlimited possibilities.

Passion gives meaning to our lives. All people have passion about something. You have been taking a journey about what it means to be a great Corporate Athlete. I'm sure it was a worthwhile experience, but the journey has only just begun. You must not only practice it, but you must also practice *all* the right strategies. You have learned strategies that will enable you to achieve your dreams. But practice alone will not perfect you. Practice alone will simply make whatever you do permanent. But *perfect practice* makes perfect. So practice all the strategies with perfection, and continue growing throughout your life. It is the quality of the commitment you make that will make you great.

I close every program and every talk I give with four phrases, and I want to share those with you now.

Commitment to Change 1: It's never too late.

I don't care where you are in life or where you are in your career, the human system will do whatever you train it to do. If you train and if you practice mentally, emotionally, physically, and spiritually, there is all the scientific evidence in the world to support the fact that you will continue growing and improving throughout your life.

Commitment to Change 2: It's never over until it's over.

We've all heard that statement, but I will present it in a little different light. We all know that in a sports event that has no clock, such as a tennis match or a round of golf, it's not over until that last point is made or that last putt is dropped, but it's true in life also. Today, however, some-one makes a mistake in business and they're reprimanded severely, or if a child fails one test, the child feels that he or she has failed the course. I challenge you to look inside your heart and soul. Have you ever failed a test? If so, I would still venture to say that you're doing all right in your life. It is the mistakes that make us what we are, not the successes. Winston Churchill said it better than I ever could: "Success is not really success, but failure is never really failure; the only thing that truly matters in life is to never, never, never give up."

Commitment to Change 3: Never lose sight of your dreams.

I believe that dreams are the essence of what it means to be here, but I must tell you to beware of the perpetual dreamer, the "woulda, coulda, and shoulda." We are all surrounded by "wouldas, couldas, and shouldas" in life, people who say, "I *woulda* done this, I *coulda* done this, I *shoulda* done this." With this attitude, these people will never achieve anything in their lifetimes because they are always looking for reasons why they didn't. The only way you will achieve your dream is to place it high on a wall or on a target and then come back and figure out the process it is going to take to get to that dream, and then learn this phrase: Savor the moment and love the battle. If you love all the battles in your life, you may just achieve that ultimate result, but if you focus only on the results, you will suffer through a lot of battles as you go through your life.

Commitment to Change 4: Never, never, never surrender your spirit.

Life is tough; there is no question about that. If we look at the totality of life as our goal, it can be overwhelming. As each of these commitments to change relates to your goals, constantly focusing on life's ups and downs, its uphill battles and downhill coasting will tear you up mentally, emotionally, and physically. It's very hard to stay in the moment once you have identified your vision, but that is exactly what you must do—stay in the moment. That's why, you see, I truly believe your journey in life is your destination.

I wish you the best on yours.

Bibliography

Acworth, I. N., M. J. During, and R. J. Wurtman. "Tyrosine: Effects of Catecholamine Release." *Brain Research Bulletin* 21 (1988): 474–477.

Ali, N. S., and R. K. Twibell. "Health Promotion and Osteoporosis Prevention Among Postmenopausal Women." *Preventive Medicine* 24 (1995): 528–534.

American College of Sports Medicine. "Physical Activity, Physical Fitness, and Hypertension." *Medicine & Science in Sports & Exercise* 25 (1993): i–x.

———. "The Recommended Quantity and Quality of Exercise for Developing and Maintaining Fitness in Healthy Adults." *Medicine & Science in Sports & Exercise* 10 (1978): vii–x.

American Heart Association. "Exercise Standards: A Statement for Healthcare Professionals from The American Heart Association." *Circulation* 91 (1995): 580–596.

Anderson, I., and P. Cowen. "Neuroendocrine Responses to L-Tryptophan as Index of Brain Serotonin Function: Effect of Weight Loss." *Advances in Experimental Medicine and Biology* 294 (1991): 245.

Astrup, A. "Caffeine: A Double-Blind, Placebo-Controlled Study of Its Thermogenic, Metabolic, and Cardiovascular Effects on Healthy Volunteers." *American Journal of Clinical Nutrition* 51 (1990): 759–767.

Behal, K. M., D. J. Schofield, and J. Canary. "Effect of Starch Structure on Glucose and Insulin Responses in Adults." *American Journal of Clinical Nutrition* 47 (1988): 428–432.

Bindoli, A., M. P. Rigobello, and D. J. Deble. "Biochemical and Toxicological Properties of the Oxidation Products of Catecholamines." *Free Radical Biology & Medicine* 13 (1992): 391.

Blair, S. N., P. V. Piserchia, C. S. Wilbur, and J. H. Crowder. "A Public Health Intervention Model for Worksite Health Promotion: Impact on Exercise and Physical Fitness in a Health Promotion Plan After 24 Months." *Journal of the American Medical Association* 255 (1986): 921–926.

Blumberg, Jeffrey G. "Dietary Antioxidants and Aging." *Contemporary Nutrition* 17, no. 3 (1992): 1.

Bowden, Jonathan. "Fat Facts and Fallacies." *Idea Personal Trainer* 6 (March/April 1995): 44.

Brand, J. C., P. L. Nicholson, A. W. Thorburn, and A. S. Truswell "Food Processing and the Glycemic Index." *American Journal of Clinical Nutrition* 42 (1985): 1192–1196.

Brand, Miller J. "The Importance of Glycemic Index in Diabetes." *American Journal of Clinical Nutrition* 59 (1994): 747S–752S.

Brand, Miller J., and K. Foster-Powell. "International Tables of Glycemic Index." *American Journal of Clinical Nutrition.* 62 (1995): 8715–8935.

Brodigan, D. "Osteoporosis: The Effect of Exercise Variables." *Melopmene Journal* 11, no. 2 (1992): 16–25.

Broeder, C. E., K. A. Burrhus, L. S. Svanevik, and J. H. Wilmore. "The Effects of Either High Intensity Resistance or Endurance Training on Resting Metabolic Rate." *American Journal of Clinical Nutrition* 55 (1992): 802–810.

Burk, C., and J. Kimiecik. "Examining the Relationship Among Locus of Control, Value, and Exercise." *Health Values* 18 (1994): 14–23.

Byers, Tim, and Geraldine Perry. "Dietary Carotenes, Vitamin C, and Vitamin E as Protective Antioxidants in Human Cancers." *Annual Review of Nutrition* 12 (1992): 139–159.

The Cost-Effectiveness of Corporate Wellness Programs. Farmington Hills, Mich.: American Institute of Preventive Medicine, 1991.

Costill, D., E. Coyle, and G. Dalsky. "Effect of Plasma FFA and Insulin on Muscle Glycogen Usage During Exercise." *Journal of Applied Physiology* 42 (1977): 695.

Craig, A., K. Baer, and A. Diekmann. "The Effects of Lunch on Sensory-Perceptual Functioning in Man." *International Archives Occupation, Environment, Health* 49 (1981): 105–114.

Cunningham-Rundles, S. "Effects of Nutritional Status on Immunological Function." *American Journal of Clinical Nutrition* 35 (May 1982): 1202–1210.

Daly, P. A., D. R. Krieger, A. G. Dulloo, J. B. Young, and L. Landsberg. "Ephedrine, Caffeine, and Aspirin: Safety and Efficacy for Treatment of Human Obesity." *International Journal of Obesity* 17, supplement 1 (1993): S73–S78.

Dawson-Hughes, Bess. "Nutrition, Exercise, and Lifestyle Factors That Affect Bone Health." In Frank Kotsonis and Maureen Mackey, eds., *Nutrition in the 90s.* New York: Marcel Dekker, 1994, pp. 99–116.

DeBusk, R. F., U. Strenestrand, M. Sheehan, and W. L. Haskell. "Training Effects of Long Versus Short Bouts of Exercise." *American Journal of Cardiology* 65 (1990): 1010–1013.

Dilman, V. M. "Pathogenic Approach to Prevention of Age Associated Increase of Cancer Incidence." *Annals of the New York Academy of Science* 621 (1991): 385–400.

DiNubile, N., and C. Sherman. "Exercise and the Bottom Line." *Physician and Sportsmedicine* 27, no. 2 (1999): 37–43.

Domel, S. B., T. Baranowski, S. B. Leonard, M. S. Litaker, J. Baranowski, R. Mullis, T. Byers, W. B. Strong, F. Treiber, and M. Levy. "Defining the Year 2000 Fruit and Vegetable Goal." *Journal of the American College of Nutrition* 12, no. 6 (1993): 669.

Dreon, D. "Dietary Fat: Carbohydrate Ratio and Obesity in Middle-Aged Men." *American Journal of Clinical Nutrition* 47 (1988): 995–1000.

Dulloo, A., and D. S. Miller. "Ephedrine, Caffeine, and Aspirin: Over-the-Counter Drugs That Interact to Stimulate Thermogenesis in the Obese." *Nutrition* 5 (1989): 7.

Eckel, R. "Insulin Resistance: An Adaptation for Weight Maintenance." *Lancet* 340 (1990): 1452.

Elmadfa, I., B. N. Both, B. Sierakowski, and T. E. Steinhagen. "Significance of Vitamin E in Aging." *Journal of Gerontology* 19, no. 3 (1986): 206.

Ernsberger, P. "The Death of Dieting." *American Health* 4 (1985): 29–33.

Fernstrom, J. D. "Tryptophan, Serotonin, and Carbohydrate Appetite: Will the Real Carbohydrate Craver Please Stand Up!" *Journal of Nutrition* 118 (April 1988): 1417–1419.

Fielding, R. A. "The Role of Progressive Resistance Training in the Preservation of Lean Body Mass in the Elderly." *Journal of the American College of Nutrition* 14, no. 6 (December 1995): 587.

Frost, H., J. A. K. Moffett, J. S. Moser, and J. C. T. Fairbank. "Randomised Controlled Trial for Evaluation of Fitness Programme for Patients with Chronic Low Back Pain." *British Medical Journal* 310 (1995): 151–154.

Gaspard, G., L. Schmal, V. P. Porcari, N. K. Beitts, A. Simpson, and G. Brice. "Effects of a Seven-Week Aqua Step Training Program on the Aerobic Capacity and Body Composition of College-Aged Women." *Medicine & Science in Sports & Exercise* 27 (1995): 5, abstract 1011.

George, C. F., T. W. Millar, P. J. Hanly, and M. H. Kryger. "The Effects of L-Tryptophan on Daytime Sleep Latency in Normals: Correlation with Blood Levels." *Sleep* 12, no. 4 (1989): 345.

Gifford, K. D. "The Mediterranean Diet as a Food Guide: The Problem of Culture and History." *Nutrition Today* 33, no. 6 (1998): 227–232.

Grediagin, M. A., M. Cody, J. Rupp, D. Benardot, and R. Shern. "Exercise Intensity Does Not Effect Body Composition Change in Untrained, Moderately Overfat Women." *Journal of the American Dietetic Association* 6 (1995): 661–665.

Grobbe, D. "Coffee, Caffeine, and Cardiovascular Disease in Men." *New England Journal of Medicine* 323 (1990): 1026–1032.

Harris, William S. "The Prevention of Atherosclerosis with Antioxidants." *Clinical Cardiology* 15 (1992): 636–640.

Hill, A., C. Weaver, and J. Blundell. "Food Craving, Dietary Restraint, and Mood." *Appetite* 17, no. 3 (1991): 187–197.

Hoeger, W. W. K., and S. A. Hoeger. *Principles & Labs for Fitness and Wellness.* Englewood, Colo.: Morton, 1997.

Holt, S., and Miller J. Brand. "Particle Size, Satiety and the Glycemic Response." *European Journal of Clinical Nutrition* 48 (1994): 496–502.

Horne, T. E. "Predictors of Physical Activity Intentions and Behaviour for Rural Homemakers." *Canadian Journal of Public Health* 85 (1994): 132–135.

Ikonian, T. "Mood Food." *Men's Fitness* 9 (August 1993): 33–35.

Ivy, J. "Muscle Glycogen Synthesis After Exercise and Effect of Time on Carbohydrate Ingestion." *Journal of Applied Physiology* 64 (1988): 1480–1485.

Jaedig, S., and N. C. Henningsen. "Increased Metabolic Rate in Obese Women After Ingestion of Potassium, Magnesium, and Phosphate-Enriched Orange Juice or Injection of Ephedrine." *International Journal of Obesity* 15, no. 6 (1991): 426.

Jenkins, David. "Health Benefits of Complex Carbohydrates and Fiber." In Frank Kotsonis and Maureen Mackey, eds., *Nutrition in the 90s.* New York: Marcel Dekker, 1994, pp. 15–24.

Jenkins, D. J. A., T. M. S. Wolever, G. S. Wong, A. Kenshole, R. G. Josse, L. U. Thompson, and K. Y. Lam. "Glycemic Responses to Foods: Possible Differences Between Insulin-Dependent and Non-Insulin-Dependent Diabetics." *American Journal of Clinical Nutrition* 40 (1984): 971–981.

Jenkins, R. R., and A. Goldfarb. "Introduction: Oxidant Stress, Aging, and Exercise." *Medicine & Science in Sports & Exercise* 25, no. 2 (1993): 210–212.

Johnson, B. "Nutrient Intake as a Time Signal for Circadian Rhythm." *Journal of Nutrition* 122, no. 9 (1992): 1753–1759.

Kelly, S. J., and K. B. Franklin. "An Increase in Tryptophan in Brain May Be a General Mechanism for the Effect of Stress on Sensitivity to Pain." *Neuropharmacology* 24, no. 11 (1985): 1019.

King, A. C., W. L. Haskell, D. R. Young, R. K. Oka, and M. L. Stedfanick. "Long-Term Effects of Varying Intensities and Formats of Physical Activity on Participation Rates, Fitness, and Lipoproteins in Men and Women Aged 50 to 65 Years." *Circulation* 91 (1995): 2596–2604.

King, A. C., C. B. Taylor, W. L. Haskell, and R. F. Debusk. "Strategies for Increasing Early Adherence to and Long-Term Maintenance of Home-Based Exercise Training in Healthy Middle-Aged Men and Women." *American Journal of Cardiology* 61 (1988): 628–632.

Kostas, Georgia G. "Fast Food Eating." *Idea Personal Trainer* 6 (January 1995): 40.

Kuczmarski, R. J., K. M. Flegal, S. M. Campbell, and C. L. Johnson. "Increasing Prevalence of Overweight Among U.S. Adults: The National Health and Nutrition Examination Surveys, 1960 to 1991." *Journal of the American Medical Association* 272 (1994): 205–207.

Kurtzam, Felice D. "Stress Eating." *Idea Personal Trainer* 6 (June 1995): 40.

Laursen, B. H. K., and E. Rhoades. "Physiological Analysis of High-Intensity Ultra-endurance Event." *Strength and Conditioning Journal* 21, no. 1 (1999): 26–38.

Lee, I., C. Hsiech, and R. Paffenbarger. "Exercise Intensity and Longevity in Men: The Harvard Alumni Health Study." *Journal of the American Medical Association* 273, no. 15 (April 1995): 1179–1184.

Lieberman, H., J. Wurtman, and B. Chew. "Changes in Mood After Carbohydrate Consumption Among Obese Individuals." *American Journal of Clinical Nutrition* 44, no. 6 (1986): 772–778.

Loehr, James E. *Stress for Success.* New York: Random House, 1996.

Loke, W. H. "Effects of Caffeine on Mood and Memory." *Physiology & Behavior* 44, no. 3 (1988): 367.

Mackey, M., and Betsy P. Hill. "Health Claims Regulations and New Food Concepts." In Frank Kotsonis and Maureen Mackey, eds., *Nutrition in the 90s.* New York: Marcel Dekker, 1994, pp. 143–164.

Maher, T. J., and R. J. Wurtman. "Possible Neurologic Effects of Aspartame, a Widely Used Food Additive." *Environmental Health Perspective* 75 (1987): 53.

Mandelbaum-Schmid, J. "Are You Addicted to Fat?" *Health* (January/February 1994): 28–29.

Mann, J. "Nutrition Options When Reducing Saturated Fat Intake." *Journal of the American College of Nutrition* 11 (June 1992), Supplement: 82S.

Maurizi, C.P. "The Therapeutic Potential for Tryptophan and Melatonin: Possible

Roles in Depression, Sleep, Alzheimer's Disease and Abnormal Aging." *Medical Hypotheses* 66 (1990): 504.

McArdle, W. D., F. I. Katch, and V. L. Katch. *Exercise Physiology: Energy, Nutrition, and Human Performance,* 3rd ed. Philadelphia: Lea & Febiger, 1991.

Miller, B. F., and C. B. Keane. *Encyclopedia and Dictionary of Medicine, Nursing and Allied Health,* 5th ed. Philadelphia: W. B. Saunders, 1993, pp. 592–593.

Miller, W. C. "Dietary Fat, Sugar and Fiber Predict Body Fat Content." *Journal of the American Dietetic Association* 94, no. 6 (1994): 612–615.

Milner, I. "Health-Food Industry Sells Supplements, Not Science." *Environmental Nutrition* 13 (January 1990): 1–3.

Mueller, W. H., and J. C. Wohleb. "Anatomical Distribution of Subcutaneous Fat and Its Description by Multivariate Methods: How Valid Are Principal Components?" *American Journal of Physical Anthropology* 54 (1981): 25–35.

Nelson, M. E., M. A. Fiatarone, C. M. Morganti, I. Trice, R. A. Greenburg, and W. J. Evans. "Effects of High-Intensity Strength Training on Multiple Risk Factors for Osteoporotic Fractures." *Journal of the American Medical Association* 272 (1994): 1909–1914.

Paffenbarger, R. S., R. T. Hyde, A. L. Wing, I. Lee, D. L. Jung, and J. B. Kampert. "The Association of Changes in Physical Activity Level and Other Lifestyle Characteristics with Mortality Among Men." *New England Journal of Medicine* 328 (1993): 538–545.

Pagan, A., and A. Bonanome. "Monosaturated Fatty Acids in Human Nutrition." *Journal of the American College of Nutrition* 11 (June 1992), Supplement: 79S.

Pate, R. R., M. Pratt, S. N. Blair, W. L. Haskell, C. A. Macera, C. Bouchard, D. Buchner, W. Ettinger, G. W. Heath, A. C. King, A. Kriska, A. S. Leoni, B. H. Marcus, J. Morris, R. Paffenberger, K. Patrick, M. Pollock, J. Ripper, J. Sallis, and J. H. Wilmore. "Physical Activity and Public Health: A Recommendation from the Centers for Disease Control and Prevention and the American College of Sports Medicine." *Journal of the American Medical Association* 273 (1995): 402–407.

Patterson, R. E., P. S. Haines, and B. M. Popkin. "Healthy Lifestyle Patterns of U.S. Adults." *Preventive Medicine* 23 (1994): 453–460.

Prasad, K., A. Kumar, V. Kochupillai, and W. Cole. "High Doses of Multiple Antioxidant Vitamins: Essential Ingredients in Improving the Efficacy of Standard Cancer Therapy." *Journal of the American College of Nutrition* 18, no. 1 (1999): 13–25.

President's Council on Physical Fitness and Sports. *The Physician's Rx: Exercise* Washington, D.C.: President's Council on Physical Fitness and Sports, 1992.

President's Council on Physical Fitness and Sports, and Sporting Goods Manufacturers Association. *American Attitudes Toward Physical Activity and Fitness: A National Survey.* Washington, D.C.: President's Council on Physical Fitness and Sports, 1993.

Pronk, N. P., S. F. Course, and J. J. Rohack. "Maximal Exercises and Acute Mood Response in Women." *Physiology and Behavior* 57 (1995): 1–4.

Pyka, G., E. Lindenberger, S. Charette, and R. Marcus. "Muscle Strength and Fiber Adaptions to a Year-Long Resistance Training Program for Elderly Men and Women." *Journal of Gerontology* 49 (1994): M22–M27.

Rasmussen O. W., S. Gregersen, J. Dorup, and K. Hermansen. "Blood Glucose and

Insulin Responses to Different Meals in Non-Insulin-Independent Diabetic Subjects of Both Sexes." *American Journal of Clinical Nutrition* 56 (1992): 712–715.

Rose, David P. "Dietary Fat, Fiber, and Cancer." In Frank Kotsonis and Maureen Mackey, eds., *Nutrition in the 90s*. New York: Marcel Dekker, 1994, pp. 1–14.

Saynor, R. "Effects of Omega-3 Fatty Acids on Serum Lipids." *Lancet* 2 (1984): 696–697.

Slattery, M. L., D. R. Jacobs, A. Dyer, J. Benson, J. E. Hilner, and B. J. Caan. "Dietary Antioxidants and Plasma Lipids: The Cardia Study." *Journal of the American College of Nutrition* 14, no. 6 (1995): 635.

Snowdon, D. A., and Phillips, R. L. "Does a Vegetarian Diet Reduce the Occurrence of Diabetes?" *American Journal of Public Health* 75, no. 5 (1985): 507–512.

Sottovia, Carla. "How Accurate Is My Body Fat Assessment?" *Idea Personal Trainer* 6 (May 1995): 18.

"Spotlight on Soy." *Tufts University Diet and Nutrition Letter* (September 1995): 12.

Stefanick, M. L. "Exercise and Weight Control." *Exercise and Sport Science Reviews* 21 (1993): 363–396.

Stephen, A. "Trends in Individual Consumpton of Dietary Fat in the United States, 1920–1984." *American Journal of Clinical Nutrition* 52 (1990): 457–469.

Tayarani, I., I. Cloez, M. Clement, and J. M. Bourre. "Antioxidant Enzymes and Related Trace Elements in Aging Brain Capillaries and Choroid Plexus." *Journal of Neurochemistry* 53, no. 5 (1989): 817.

This Is Corporate Wellness—and Its Bottom Line Impact. Farmington Hills, Mich.: Wellness Councils of America, 1991.

Tremblay, A., N. Lavalle, N. Almeras, L. Allard, J. Despres, and C. Bouchard. "Nutritional Determinants of the Increase in Energy Intake Associated with a High-Fat Diet." *The American Journal of Clinical Nutrition* 53 (1991): 1134–1137.

Tucker L., and M. Kano. "Dietary Fat and Body Fat: A Multivariate Study of 205 Adult Females." *American Journal of Clinical Nutrition* 56 (1992): 616–622.

U.S. Department of Agriculture and U.S. Department of Health and Human Services. *Nutrition and Your Health: Dietary Guidelines for Americans*, 4th ed. Washington, D.C.: U.S. Department of Agriculture, 1995.

Wahlqvist, Mark L. "New Directions in Food-Health Research." In Frank Kotsonis and Maureen Mackey, eds., *Nutrition in the 90s*. New York: Marcel Dekker, 1994, pp. 117–132.

Weingarten H., and D. Elston. "The Phenomenology of Food Cravings." *Appetite* 15 (1990): 231–246.

Wiginton, Kristin. "Shame and Psychosocial Health: Considerations for Health Education." *Journal of Health Education* 30, no. 1 (1999): 30–35.

Willett, W. C. "Diet and Health: What Should We Eat?" *Science* 264 (April 22, 1994): 532–537.

Williams, Roger R. "Diet, Genes, Early Heart Attacks, and High Blood Pressure." In Frank Kotsonis and Maureen Mackey, eds., *Nutrition in the 90s*. New York: Marcel Dekker, 1994, pp. 25–44.

Williford, H. N., L. A. Richards, M. S. Olson, D. L. Blessing, and J. Brown. "Training Responses Associated with Bench Stepping and Running in Women." *Medicine & Science in Sports & Exercise* 27 (June 1995 supplement): abstract 1125.

Wurtman, R. "Food and Mood." *Nutrition Action* 19, no. 7 (1992): 1, 5–7

Wurtman, R. J. "Dietary Treatments that Affect Brain Neurotransmitters." *Annals of New York Academy of Sciences* 499 (1987): 179–190.

Young, S. N. "Acute Effects of Meals on Brain Tryptophan and Serotonin in Humans." *Advances in Experimental Medicine & Biology* 294 (1991): 417.

Credits

Grateful acknowledgment is made to ESHA Research for its software in nutrition analysis.

Pages 64–65: Body Mass Index data from the Surgeon General's Report on Nutrition and Health (1988), U.S. Department of Health and Human Services, p. 284.

Page 66: Bray & Gray, Waist-to-Hip Circumference Ratio (WHR) Norms for Men and Women. *Western Journal of Medicine,* Obesity, Part I, Pathogenesis, 149 (1988):432.

Page 163: Table 13.1 modified from Rockport Fitness Walking Test. Copyright © 1993, The Rockport Company, Inc. All rights reserved.

Page 163: Table 13.2 from *The Aerobics Program for Total Well-Being* by Kenneth H. Cooper, M.D., M.P.H. Copyright © 1982 by Kenneth H. Cooper. Used by permission of Bantam Books, a division of Random House, Inc.

Page 165: Table 13.4 from *The Physical Fitness Specialist Certification Manual,* The Cooper Institute for Aerobics Research, Dallas, Texas, revised 1997. Used with permission.

Page 166: Table 13.5 from *Principles & Labs for Fitness & Wellness,* 5th ed., by Werner W. K. Hoeger and Sharon Hoeger. Copyright © 1999 Morton Publishing Co. Reprinted with permission.

Index

About the Authors

Jack Groppel, Ph.D., is a partner in Orlando-based LGE Performance Systems. Groppel travels more than 150,000 miles every year, delivering speeches and conducting Mentally Tough training programs, workshops, and clinics. He also is a regular speaker at Peter Lowe International Success Seminars. In addition, Groppel is an instruction editor for *Tennis* magazine, a fellow in the American College of Sports Medicine, and a certified nutrition specialist. He has also been chairman of the Sports Science Committee of the U.S. Tennis Association for more than a decade. To learn more about LGE's systems of Corporate Performance Training, call 1-800-543-7764 or investigate their Web site (www.mentallytough.com).

Bob Andelman is the author or a collaborator of six books, including *Built from Scratch: How a Couple of Regular Guys Grew the Home Depot from Nothing to $30 Billion; Mean Business: How I Save Bad Companies and Make Good Companies Great; The Profit Zone: Lessons of Strategic Genius from the People Who Created the World's Most Valued Companies;* and *Stadium for Rent: Tampa Bay's Quest for Major League Baseball.* Andelman lives with his wife and daughter in St. Petersburg, Florida.